A KIND OF LIFE IMPOSED ON MAN: VOCATION AND SOCIAL ORDER FROM TYNDALE TO LOCKE

PAUL MARSHALL

A Kind of Life Imposed on Man:
Vocation and Social Order
from Tyndale to Locke

UNIVERSITY OF TORONTO PRESS
Toronto Buffalo London

© University of Toronto Press Incorporated 1996
Toronto Buffalo London
Printed in Canada

ISBN 0-8020-0784-8

Printed on acid-free paper

Canadian Cataloguing in Publication Data

Marshall, Paul
    A kind of life imposed on man : vocation and social
    order from Tyndale to Locke

    Includes bibliographical references and index.
    ISBN 0-8020-0784-8

    1. Vocation – History – 16th century.
    2. Vocation – History – 17th century.
    I. Title.

    BV4740.M3 1996   274   C96-930013-1

University of Toronto Press acknowledges the financial assistance to its publishing
program of the Canada Council and the Ontario Arts Council.

This book has been published with the help of a grant from the Humanities and
Social Sciences Federation of Canada, using funds provided by the Social Sciences
and Humanities Research Council of Canada.

To Diane, in gratitude

... vocation or calling is a certain kind of life ordained
and imposed on man by God for the common good.

William Perkins, 'A Treatise of the Vocations'

Contents

Acknowledgments

While this study concludes by describing the decay of a genuine sense of calling, the process of writing it has helped to confirm for me that vocations are still present in the world of scholarship. Many people have given time and energy to help further another's work. The staff of the libraries at York University and the University of Toronto, and of the British Library and the Bodleian have always been most courteous and helpful. Dorothe Rogers and Carroll Guen coped almost uncomplainingly with my awful scrawls, while Christiane Carlson-Thies and Al Wolters helped by their translations. I would also like to thank the late Bernard Zylstra, who first stimulated my interest in Locke and who was a guide in my earliest struggles with political and legal theory. Lee Hardy, Martin Marty, Oliver and Joan O'Donovan, John Sommerville, Gustav Wingren, Mark Goldie, John Yolton, and the late George Grant and C.B. Macpherson kindly offered advice and criticism at various points. In this study's earlier incarnation as a dissertation it benefited immeasurably from the work of Virginia McDonald, Ross Rudolph, and, above all, the comments and challenges of Neal Wood. The Canada Council and the Social Sciences and Humanities Research Council of Canada provided indispensable support in the form of doctoral fellowships and a research grant, while the Institute for Christian Studies granted leave time that it could ill afford to give.

A KIND OF LIFE IMPOSED ON MAN: VOCATION AND SOCIAL ORDER FROM TYNDALE TO LOCKE

1

Introduction:
The Importance of a Calling

VARIATIONS ON A THEME FROM MAX WEBER

This study traces understandings of vocation in England from the Reformation to the end of the seventeenth century and tries to show some of the implications of this history for political and social theory. Before embarking on the study, I would like to suggest some reasons why it is worth doing. Vocation, or calling – the idea that people are called by God to a specific mundane work or duty as a sphere and means of religious obedience – is, at first glance, peculiarly a theological notion. Despite this fact, the concept has tended to draw the attention of sociologists, economic historians, and political theorists more than of theologians *per se*. It has done so because it was through an idea of calling that everyday work acquired religious significance. The peasant and the merchant came to be seen as doing God's work just as much as the nun, the priest, and the magistrate. The idea served as a baptism of the world of work by the church. Hence, views of calling came to form the core of much of the economic and social theory of Protestantism at a time when such theory was culturally and politically important. It was the realization of this significance that caused Max Weber to make calling one of the foci of his celebrated studies of 'the Protestant ethic' and the 'spirit of capitalism.' The themes that Weber elaborated are also significant in four other areas of current concern. These are the relation between Renaissance and Reformation social thought; the nature of the competing political forces in England's mid-seventeenth-century upheavals – particularly those concerning Puritan social views; the interpretation of seventeenth-century political theory, notably that of John Locke; and contemporary theological discussions of the relation of vocation to the existing social order, which parallel debates between the Levellers and their opponents during the Civil War. I will outline the discussions in these areas briefly, concentrating on Weber's work since he set the parameters of much of the subsequent discussion.

At times it seems doubtful that anything new can be said on the subject of the 'Protestant ethic' and the 'spirit of capitalism.'[1] In some circles the debate which was sparked by the thesis is regarded as closed; closed because Weber's views are held to have been definitely disproved. For example, thirty years ago G.C. Homans said that Kurt Samuelsson's *Religion and Economic Action* 'does not just tinker with Weber's hypothesis but leaves it in ruins.'[2] Yet, despite this and other such conclusions that the Weber thesis has been either 'proved' or 'discredited,' the controversial literature continues to increase and many historians and social scientists apparently still feel compelled to offer some sustained verdict on the matter.

It is important to see the 'Weber thesis' in terms of his larger enterprise.[3] If this is not done then its content, intent, and significance will be lost. The *Protestant Ethic* was not an isolated study. It was followed by, and was part of, the much wider comparative research which produced Weber's major studies of China, India, and ancient Israel.[4] On the basis of this massive work, he sought to develop a theory of religion and society that would account for the formative place that religion occupied in the generation and establishment of patterns of social action. Weber's concern was to understand the modern world, particularly the Western world, as a whole. His problem was Western civilization, Western culture, and, more especially, Western rationality – what forces brought them into being; what modernity is and how it came to emerge in the social and cultural evolution of mankind. His work on the 'Protestant ethic' and his comparative research into similar problems in other religions and cultures indicated that one of the major clues to this development lay in the realm of religion. There he tried to show that Protestantism, by legitimizing and imposing an ethic of individual rational achievement in this world not just on an élite but on all, or at least the great majority, of a population, was a positive factor in the emergence of a capitalist economy. His work on India and China brought some confirmation in that it appeared that religious factors had hampered a similar development in the East.

The use of the word 'capitalist' may be a little misleading here. In the original text of the two parts of his famed study, Weber outlined his purposes in a more subtle, complex, and, indeed, different way from that usually attributed to him.[5] As Benjamin Nelson notes,

Weber was intent on countering the following theses of theological and other partisans:

1. The thesis of Protestant polemicists that the secularization of the modern world was due to the 'rationalism' and secularism of the French Enlightenment *philosophes* who had been bred in Catholic 'culture areas.'
2. The thesis of the Catholic polemicists that the secularism of the modern world had begun with Protestantism itself in the 'rationalism' growing out of Luther, Calvin, and the Protestant scholastics.[6]

What he wished to show was that the 'rationalized economic cosmos of the nineteenth and twentieth centuries' was not a product of these 'rationalisms' or even of any 'rationalism' at all. As Ralph Hancock puts it, 'the motives behind modernity are not fully rational.'[7] Weber wished to show that it was the product of an 'irrationalism,' that it was a by-product of a view of *vocation* which had spiritual ends and spiritual roots. As Weber suggests: '*one may ... rationalize life from fundamentally different basic points of view and in very different directions* ... the idea of a calling and the devotion to labor in the calling ... is ... irrational from the standpoint of purely eudaemonistic self-interest, but ... still is one of the most characteristic elements of our capitalistic culture. We are here particularly interested in the origin of precisely the irrational element which lies in this, as in every conception of a calling' (emphasis added).[8] He was interested in how callings lay at the root of the difference between what he called a 'traditional order' and a 'legal-rational' one.

In his investigations he took over the notion, earlier propounded by Werner Sombart, of a 'spirit of capitalism.'[9] This 'spirit' was characterized by the rational utilization of resources for the purpose of accumulation and gain, but with little regard to any questions of pleasure in or consumption of goods which are so gained. It was marked by calculation and behaviour that was specifically and systematically 'oriented by deliberate planning, to economic ends.' Weber regarded this as a modern development that was not present in earlier capitalism, which had been of a more adventurous, less thrifty, less rational type. The distinguishing mark of this modern capitalism he described as 'identical with the pursuit of profit, and forever *renewed* profit, by means of continuous, rational ... enterprise.' He, of course, acknowledged that capitalism in some form or other had existed 'in all civilized countries of the earth,' that 'there were at all times bankers and merchants.' But he maintained that 'a rational capitalistic organization of industrial labour was never known until the transition from the Middle

Ages to modern times took place.'[10] Weber used Benjamin Franklin to typ-ify this 'spirit of capitalism,' where infractions are seen not just as 'foolish-ness but as forgetfulness of duty.'[11] Having identified the 'spirit' of modern capitalism, he now sought for an answer to the question of how such a way of approaching and utilizing the world had arisen.

In order to help answer this question, Weber further identified what he thought was another feature, the 'Protestant ethic,' which preceded and in some fashion gave impetus to the spirit of capitalism. This 'Protestant ethic' was particularly developed in Calvinism and was centred on a view of call-ing – the idea that one's faithful following of a job or trade was the focus of one's obedience to God. In the calling the world is accepted and sanctified, and, hence, religious energy and asceticism, hitherto finding their highest expression in a monastic life, now find expression in the world of a trade. Thus people pursue their work diligently and systematically, but without seeking to live luxuriously. 'The moral conduct of the average man was thus deprived of its planless character and subjected to a consistent method.'[12] He maintained that 'An unbroken unity integrating in system-atic fashion an ethic of vocation in the world with assurance of religious salvation was the unique creation of ascetic Protestantism alone. Further-more, only in the Protestant ethic of vocation does the world, despite all its creaturely imperfections, possess unique and religious significance as the object through which one fulfills his duties by rational behavior according to the will of an absolutely transcendental God.'[13] He believed that such an ethic was particularly prevalent in Calvinism, especially the Puritanism of seventeenth-century England. This, he thought, was due to the fact that Calvinists felt that diligence (and perhaps success) in one's calling was a proof (to oneself) of one's election. The overall result of this ethic was that large groups in the population now systematically organized their life around their work and rationalized their work. Furthermore, now they worked not just to satisfy needs, but because it was a duty.

Not only did Weber see in this 'worldly asceticism' a peculiar feature of Protestantism; he also saw a similarity between this view and that of the 'spirit of capitalism.' He concluded that the former 'must have been the most powerful conceivable lever' for the latter.[14] In his own words: '[Puri-tanism] alone created the religious motivations for seeking salvation prima-rily through immersion in one's worldly vocation ... The inner-worldly asceticism of Protestantism first produced a capitalistic state, although unintentionally, for it opened the way to a career in business, especially for the most devout and ethically rigorous people.'[15] Hence Weber thought that the 'Protestant ethic' had been a lever, or a sort of midwife, to the birth of the 'spirit of capitalism.' He was not saying that the two were identical or that Protestants advocated money making. In fact, he maintained, 'examples of the condemnation of the pursuit of money and goods may be gathered without end from Puritan writings.'[16] What he was interested in showing was how the Protestant ethic of vocation and worldly asceticism had helped shape the later, more directly acquisitive, virtues of the 'spirit of capitalism.' It was not part of his argument that Calvinists were inclined to capitalism. Rather, he maintained that they unwittingly smoothed its path.[17]

It is also important to recognize that Weber saw Protestantism as only one factor in the development of the 'spirit of capitalism,' and perhaps a contingent factor at that. He maintained that he had no intention: 'of maintaining such a foolish and doctrinaire thesis as that the spirit of capitalism could only have arisen as the result of certain effects of the Reformation, or even that capitalism as an economic system is a creation of the Reformation ... we only wish to ascertain whether and to what extent religious forces have taken part in the qualitative formation and the quantitative expansion of that spirit over the world.'[18] Moreover, he noted, 'it would also further be necessary to investigate how Protestant Asceticism was in turn influenced in its development and its character by the totality of social conditions, especially economic ... it is, of course, not my aim to substitute for a one-sided materialistic an equally one-sided spiritualistic causal interpretation of culture and history.'[19]

The factors which Weber thought linked the 'Protestant ethic' with the 'spirit of capitalism' were neither logical nor theological ones; that is, it was not that a commitment to capitalism was somehow the logical working out of Protestant assumptions. Rather, the connecting factor that he emphasized was a *psychological* one. That is why he focused primarily not on systematic theological works but on 'counselling manuals' such as Richard Baxter's *Christian Directory*. While Weber was never very explicit on this point, the nature of his language indicates the sort of connection he had in mind. He wrote of 'the unprecedented inner loneliness of the single individual,' 'the elimination of magic from the world,' 'antagonism to sensuous culture,' and 'disillusioned and pessimistically inclined individualism.'[20] He emphasized that 'Calvinism ... caused very specific psychological premia to be placed on the ascetic regulation of life.' These 'did not exist consciously in every individual's mind in such absolute consistency and intellectual awareness. Rather, the individual grew up in the atmosphere created by these religious forces.' 'There emerged a "habitus" among individuals ...'[21] Hence Weber asserted that the 'inner-worldly ascetism' connected with the Protestant doctrine of vocation created a disposition towards continual, limitless, rational, restless labour, a disposition that persisted, and provided an impetus for the rational 'spirit of capitalism,' even after the religious spirit and teaching which had given birth to it had passed away.

He was not the first to express such a view, but his work was the most systematic and the best argued, even though it was merely a series of journal articles. His writings provoked a storm of criticism, and historians and economists, sociologists and theologians, political scientists and philosophers, Christians and non-Christians, Catholics, Protestants, Jews, capitalists, and socialists all entered the debate from a variety of angles and with a variety of intents. Within fairly short order, academically speaking, Weber was criticized by Rachfall, Holl, Sombart, Brentano, See, Robertson, Fanfani, and Hyma, all in major works on the subject. Ernst Troeltsch and, to a lesser degree, R.H. Tawney, defended Weber's views in equally weighty tomes. The criticism and counter-criticism have continued to this day.

THE CALLING SPREADS

A discussion closely related to the Weber thesis concerns the respective impact of Renaissance and Reformation views. Increasing numbers of scholars express the view that humanist and evangelical social teachings represented just two phases of much the same phenomenon. This position has been argued recently by Quentin Skinner and Margo Todd. They maintain that most teachings during the English Reformation only further developed the views of humanists such as More and Starkey, and that there were close spiritual connections between humanism and the Puritan movements.[22] Another related debate which, at least in Britain, generates as much heat as the Weber thesis concerns the background to the English Civil War. This debate involves a host of interrelated questions as to whether the English conflict was primarily constitutional, political, regional, national, religious, or economic in nature, or simply an unforeseen muddle. The fact that it appears to have been a combination of all these does not help us much unless we know something of the nature and the relative strengths of these features. Other related questions touch on the differences, if any, between 'Anglicans' and 'Puritans.' Were the Puritans, assuming they existed as an identifiable group, more open to social mobility? What were their attitudes to the poor and to those who worked with their hands? What was the relation between their religious beliefs and their political ambitions? Were they more disposed to the rational organization of life than were 'Anglicans'? As Patrick Collinson has noted, 'the saints of the seventeenth century have been invested with an almost cosmic significance as in some sense the mediators of nothing less than the transition from traditional to modern society, the agents of rationalisation ...'[23] The nature of this debate is perhaps even harder to describe briefly than is the Weber thesis. Here we may just note that there is disagreement over each of the questions just posed, and over how the questions are posed.[24]

Debate about social groupings in seventeenth-century England has become extended to the question of how to understand various political theorists of the age. C.B. Macpherson outlined what he described as a common thread of 'possessive individualism' which underlay much seventeenth-century political thought and which was typical of an emerging 'market society.'[25] The theorists' religious views, while seriously held, were really only historical relics which obscured the real function, and perhaps the intent, of what they said. Many criticisms have been levelled at Macpherson's work. John Dunn took Macpherson to task, especially for his interpretation of Locke.[26] Dunn maintains that Locke's possessiveness, his individualism, and his equation of industry and rationality stemmed from his adoption of a Puritan view of calling wherein work was a God-given task with little orientation towards economic benefits. Thus, for Locke, each person was and had to be responsible for his or her own work. This religious stress produced an intensely private and individual view of labour and its benefits.[27]

Finally, the actual normative import of Reformed doctrines of calling has become a live issue in theological circles. Variations on sixteenth- and seventeenth-century views have long remained influential in conservative Protestantism. In the twentieth century, such views have come under attack for their alleged fusion of God's vocational will with existing roles in the current social order, sometimes via a doctrine of creation ordinances. This was a major debate between Karl Barth and Emil Brunner, and the issue has since been revived, notably by Jacques Ellul and Miroslav Volf.[28]

THIS STUDY

Since these debates are important to understanding the sixteenth and seventeenth centuries, and since the matter of calling is important to understanding these debates, it is surprising that, while there have been many studies on some particular aspects of the matter, there is no overall history of views of calling.[29] This is a lack which the present study seeks to rectify. In looking at sixteenth- and seventeenth-century views we find that there were in fact few systematic elaborations of the doctrine. After the 1550s, apart from the better-known treatises by William Perkins, George Swinnock, and Richard Steele, there is only an exposition by Bishop Robert Sanderson. Nevertheless, the concept is widespread in these centuries: many people consistently worked with the notion without having a very clear sense of what they were saying nor what it might imply. They often thought that they were reiterating a well-established view when in fact they were saying something quite different. Post-Restoration divines assumed that they were repeating the views of a century earlier; but meanwhile, several subtle and not-so-subtle shifts of meaning had taken place. Consequently, the story of callings becomes less an exposition of texts and more an uncovering of the assumptions implicit in different ways of using words. This endeavour in turn requires examination of a relatively large number of texts which reveal only shades of meaning. However, such an exercise does allow longer-term deep-seated changes of outlook to be revealed.[30]

As I try to give this history, I also seek to show what it implies for these ongoing debates. We find (in chapter 3) that the Reformation did introduce a new understanding of calling, one which placed everyday human work at the centre of religious concerns. The fact that this feature was peculiar to Protestantism rather than to humanism more generally suggests that we should take care not to conflate the two movements. In the post-Reformation period (chapters 4 and 5) we find that 'the hotter sorts of Protestants' (Puritans) tended to have more developed vocational views and to devote more attention to introducing religious rigour into the world of work. By the late seventeenth century, the views of latitudinarians and Nonconformists were becoming similar. In this sense there was a 'Protestant work ethic,' or rather an ethic of rationalizing work, but it often differed from that suggested by Weber.

Vocational ideas underwent some major transformations in the course of the English Civil War (chapter 6). Throughout the previous century, the doctrine of vocation had often been used to justify submitting to, and requiring submission to, established political authorities. However, the Levellers used a revised view of vocation founded on necessity as one means of justifying widespread political involvement. In their turn the Diggers gradually abandoned the notion of calling, as even in radical forms it still seemed to imply divine warrant for the existing social order. As well as helping us to understand the nature of Leveller and Digger views, this discovery brings out some features relevant to twentieth-century theological disputes. For one thing it shows that these disputes are not as new as their protagonists think: they had counterparts in the sixteenth- and seventeenth-century discussions of grounds for rebellion. It also shows that the social implications of a doctrine of work as situated calling necessarily have a conservative cast. If we wish to avoid such implications then we need a major reworking of what is meant by vocation.

As Dunn notes, the conception of calling lay near to the heart of Locke's concerns and was a key feature of the individualism that pervaded his writings. But Locke's view cannot simply be related to a generalized doctrine of calling, since by this point the doctrine had several possible meanings. His was a blend of various elements, but was most akin to the latitudinarian view (chapter 7). Callings were only one part of and not the centrepiece of Locke's understanding of labour, however. He also drew on developing economic theory to shape a more technical view of labour and a labour theory of value. His view of work was an unusual and precarious synthesis which treated it both as a means of sanctification and as a factor of production.

Before turning to sixteenth-century England and the entrance of a full-fledged doctrine of vocation, I first set the stage by surveying views of work and vocation up to that point (chapter 2). This involves a rapid survey of biblical and other ancient views, of patristic and medieval ideas, and of the thinking of Luther and Calvin.

2

Freedom, Necessity, and Calling: From the Ancient World to the Reformation

Vocation

In the Old Testament, the Hebrew words which have been translated into English as variants of 'call' usually have meanings similar to the common English 'call' – the call of an animal (Ps. 147:9), to call on the Lord (Ps. 79:6; Gen. 4:26) and so forth.[1] There is also a sense of calling as a particular task, such as service of the king (1 Sam. 8:16; 1 Chron. 4:23), superintending labour (2 Kings 7:12), slave labour (Gen. 29:11), labour in the fields (1 Chron. 27:26), or the practice of a craft (Exod. 31:5; 35:21; 1 Kings 7:14). Its meaning was not that of a divinely given vocation, such as we find later in Puritanism, but rather was derived from the fact that in Hebrew 'to call' came to mean 'to name.' So, in Genesis 1:5, we find that 'God called the light Day.' In a Hebrew view, this naming did not mean merely attaching a label: to be called something was to *be* something.[2] Hence tasks could be callings. They could tell what a person was. One could describe people in terms of tasks and thus 'call' them.

This ordinary word was given special significance when it was God who called as part of the plan of salvation. God appointed people to a particular task or gave them the capability for some particular purpose in the divine plan (e.g., 1 Sam. 3:4). Hence, God called Israel to be His people and to dwell in righteousness (Isa. 42:6; 43:1; Joel 2:32). When God called Israel to be His people, then they *were* His people. That was then their name, their identity; they were called His people. In this way, Israel found its identity in terms of God's plan, as His chosen, His called. This same view was extended to particular offices within God's work in history.

The words in the New Testament translated in English as 'call' or 'calling' also have a breadth of meaning. The principal words are *kalein* (call), *klesis* (calling), and *kletos* (called) and their various compounds.[3] There are three types of use. One meaning was a general usage of the type of to call by name (Matt. 2:23; Luke 1:32); to call upon (Rom. 10:14; Acts 2:21; 9:21; 1 Pet. 1:72); to invite (Matt. 9:13; 22:3; 1 Cor. 10:27; Rev. 19:9). This was also a use similar to that in the Old Testament where we have the fusing of naming and being. So in 1 John 3:1 we read, 'See what Love the Father has bestowed upon us that we should be called the children of God,' and in Luke 1:32, 'He will be called the Son of the Most High.' In both these instances the meaning is almost as clear if we substitute conjugations of 'to be' for 'to call.'

There was also a specific use which referred to God's dealing with humankind. The disciples were *called* by Jesus to follow Him. Israel was *called* of God. This use led to a technical soteriological application of the term by Paul. For Paul the term included the basic ideas of invitation and summons. One can distinguish an 'external call' and an 'effectual call.' The former is based on Matt. 22:14: 'Many are called, but few are chosen.' This external call is a universal call for all people everywhere to repent. As people are sinners and blind to God, they reject this call. The 'effectual call' is that by which God invites people and *causes* them to be drawn to Him. When the term 'calling' is used in the New Testament with regard to salvation it is usually in the sense of 'effectual calling' (cf Rom. 1:67; 8:30; 1 Cor. 1:9; 1:26; Gal. 1:6, 15; 1 Thess. 2:22; 5:25; 2 Thess. 2:14; 1 Pet. 2:9; 5:10; 2 Pet. 1:3). This calling was a calling to fellowship with Jesus Christ (1 Cor. 1:9), to peace (1 Cor. 7:15), to holiness (1 Thess. 4:7), to hope (Eph. 4:4), to eternal life (1 Tim. 6:12), to God's Kingdom (1 Thess. 2:12). In fact, the church itself was called (Heb. 11:8), which is the origin of *ecclesia*.

A further use was an extension and more general category of the above. It occurred when God called people to particular duties for particular purposes. Being called to salvation was one of these purposes. But one could also be called to specific roles within the plan of salvation – for example, suffering (1 Pet. 2:20). Or one could be called to a particular office, as Paul was called to be an apostle (Rom. 1:1; 1 Cor. 1:1). It should be borne in mind later when we discuss the understanding of calling within Protestantism that, for most of the figures we discuss, as for the New Testament, the predominant use of 'calling' was in the sense of the external or the effectual call, the call to salvation.

Having dealt with these several meanings of the word calling, we can now ask if there is any biblical (specifically Pauline) use of calling in the

sense of a Christian's station and work in the world. When the other meanings have been addressed we find that the only possible source for such a
view of calling is Paul's admonition in 1 Cor. 7:20, where he wrote, 'Let
every man abide in the same calling wherein he was called' (King James
Version). This is a verse in which Luther had translated *klesis* as *Beruf* and
from which he and Calvin developed a notion of 'worldly calling.' An exegesis of calling as external conditions comes from reading the verse in the
light of those that follow it. Verse 21 reads, 'Were you a slave when you
were called ...' However, the verse can equally well be read in terms of the
verses which *precede* it, where Paul discusses circumcision and its unimpor-
tance for the Christian. In this case one's calling would relate to one's position as circumcised or uncircumcised, and Paul would be advocating that
no one seeks to change *this* circumstance. Abiding in the calling would
hence have meant not placing too much emphasis, positive or negative, on
Jewish ceremonial law, but rather staying in the same relation to that law as
when one became a Christian.

Another exegesis is that Paul was concerned to show that the state of
one's foreskin was ultimately *unimportant* (vv 18, 19), and that one's occupation was ultimately *unimportant* (vv 21–4). Hence in verse 20 he would
have been concerned to tell Christians to abide in their calling *as Christians*
rather than be overly concerned with any of these external conditions. This
exegesis fits closely with Paul's statements in 1 Cor. 1:26–30: 'For consider
your call, brethren; not many of you were wise according to worldly standards, not many were powerful, not many were of noble birth; but God
chose what is foolish in the world ...' This interpretation of calling is not
difficult to square with other meanings in the New Testament. However,
the interpretation of calling as 'external conditions' would mean that Paul
was using *klesis* in a sense used *nowhere else* in the New Testament. Indeed,
it would be a usage without parallel in the Greek of the period. He would
have to have been coining a new term. In view of the lack of any parallels,
both within and outside the New Testament, I, along with most recent
commentators, conclude that the exegesis of calling as one's social position,
occupation, or indeed anything external, is untenable.[4] This means that the
Bible does not contain a notion of vocation or calling in one of the senses in
which these terms were used in Reformation theology.

Work

While there is no 'Protestant' understanding of 'vocation' in the Bible,
there is a strikingly positive appreciation of work. The books collected in

the Bible give a markedly different evaluation of work from that found in ancient and medieval culture.[5] In Genesis the curse that was given as a consequence of the Fall was not the imposition of work itself, but only the fact that work would now become harsh and painful. Before the Fall work seems to have been considered one of the blessings. Indeed, the task given to Adam and Eve – 'Be fruitful, multiply, fill the earth and conquer it. Be master of the fish of the sea, the birds of heaven and all living animals on the earth' – seems to imply that the purpose and identity of humankind was closely tied up with work (Gen. 1:18, Jerusalem Bible). In fact, the earlier chapters of Genesis focus particularly on the development of human culture and the place of work in that culture. They recount the beginning of cities, the development of herding and nomadic life, music, tools, tilling the soil, hunting, and the development of bricks and tar.[6] Later, Exodus describes particular work skills as being directly inspired by the Spirit of God:

the Lord has called by name Bezalel ... and he has filled him with the Spirit of God, with ability, with intelligence, with knowledge, and with all craftsmanship, to devise artistic designs, to work in gold and silver and bronze, in cutting stones for setting, and in carving wood, for work in every skilled craft. And he has inspired him to teach, both him and Oholiab the son of Ahisamach of the tribe of Dan. He has filled them with ability to do every sort of work done by a craftsman or by a designer or by an embroiderer in blue and purple and scarlet stuff and fine twined linen, or by a weaver – by any sort of workman or skilled designer. (Exod. 35:30–5, Revised Standard Version)

Even God is described by analogy to human work, as the one who makes, forms, builds, and plants (Gen. 2:4, 7, 8, 19, 23). The prophetic literature contains the expectation that the new heavens and new earth will include work. Isaiah prophesies that

They shall build houses and inhabit them;
they shall plant vineyards and eat their fruit.
They shall not build and another inhabit;
they shall not plant and another eat;
for like the days of a tree shall the days of my people be,
and my chosen shall long enjoy the work of their hands.   (Isa. 65:21–2)[7]

And when we read that 'they will beat their swords into ploughshares and their spears into pruning hooks' (Mic. 4:35), we should remember not only the destruction of implements for war but also the (new) creation of implements for work.

In the New Testament the apostles were mainly of humble background and sometimes returned to their work after being called by Jesus. Jesus himself was a carpenter for all but the last few years of his life. His parables continually referred to the day-to-day realities of work – to sowing, vineyard labour, harvesting, house building, swine tending, and women's sweeping of their houses.[8] Similarly, the writings of the Apostle Paul contained a sustained polemic against idleness and many exhortations to work.[9] He did not distinguish between physical and spiritual work and used the same terms to refer to the labour by which he earned a living as to his apostolic service.[10] Often it is difficult to know to which he was referring. The work he considered was not limited to liberal pursuits; in fact, it was manual labour which most often drew his attention. When he outlined the service of the 'new man ... created after the likeness of God,' he urged him to 'do good work with his hands.' Paul himself worked with his hands to avoid being a burden to the church and in order to support others.[11] His often-quoted declaration 'if anyone does not work, let him not eat' was not an expression of callousness towards those who could not support themselves; the complex church system of deacons, collections for the poor, and sharing of goods that he encouraged shows that this was not the case. Paul was concerned not with those who could not find work, but with those who could and yet refused to share burdens. He was asserting that a life of leisure or one solely devoted to religious contemplation was a deficient life – that all members of the church should be involved in useful activity.[12] A similar positive evaluation of work is present even in the book of Revelation. Here 'the holy city, the New Jerusalem ...' is portrayed 'as a bride adorned ...' No longer is paradise pictured as a garden, as at the beginning, but as a city, the creation and culmination of human work and culture. The bride is no longer naked, as with Eve and Adam, or using primitive fig leaves to cover shame, but is adorned and clothed, wrapped about with what hands can make (Rev. 21:2).

THE ANCIENT WORLD

The biblical teaching is strikingly different from the attitudes of the educated in the Greek and Roman world. Most of the discussions that we have are from those who were more philosophically inclined; there isn't too much of a record from the ones who actually did most of the tasks.[13] Given this restriction, it is clear that the educated viewed what we now call work with some disdain, a disdain which extended to those who were involved in it. One type of work which drew widespread condemnation was that of the artisan. Xenophon's Socrates said that 'the illiberal arts [*banausikai*], as they are called, are spoken against, and are ... held in utter disdain in our states ... [they] ... leave no spare time for attention to one's friends and the city ... In fact, in some of the states, it is not even lawful for any of the citizens to work at illiberal arts.'[14] Aristotle wanted citizens to cultivate leisure, as 'leisure is a necessity, both for growth in goodness and for the pursuit of political activities.'[15] Isocrates held that citizenship rights should be restricted to those 'who could afford the time and possessed sufficient means.'[16] Later, Cicero used *sordidi* to describe the occupation of artisans, while the writers at the end of the Roman Republic had an ideal of *otium* (leisure) *cum dignitate.*[17]

At times there was a different view concerning agriculture. Xenophon thought that 'even stouthearted warriors cannot live without the aid of workers ... those who stock and cultivate the land'; Aristotle believed that the 'best kind of populace is one of farmers'; Cicero found 'none is better than agriculture ... none more becoming in a free man.'[18] The reason for this duality is contained in Cicero's qualifier 'in a free man.' Doing something with one's hands was not itself necessarily degrading. Homer's Odysseus could build his own boat, and Penelope could spin and weave; Paris of Troy helped build his own house, while Nausicäa did her brothers' laundry.[19] But this activity was freely chosen; it was independent. What was rejected was work based on dependency and necessity – the absence of autonomy (*autarkeia*). Freedom at the time of Aristotle consisted of 'status, personal inviolability, freedom of economic activity and right of unrestricted movement.'[20] Slaves, the majority of the population, lacked all of these, and artisans, while under contract, lacked the last two. Hence Aristotle thought that craftsmen were really part slaves, and therefore less than fully human. In his 'ways of life,' he did not mention the craftsmen because it was obvious to him that they were not free.[21]

This concern with absence of necessity carried over into attitudes towards farming. Aristotle ranked shepherds high because 'The laziest are shepherds; for they get their food without labour [*ponos*] from tame animals and have leisure [*skholazousin*].'[22] Hesiod praised farming, but advised his brother: 'Make haste, you and your slaves alike ... set your slaves to winnow Demeter's holy grain ... put your bondman out of doors and look out for a servant girl with no children ... let your men rest their poor knees.'[23] No poor peasant this who must do his own work. Those who praised agriculture assumed that the actual labour was done by slaves and servants. Their praise was for landowners as the backbone of the political order.

These views permeated the language itself. The word for leisure was *skole*, but there was no word for work. Work was referred to as 'unleisure,' *ascolia*. Latin was similar in its use of *otium* and *negotium*.[24] Unlike the modern age wherein we, as Weber pointed out, live to work, the Greek or Roman who could do so worked to live. Life revolved around leisure. Work, although necessary, was peripheral to real human concerns. Work formed only a base, a substratum, upon which genuine human activities could flourish.

Some exceptions to this disdain for work occurred in the Stoics. Chrysippus reversed Aristotle's treatment of the servant in terms of the slave. He thought that slaves were like servants except that they were hired for life. Stoic philosophy gave work a value of its own and held that it did not exclude one from a virtuous life.[25] For example, Seneca thought that nobility of mind could be found in all classes, for 'Socrates was no aristocrat. Cleanthes worked at a well and served as a hired man watering a garden. Philosophy did not find Plato a nobleman; it made him one.' Everyone could enter the 'households ... of noblest intellects.' But, even in his scheme, this only meant that such work was not a barrier to a higher life. Philosophical activity was still the best sort of life; Seneca was saying only that a wider range of people could now enter into it. Beyond that, he thought that the 'common sort' of arts were 'concerned with equipping life; there is in them no pretence to beauty or honour.'[26]

THE ADAPTATION OF CHRISTIAN TEACHING

Work and Contemplation: The Two Lives

In the first century after the apostles, Pauline views continued to set the pattern for the Christian church – a strong commendation of work, but with no specific doctrine of calling.[27] Gradually, however, the Church Fathers began to draw more heavily on Greek and Roman motifs than on specifically biblical teaching. In the early part of the fourth century, Eusebius propounded a doctrine of two lives: 'Two ways of life were thus given by the law of Christ to His Church. The one is above nature, and beyond common human living ... permanently separate from the common customary life of mankind, it devotes itself to the service of God alone ... Such then is the perfect form of the Christian life.' The other is 'more humble, more human, permits man to join in pure nuptials, and to produce children ... it allows them to have minds for farming, for trade, and the other more secular interests as well as for religion ... a kind of secondary grade of piety is attributed to them.'[28]

This pattern shaped much of subsequent Church thinking. So, for example, Augustine had praise for the work of farmers, craftsmen, and even for merchants. He thought that 'Christians will not refuse the discipline of this temporal life.' However, he tended to view this life as a *school* for life eternal. One other analogy he used was that of a wayside inn: 'Thou art passing on the journey thou hast begun, thou hast come, again to depart, not to abide ... this life is but a wayside inn. Use [it] ... with the purpose not of remaining but of leaving them behind.' In this conception, one could 'use' (*uti*) worldly goods, but one could 'enjoy' (*frui*) spiritual goods.[30] Augustine distinguished between an 'active life' (*vita activa*) and a 'contemplative life' (*vita contemplativa*). The contemplative life was akin to Aristotle's *bios politikois* and was shaped by Greek and Roman views. The *vita activa* took in almost every kind of work, including studying, preaching, and teaching. The *vita contemplativa* was reflection and meditation upon God and His truth. While both kinds of life were good, the contemplative life was of a higher order. At times it might be necessary to have the active life, but, wherever possible, one should choose the other: 'the one life is loved, the other endured.' 'The obligations of charity make us undertake righteous business [*negotium*]' but 'If no one lays this burden upon us, we should give ourselves up to leisure [*otium*] to the perception and contemplation of truth.'[30]

Thomas Aquinas also took the world and all its work with the utmost seriousness. He was a member of a largely urban order, the Dominicans, and he sought to find the place of each human concern in the overarching order of God's creation. For him the division of labour was a manifestation that all were members of the one body; he even compared God to a master craftsman.[31] However, he also employed Augustine's distinction between the *vita contemplativa* and the *vita activa*. Although he gave everything its place, yet some things had a higher place than others. The *vita contemplativa* was 'oriented to the eternal' whereas the *vita activa* was required only because of the 'necessities of the present life.' The active life was connected to the needs of the human body that humans and animals had in common. It was good if it was necessary, but if one could stay alive without it then so much the better; it might even function only as a last resort. While both lives had their place, the active life was bound by necessity and only the contemplative life was truly free. In short, 'the life of contemplation' was 'simply better than the life of action.'[32]

Similarly, the divines of medieval England taught that the highest form of piety was a forsaking of the world and consequent voluntary poverty. The states closest to perfection were those of the nun, friar, or monk.[33] But this elevation of a life beyond the world and the commendation of the poor did not mean that work was rejected. On the contrary, idleness was castigated and work was acclaimed, with the proviso that continual contemplation of the divine was not held to be idleness. The higher place given to voluntary poverty and the *vita contemplativa* did not mean that work *per se* was of no value.[34] The two could, and usually did, go hand in hand. However, the high calling, the truly religious vocation, was one of contemplation, and other work, especially manual work, had lesser and derivative value. Religious energy would not be focused in one's occupation unless one had a religious vocation, but one had still to work and not dissipate one's life. Thomas Beton said that each must have a 'good occupation against sloth.' Each must 'be quick in such deed doing ... leaving all other occupations.' Above all one had to 'beware of idleness the which is mother of all sin and uncleanness, so do that by your office that ye be called to, or by prayer, reading, writing, living or other handworks doing.'[35] The Dominican John Bromyard, chancellor of the University of Cambridge in the late fourteenth century, delineated the classes of society and found one extra: 'The Devil ... finds a certain class, namely the slothful, who belong to no order ... they shall go with their own Abbott, of whose order they are, namely the Devil, where no Order exists, but horror eternal.' The early-fourteenth-century priest Nicole Bozon propounded the same message. Indeed, so intent was he on driving home his point that he bolstered his argument with wholly spurious Scripture references: 'For nothing in this life is worth so much for body and soul as well ordered work. As to which Holy Scripture describes work in this fashion: "Work is the life of men, and keeper of health. Work drives away occasion for sin, and makes a man rest himself; it is the relief of langour, a stay to idleness, safety of the people, sharpener of all the senses."'[36] Such work included manual labour. The preachers did not sneer at *servilia opera*. *Piers Plowman* was a homily centring on just this theme and, except for its epic proportions, was representative of the pulpit teaching of the day. Ralph of Acton spoke of humble labour as being 'canonized.' 'Labour of the hands confers four benefits; It destroys vices; it nourishes virtues; it provides necessaries; it gives alms.'[37]

In the sermons and writings of the fourteenth and fifteenth centuries, we also frequently encounter the view that God was 'cleping' (calling) people to various estates. Thomas Wimbledon spoke of God as 'cleping' (calling) men to a 'state' and Thomas Beton spoke of a 'calling' to an office. William Caxton spoke of men 'of noble name and vocation.'[38] However, with the doubtful exception of Caxton, this was not a view of calling like that held by Luther or later English reformers. This medieval conception was that God appointed – 'called' – men to a particular *estate* in society. This did not imply that the work of an estate was itself a calling, the focus of the divine command, but merely that it was a place where God had commanded people to be to serve him. It merely reinforced the belief that God had appointed the orders of society and commanded each to serve in their due degree.

Exceptions to the Two Lives

There were exceptions to the conception of the two lives and, paradoxical though it might appear, it was in some of the most mystical and heterodox of medieval figures that we find the highest appreciation of the active life. Meister Eckhart shows this in two ways: one in his understanding of calling; the other in his consideration of the relative merits of work. In his sermon 'The Contemplative and the Active Life,' Eckhart discussed the familiar biblical story of Mary and Martha.[39] The evangelist Luke recounted the story thus: 'Mary ... sat down at the Lord's feet and listened to him speaking. Now Martha, who was distracted with all the serving, said, "Lord, do you not care that my sister is leaving me to do the serving all by myself? Please tell her to help me." But the Lord answered: "Martha, Martha," he said, "you worry and fret about so many things, and yet few are needed, indeed only one. It is Mary who has chosen the better part; it is not to be taken from her."'[40] Medieval authors had generally used this text to assert the superiority of the *vita contemplativa*. Eckhart, however, took a more sympathetic view of Martha's predicament.[41] He used the word 'calling' to refer to Martha's activity: 'One [means] ... without which I cannot get into God, is work, vocation, or calling in time ... Work is the outward practice of good works but calling implies the uses of discrimination.'[42] This very use of the word 'calling' already implied an elevated view of Martha's work – 'He who works in the light rises straight up to God without let or hindrance: his light is his calling, and his calling is his light. This was the case with Martha.'[43] Indeed, he said, 'temporal work is as good as any communing with God, for it joins us as straitly to God as the best that can happen to us, barring the vision of God in his naked nature.'[44] Such works were 'just as good and unite us as closely to God as all Mary Magdalene's idle longings.'[45] Eckhart maintained that it was the nature and purpose of our occupations that they lead us to God: they were, in fact, the reasons that we are on this earth: 'We are brought forth into time in order that our sensible worldly occupations may lead us nearer and make us liker unto God.'[46]

Similar themes occurred in the writings of the Dominican Johann Tauler. In his sermons on 'Vocation' he was at pains to show that Jesus' rebuke to Martha was 'not because of the things she did, for these were good and sanctified; but because of the ways in which she did them, with too much worry and anxiety.'[47] The model that Tauler employed in comparing the two lives was the body. He stressed that in this body all parts are required and that no part 'should usurp the name or office of another.' This analogy is in itself unremarkable in medieval writing, but what is unusual is the way Tauler treats the *vita activa* and the *vita contemplativa* as *parts* of a body. 'To abide in one's calling' meant that one should *not* aspire to contemplation or a monastic estate. In this context his assertion that it is the same spirit that gives each task is a form of spiritual levelling. Tauler described a variety of ways of serving and knowing God: one was 'external works': 'he knows all the secrets of commerce.'[48] He criticized those who thought such an estate was 'an obstacle for his perfection,' for it was 'certainly not God who has put this obstacle.' He condemned 'all those who would stop at contemplation, but scorn action.'[49]

But Tauler and Eckhart were exceptions. Basic to the pattern of medieval Christianity was a conception according to which the only true Christian calling, or, at least, the highest calling, was a priestly or monastic one. In fact the term 'calling' or 'vocation' was used only to refer to such pursuits. Karl Barth's summary is quite accurate: 'According to the view prevalent at the height of the high Middle Ages [secular work] only existed to free for the work of their profession those who were totally and exclusively occupied in rendering true obedience for the salvation of each and all. There could be no question of "calling" for Christians in other professions.'[50]

CONTINENTAL REFORMERS

Luther

Luther broke with traditional translation when at Ecclesiasticus 11:20 and 21, and 1 Cor. 7:20 he used *Beruf* in his German Bible. Earlier commentators had understood Ecclesiasticus as *Werk* or *Arbeit*. In medieval times

Beruf was restricted largely to referring to calling someone to a clerical position.[51] In introducing this novel translation, Luther took a word previously used only for a priestly or monastic calling and applied it to all worldly duties. Hence, he implicitly maintained that the role of husband, wife, peasant, or magistrate was a particular duty given by God.[52] Luther denied that there was anything special about the priestly estate: 'Therefore all Christian men are priests, the women priestesses, be they young or old, masters or servants, mistresses or maids, learned or unlearned. Here there are no differences unless faith be unequal.'[53] As all people were now seen equally as priests, there was nothing especially spiritual about the traditional priestly estate: 'Therefore the estate [*Stand*] of a priest is nothing else in Christendom than an office ... Hence it follows from this that layman, priest, prince, bishop, and as they say, spiritual and worldly, have no other difference at bottom than that of office and work, not of estate, for they are all of the spiritual estate, truly priests, bishops and popes ...'[54] Here Luther appropriated the religious aura which surrounded the clerical vocations and permeated all worldly tasks with it. To work in one's estate was a divine calling. He not only extended the notion of calling but also *focused* it in terms of estate (*Stand*). One's estate was one's divine appointment to serve God in the particular duties of the office that the estate required. If some objected that they had no calling, Luther replied 'how is it possible that you should not be called. You will also be in some estate, you will be a husband, or wife, or child, or daughter, or maid.'[55] Hence 'everyone should take care, that he remains in his estate, looks to himself, realizes his calling, and in it serves God and keeps his command.'[56]

This fusion of estate, office, and calling was the core of Luther's view of calling. Estates were the locus of one's office and hence were callings. After 1522 Luther used *Beruf* synonymously with estate (*Stand*), office (*Amt*), and duty (*Befehl*).[57] All work in the world, not just some particular offices, was understood as immediately divinely appointed; one was called to it. The type of work varied according to one's office; one's office was determined by one's estate; one's estate was given by God, and it was one's existing social situation. The calling was hence a definite divine commandment to work diligently according to one's given social position. No calling was more spiritual than any other. This extension of vocation meant that work was elevated. For Luther work was part of God's creation: it was instituted not just because of sin but even before the Fall. So Adam had 'work to do, that is ... plant the garden, cultivate and look after it.'[58] Work was honourable and a blessing.[59] Work had fallen under the curse of sin and so was wearying and disappointing, hence it always involved toil and trouble.[60] But the Christian had to see work beyond the curse, for man was blessed when he worked industriously.[61]

A distinction which arose later concerned callings *as* one's *estate*, which was hence seen as a divinely appointed sphere of work, and calling *as* a *duty* to serve God which is to be carried out *in* one's particular *estate*. This distinction was foreign to Luther, but still his conception of calling was one of duty rather than position. What he usually had in mind when he spoke of calling was a call to service that came to a Christian *within* the midst of his or her sphere of work. Vocation was hence seen primarily as a summons to work for a neighbour's sake within one's estate.[62] In this sense, *a vocation could be distinguished from one's immediate work*: 'the eyes of God regard not works but our obedience in them. Therefore it is His will that we also have regard for His command and vocation.'[63] Vocation required a right use of one's office. For Luther, those who were not Christians could not have a calling, for they lacked faith, which alone was pleasing to God. Some inconsistencies appear, but, when he picked his words carefully, Luther treated callings as matters for Christians only. A calling was not just the work of some social ranking but a faithful Christian obedience to God *in* such work.

Calvin

When Calvin used the term 'calling' he usually meant a calling to salvation, or else a calling to the ministry. But he also developed a conception similar to Luther's. He thought that 'In the Scriptures "calling" is a lawful way of life, for it is connected with God, who actually calls us.'[64] One way in which he differed from Luther was that he tended to identify a calling with *work itself*, rather than see it as something which comes *into* work. God 'has appointed duties to every man in his particular way of life ... He has named these various kinds of livings "callings."'[65] For Luther, we obey the divine call when through faith we serve God in our estates. For Calvin the work of the calling was the work of the 'estate' itself and so was itself an obedience to God.[66]

Calvin had a similar conservatism to Luther in relating the calling both to the given orders of society and to the particular station that a Christian was in. But he also, like Luther, thought that some occupations could not really be from God and, hence, could not really be vocations. In fact, he could be quite sarcastic: 'A monk ought to remain in his cloister like a pig in his trough, for that is his vocation ... Let a brothel keeper ... ply his trade ... let a thief steal boldly, for each is pursuing his vocation.'[67] Not all occupations were callings but only those which were lawful and genuinely useful ways of life. But Calvin's view was not as static as Luther's. One's given social position was not quite so normative, limiting, or all-encompassing. Although he still emphasized that one should stay in a calling, he did not regard this as an iron rule but only as a caution to prevent undue 'restlessness.'[68] Indeed, his use of the word 'adopted' to describe the calling that one already occupied seems to imply a definite choice. For Calvin, a Christian might, with 'proper reason,' change a calling and choose another. A certain voluntarism in deciding on the Lord's calling was appearing. It was, as Troeltsch said, 'a freer conception of the system of callings.'[69]

A further feature of Calvin's work was his stress on the *utility* of callings. He emphasized the 'advantage,' 'utility,' 'profit,' and 'fruit' of Christian works. Certainly he was not concerned with these fruits in terms of worldly success, but he stressed that things of importance are always *for* something.[70] Speaking of his own work, he wrote 'I do not demand at all that people agree with me on my opinion or my say so, except upon condition that they first recognize that what I teach is useful.'[71] Of callings he said, 'It is certain that a calling would never be approved by God that is not socially useful, and that does not redound to the profit of all.'[72] Biéler summarized his position thus: '"God has created man," Calvin says, "so that man may be a creature of fellowship." ... Companionship is completed in work and in the interplay of economic exchanges. Human fellowship is realized in relationships which flow from the division of labour wherein each person has been called of God to a particular and partial work which complements the work of others. The mutual exchange of goods and services is the concrete sign of the profound solidarity which unites humanity.'[73]

This stress permeated Calvin's teachings on social relations. He advised ministers to be aware of the conduct of business around them so that they would be in a position to give advice and counsel which was both pertinent and realistic. Indeed, it was on Calvin's own initiative that cloth manufacture was introduced into Geneva to provide work for the poor and unemployed.[74] In this context it is also worth noting Calvin's exegesis of the parable of the talents (Matt. 25:14–30). Before Calvin the talents of gold, which one should use to glorify God, were seen as spiritual gifts and graces that God had bestowed on Christians. Calvin made a revolutionary change in interpretation when he understood the talents in terms of one's calling and in terms of people's 'talents'; the particular instance he considered was trading (*negotiari*). Calvin stressed the *historical* nature of these gifts and talents and in doing so helped shape the modern meaning of the word 'talent.'[75]

This awareness of usefulness led to an equal emphasis on the importance of useful *activity*. Calvin asserted that the contemplative life was not better.[76] In fact his God was very active; He was 'not such as is imagined by the sophists, vain, idle and almost asleep, but vigilant, efficacious, operative, and engaged in continual action.'[77] One need not believe that people make God in their own image to see here a remarkable picture of Calvin and his followers. For Calvin, God put us here to work: '*sei deo creatum esse ut laboret,*'[78] and 'The nature of the Kingdom of Christ is that it everyday grows and improves.'[79] This activity was not restricted to the church or to pious duties, but encompassed the whole creation; its purpose was 'to establish the heavenly reign of God upon earth.'[80] These twin stresses on utility and activity gave Calvin's doctrine of callings a markedly different ethos from Luther's. While both stressed quiet, unassuming labour and abiding in one's calling, for Calvin, in the heart of a bustling city, the whole tenor of callings was much more aggressive and busy. His readers and hearers were to work, to perform, to develop, to progress, to change, to choose, to be active, and to overcome until the day of their death or the return of their Lord.

3

Reform, Estate, and Calling:
The More Circle and the
Early Protestants

Perhaps the first thing one notes on reading the writings of the circle around Thomas More is their leisured and irenic tone. They are a far cry from the earthy, almost grubby, style of the Protestant reformers.[1] Some reasons for this tone become clearer if we consider aspects of their views of learning, virtue, work, and contemplation. Thomas Lupset revived the discussion of active and contemplative lives, although in an altered garb. In his 'Treatise of Charity' he criticized covetousness and worldliness, but he thought of worldliness not only as the self-seeking which he attacked, but also as a concern for this world rather than the next one. The distinction he developed was not one of greed versus charity, but a more Stoic one of 'worldly passion' versus 'rest.' Of 'ambitious' men, he claimed that 'sleeping and waking these men's minds roll without taking rest.'[2] He denounced 'the love of this carcass, and of this life' and said 'Our master Christ teaches us to hate this life, and to set our body at nought.' 'Now then, to get this rest, that thereby we may get charity, we must cast away the love of this life.' 'The quick living soul, that quietly resteth in the love of God, driveth from him ... all these unquiet passions.' The rest he had in mind was like the 'rest that angels in heaven have ... not to be moved or stirred with these passions, of loving, of hating, of being pleased, of being diseased, of trusting, of lusting, of abhorring, of coveting, of refusing, of rejoicing, of lamenting, of innumerable such other, that scourgeth and whippeth man's mind by reason of the corrupt affection and love that he beareth in his itching body ...'[3] Lupset cautioned that 'it is not forbid to eat, to drink, to have and get wherewith such sustenance may be maintained,' but he noted that 'it is plain contrary to the will of God, that we should with any great intention, solicitude, or carefulness, of mind, prosecute these bodily necessities.'[4] Later, he distinguished between the duties of body and soul.[5] His views were blurred a little by the fact that he was principally criticizing worldliness understood as ambition, or gluttony. But he did go beyond just this juxtaposition.[6] A year later, in 'An Exhortation to Young Men,' he advised his reader, Withypool, 'first to care for your soul, next to care for your body, and thirdly to care for the goods of this world.'[7]

In Thomas Starkey's famous *Dialogue between Pole and Lupset*, Starkey has Pole say: 'the perfection of man resteth in the mind and in the chief and purest part thereof, which is reason and intelligence, it seemeth without doubt that knowledge of God, of nature, and of all the works thereof should be the end of man's life.'[8] 'Lupset,' who appeared to speak for Starkey here, responded that contemplation was not enough but that one should also be active in the affairs of the commonwealth. He used Aristotle to show that 'the perfection of man ... stand[s] jointly in both, and neither in the bare contemplation and knowledge of things separate from all business of the world, neither in the administration of matters of the commonweal'[9] and held that 'it is not sufficient, a man to get knowledge and virtue ... but chiefly he must study to commune his virtues to the profit of other. And this is the end of the civil life.'[10] Despite this exhortation that knowledge must be used by the educated man in the commonwealth, 'Lupset' still cautioned that 'high philosophy and contemplation of nature be of itself a greater perfection of man's mind, as it which is the end of the active life, to the which all men's deeds should ever be referred,' but he acknowledged 'meddling with the causes of the commonwealth is more necessary and ever rather first to be chosen as the principal mean whereby we may attain to the other.'[11] This view was similar to those of Augustine and Thomas Aquinas, or Cicero and Seneca. The active life was good, was necessary, and one might be called to it rather than to study or contemplation. However, the active life was only to provide 'good and politic order,' 'quietness and tranquillity' so that all might 'attain to their natural perfection.'[12] The active life was subordinate to and served the contemplative life. The contemplative life remained the highest perfection.

In Thomas More's *Utopia*, the inhabitants worked for six hours, three in the morning, three in the afternoon, with a two-hour lunch break. They slept for eight hours, and the rest of the time was 'left to every man's discretion, not to waste in revelry or idleness, but to devote the time free from work to some other congenial occupation according to taste.'[13] For 'the authorities do not keep the citizens against their will at superfluous labor since the constitution of their commonwealth looks in the first place to this sole object: that for all the citizens, as far as public needs permit, as much time as possible should be withdrawn from the service of the body and devoted to the freedom and culture of the mind. It is in the latter that they deem the happiness of life to consist.'[14] There was also a strange class of people 'who for religious motives eschew learning and scientific pursuits.' This type did good works, looking after invalids, digging ditches, and so on. In short 'they behave as servants ... and more like slaves ... they leave leisure for the others and yet claim no credit for it.'[15] Apart from their own peculiar characteristics, these people are of note for the way More compared them – 'like slaves' – and the way he characterized what they gave to others – 'leisure.' None of this means that More or those around him excused idleness, for their works repeatedly condemned this vice.[16] However, they had a particular conception of what idleness was, for the highest virtue consisted of a life of reason, a life they often characterized as 'leisure.' In this sense 'leisure' was the highest of all.

When the members of More's circle contrasted the contemplative and the active life, their principal understanding of action reflected not Martha, who served in the kitchen, but politics, particularly that of the wise counsellor who advised the sovereign out of the depth of his learning. Their ideal centred on the importance of education; the highest life was the life of reflection and reason; the ideal type was the cultured, pious gentleman and adviser; the life of action was epitomized by the wise counsellor.[17]

More's conception of piety and spirituality is also worthy of note in this context. As Richard Sylvester concluded: 'The spiritual life should be mixed with the public life. Each drew strength from the other and man's proper condition was the mingled state.'[18] However, even here there is a difference from the Protestant view. More sought balance between two modes of life: the public life was almost on a par with the spiritual, but the public was not itself the spiritual.[19] The view developed by the Protestant reformers was that all works were equal as service to God; that all works done in faith were themselves spiritual works; that the world itself was the locus of piety.

The members of More's circle were usually advocates of reform. They suggested remedies for the poor and condemned idleness, oppression, and covetousness.[20] However, there was a note of élitism in their reform program. They emphasized change from the top down, with the emphasis on wise and educated rulers, counsellors, and magistrates. The behaviour of the rest of the populace was presumed to be largely dependent on the virtue and wisdom of these rulers. While they exhorted each person to do his or her duty, there was none of the widespread emphasis on the gifts and labour of all in their callings that pervaded Protestant writings.

THE EARLIEST PROTESTANTS: TYNDALE AND FRITH

In 1530 a list of heresies was proscribed. The proscription was aimed particularly at William Tyndale and Simon Fish, noted for his agitation on behalf of the poor. The opinions condemned as heretical concerned the following views: 'Every man is lord of another man's good'; 'He that is rich, and liveth of his rents, may not use or spend his goods as he will, but the goods belong as well unto the poor as to thee'; 'God hath not given riches to the rich man for to boast and brag therewith ... but to the intent they should be servants to all the world'; 'A man shall be reproved for no other thing at the day of judgement, but for forgetting the poor.'[21] There was nothing particularly remarkable about the sentiments condemned. They asserted the doctrine of stewardship, the necessity of caring for the poor, and the fact that each was, as a member of the body, to serve the other parts. The fear seemed to stem from the fact that Tyndale, among others, was unusually blunt in expressing these sentiments, particularly in a country already agitated by events in Germany. Tyndale's words were striking: 'If thy brother ... therefore need, and thou have to help him ... but withdrawest thy hands from him ... thou ... art a thief.'[22] Even this view could be found in Thomas Aquinas; but at times Tyndale took this argument beyond powerful rhetoric on the analogy of the body and revealed some radical implications of the doctrine of the priesthood of all believers. He maintained that 'Every Christian man to another is Christ himself ... To thy neighbour owest thou thine heart, thyself, and all that thou hast and can do,' and he drew the stark conclusion: 'In Christ *we are all of one degree, without respect of persons*'[23] (emphasis added). It is clear that Tyndale did not wish to take away degree in society, but his formulations of the equality of believers before God provoked misunderstanding in 1527. Indeed his vocabulary implied remarkably levelled relations between people. While he spoke of the duty of rich and poor, gentle and labourer, yet, when he considered what was owed one to another, his language was usually of brother to brother, sister to sister, and neighbour to neighbour.

Another of the articles of heresy touched directly on callings. Article 22 condemned the view that 'There is no work better than another to please God; to pour water, to wash dishes, to be a souter [cobbler], or an apostle, all is one; to wash dishes and to preach is all one, as touching the deed, to please God.' This appeared to be aimed at Tyndale's assertion, later quoted by William Perkins, that 'if thou compare deed to deed, there is difference betwixt washing of dishes, and preaching of the word of God; but as touching to please God, none at all: for neither that nor this pleaseth, but as far forth as God hath chosen a man, hath put his Spirit in him, and purified his heart by faith and trust in Christ.'[24] Tyndale related this service to degree in society. You had to do 'whatsoever cometh into thy hands ... as time, place and occasion giveth, and as God hath put thee in degree, high or low.' 'Knowest that God hath put thee in that office; submittest thyself to his will.' Each work was of equal value because God was principally concerned with 'how thou acceptest the degree that he hath put thee in, and not what degree thou art ...'[25] The chief concern was accepting one's estate. One must not seek another or desire a change. This did not mean that change was impossible, for if a person will 'wait on the office wherein Christ hath put him ... If ... he patiently therein abide,' then God may 'promote him and exalt him higher.' But one could not be one's own promoter. Each must accept his or her lot, letting providence have its way. Work must be willing and earnest. Even earning a living was not enough: '"If I do it against my will ..." that is, if I do it not of love to God, but to get a living thereby, and for a worldly purpose, and had rather otherwise live, then do I that office which God hath put me in, and yet not please God myself.'[26] This view was reminiscent of Luther, but it lacked some of his subtlety. In particular, Tyndale did not distinguish vocation and office from the particular social station in which they were manifest. One could 'do ... [an] office ... and yet not please God.' This conception of office was of something immanent within the social order.[27]

John Frith's views were similar to Tyndale's.[28] He emphasized the 'parable of the rich man ... which ... fared delicately in this world, and after was buried in hell' and urged each and every person to 'get to some occupation and work with thine own hands.'[29] When he considered the poor, he was more inclined than Tyndale to restrict alms giving to those who were idle only through physical defect. But he urged generosity to those who qualified, for the 'rich man was not damned because he despoiled another man's, but because he did not distribute his own.'[30] His intent in controlling alms giving was really to cut out 'idle-bellied' 'bishops, abbots, and spiritual possessionaries' who were 'double thieves and murderers.' His spleen was vented on orders of begging friars. Frith maintained that none, including friars, should be idle, and that the mundane works of all people were as good as prayers or preaching. To forestall criticism, he recounted the tale of Mary and Martha: 'Now if they object that they live in contemplation, and study of Scripture, and say that they ought not to be let from that holy work, for Christ said, that *Mary* had chosen the best part which should not be taken from her,' and immediately went on to tell the story of the holy abbot St Silvane who caused his monks 'to labour for their living' as well as pray.[31] One religious man came to the abbey and asked why the monks 'gave not themselves to holy contemplation, seeing that Mary had chosen the better part.' The abbot sent him to a cell to contemplate and did not call him when the other monks sat to dinner. When the man was hungry and asked why he had not been summoned, the abbot replied, 'I thought you had been all spiritual and had needed no meat.' If he was to eat, he must work. Frith's notion of vocation had elements absent in Luther and Tyndale.[32] His view was related less to a station in society and more to a notion of stewardship. He focused less on degree than on the use of gifts and talents employed for one's neighbour. His attention was on activity itself rather than on the place where it happened. Consequently, he was less critical of monastic orders. Rather than eliminating monasticism, he wished to reform it so that monks had a vocation of service to the needy.[33]

Neither Tyndale nor Frith used the terms 'vocation' or 'calling' to refer to the pursuits that they discussed. Tyndale preferred 'state,' 'degree,' 'place,' or 'office.' His 1534 translation of 1 Corinthians 7:20 read, 'in the same state wherein he was called.' However, their views were strikingly similar to the views of those who later did use such terminology, and they were a departure from the ideas then prevalent in England. The life of contemplation and leisure was denied, the two lives were combined, and everyday labour was elevated as a vocation on a par with prayer or preaching. But these early reformers merged the divine calling with the particular social setting in which it was manifested. Callings were conflated with the estates and degrees of society.

THE COMMONWEALTH PARTY

It was in the 'Commonwealth Party' that the idea of calling flowered in England. It formed the core of the party adherents' views on social duty, and then became widespread throughout the country.[34] In his *Voice of the Last Trumpet*, which called 'all Estates of men to the Right Path of their Vocation,' Robert Crowley, preacher and publisher, gave advice to 'twelve sorts of men,' including beggars, servants, yeomen, priests, learned men, lawyers, merchants, poor men, gentlemen, magistrates, and women [*sic*]. All had and occupied callings and were to be devoted to them.[35] He gave advice on how these people were to serve their neighbours and the Commonwealth, and on how they could avoid self-seeking:

First Walk in thy vocation,
And do not seek thy lot to change,
For through wicked ambition,
Many men's fortune hath been strange.

Even beggars were advised to 'Content thyself with that degree, / And see thou walk therein upright.'[36] On this basis he denounced all who sought to change or go beyond their vocation. This involved necessary submission from all inferiors. But he also used the doctrine of vocation to castigate those who sought to increase their estates, enclose, raise rents, buy more land, or in any way add to, rather than help overcome, the burdens of the poor.[37] Crowley maintained such views so consistently that in 1566 he was charged before Archbishop Parker with 'Anabaptistical opinions.'[38] He pictured the man who 'lieth in wait with the rich men of the villages or granges, in secret corners to slay the innocent. His eyes are fixed on the poor; he lieth await even as a lion in his den.' Merchants who bought farms drew particular condemnation. Crowley imagined that

merchants would meddle
with merchandise only
And leave farms to such men
as must live thereby
Then were they most worthy ...[39]

Such merchants had 'left their offices.' Any scheme of rationalizing agriculture or any desire for advancement drew his ire and condemnation. The ambitious merchant was thus castigated:

what shouldst thou desire more,
Or of higher estate to be
Let it suffice thee to marry
Thy daughter to one of thy trade ...
And let thy sons every one
Be bound prentice years nine or ten ...
To learn some art to live upon:[40]

As for the covetous: 'Your greedy gut could never stint, / Till all the good and fruitful ground, / were hedged in within your mound.' They were 'Cormorants, greedy gulls ... churlish chickens.'[41]

Crowley was the strongest exponent of such sentiments, but his fellow preacher, Thomas Lever, was almost as stringent. He took the example of rich men whom God had endowed with great riches, but who could 'not be content with the prosperous wealth of that vocation to satisfy themselves ... but ... must abroad in the country to buy farms out.' Such people were 'never ... content with their vocation, but ... at a beck of their father the devil.'[42] Bishop Hugh Latimer echoed these sentiments. He took pains (as did Crowley and Lever) to protect himself from charges of communism. He combined these views in his social theory: 'God is not my God alone, he is a common God ... I cannot say, "This is my own"; but I must say, "This is ours." For the rich man cannot say, "This is mine alone, God hath given it unto me for my own use." Nor yet hath the poor man any title to it, to take it away from him ... when God rendeth me much, it is not mine, but ours.'[43]

These themes pervaded the sermons of Bishops Thomas Becon, John Hooper, John Bradford, and Roger Hutchinson.[44] They all also placed high stress on the virtues of labour. Crowley thought idleness 'the gate of all mischief.' Latimer even gave, for him, uncharacteristic support of the poor laws: 'Therefore those Lubbers which will not labour, and might labour, it is a good thing to punish them according to the King's most godly statutes.' He held that 'we must labour and travail; as long as we be in this world we must be occupied.'[45] Thomas Becon believed that 'no man in a Christian commonwealth ought to be idle, but to do some good thing unto the glory of God, and to the relief of the poor, be he never so rich and wealthy.' 'Our Saviour Christ was a carpenter. His apostles were fishermen. St. Paul was a tent-maker ...'[46]

The core of the Commonwealth divines' view of labour, poverty, oppression, degree, and duty, as well as of the structure of society itself, was a view of calling. The majority gave specific attention to the notion.[47] However, in spite of this, they were usually quite vague about its nature. Thomas Becon spoke of it as 'the manner of life unto which God hath called thee ...' or else as 'every kind of life in which we exercise faith and charity.' He also thought of it as a political commission as by 'common consent (as mayors and other officers).' Apart from these, he spoke of callings as 'certain honest and godly states and degrees wherein thy people should live.' He distinguished a 'general' and a 'particular' calling, a terminology later to become common; but for him the general was the call to salvation and the particular was 'any manner of benefit, office or ministration.'[48] Hooper thought of vocations as offices, and he spoke of 'public' and 'private' ones. He even spoke of 'the vocation of bawds, idolators ... etc.' Hutchinson spoke of offices and occupations. He maintained that God 'alloweth every man one vocation, one office and occupation, not many; for he saith *in vocatione*, "in his vocation," not "in his vocations."' Latimer distinguished a general vocation from a special one. The former was like that of a fisherman; the latter was a particular spiritual task such as evangelism. Crowley appeared to equate a calling with an estate, and he continually urged labour *in* rather than *at* a calling. However, he occasionally broke with this pattern, maintained 'that thy calling is to do service,' and emphasized particular duties and offices.[49] These examples could be multiplied, producing an array of confused conceptions. Rather than try to outline this diversity, which has few consistent patterns, I conclude with some observations on the general trends of early-sixteenth-century views.

CONCLUSIONS: THE DIFFERENCES OF HUMANIST AND EVANGELICAL

The more radical Protestants were more stringent critics of social injustice and made a more wholehearted plea for the poor than did their theological adversaries.[50] Indeed, there appears to be a correlation in that the more radically Protestant a figure was, the stronger his social criticism was likely to be. In addition, the reformers' elevation and sanctification of the labours of all people, as well as their view that while all estates were in hierarchy, all callings were equal, not only contained implicit subversive tendencies but also, in their own hands, were put to use as tools for criticizing oppression.

Their criticism has often been described as 'medieval' or reactionary; and since much of their verbal assault was medieval in tone, there is something to such labels.[51] However, much more needs to be said. One Protestant innovation was the doctrine of calling, a distinctly unmedieval notion. This conception not only directed attention to work as the centre of spirituality, but also, by asserting that all works were equally pleasing to God, undercut some of the basis of hierarchical order. While the reformers certainly did not want to upset degree, they introduced the element of brother to brother and sister to sister into the scheme of master and servant, ruler and subject. This shift was neither conservative, with some exceptions, nor medieval; yet it formed the core of early Protestant social theory.

In England, views of vocation of the general type that Luther had propounded became accepted by Protestants. However, in this acceptance certain elements were lost. The result was an uneasy fusion of the medieval hierarchical doctrine of estates with a newer equalitarian doctrine of calling. To a large degree a calling became viewed as something immanent in society rather than as a call to specific duties which come to one in a social position. Consequently, it was repeatedly emphasized that everybody had to remain in his or her calling and estate.[52] The Protestants associated the centrality of work and the equality of callings with conceptions of submission, degree, mutuality, and charity in an organic picture of the commonwealth. In general a calling was what each person had by virtue of being a member of society. But now all social stations and all types of work were equal before God and required equal human devotion. The doctrine of the two lives was abandoned. Contemplation and leisure were dethroned, while work – especially the labour of the hands – was uplifted. All work was directly a divine task.

This development shows some essential differences between humanist and Protestant, or evangelical, figures. Recently, the originality of Protestantism has been downplayed, and these groups have been seen as essentially two phases of one overall movement. Quentin Skinner concluded that the Commonwealth Party merely took up and developed the questions set by the humanists and emphasized that there was 'a close spiritual connection between humanism and the puritan movement.'[53] In his view evangelical doctrines were relatively sterile in their original social import. More recently, Margo Todd has maintained that all the social principles of Protestantism, including Puritanism, can be found in their inheritance from Christian humanism.[54] However, these studies seem to have mistakenly aggregated two distinct movements, for in comparison with the More circle, the Protestants were hectic and busy.[55] The Protestant vocabulary of and emphasis on callings, on the equality and dignity of all types of labour, and on the superiority of labour over a contemplative form of life had no humanist counterpart.[56] The Protestant pattern of reform was to call all persons to their duty, and to drive them to labour in their estate and calling. The humanist pattern was one of the education of the ruler and the elevation of the wise and virtuous to positions of authority, a pattern the humanists themselves sought to exemplify.[57]

4

Work, Rationality, and Calling: Puritans and Nonconformists

'ANGLICANS' AND 'PURITANS'

In comparing the development of views about calling we need to have some means of classifying the proponents of various tendencies. This brings us to the vexed questions of the views held by 'Puritans' and the meaning, if any, of the term 'Puritan.' Thirty years ago Perry Miller remarked that 'Most accounts of Puritanism, emphasizing the controversial tenets, attribute everything the Puritans said and did to the fact that they were Puritans; their attitudes towards all sorts of things are pounced upon and exhibited as peculiarities of the sect, when as a matter of fact they were normal attitudes of the time.[1] While Miller had the American context in mind, the same caveat can be applied to contemporary studies of English Puritanism. In addition, the very term 'Puritan' has long been a controversial one. Indeed, some have suggested that it be abandoned altogether. However, as Margo Todd has pointed out, historians who avoid the term usually end up using substitute terms to do substantially the same duty.[2] For instance, Conrad Russell maintains that the 'custody battle' over the Church of England 'cannot be described as one between "Anglicans" and "Puritans" without begging every question which was at issue. This is because the division was one 'between rival claimants to the title of orthodox' in which the label 'Puritan' was a 'polemical weapon' to 'deny orthodoxy' to those so labelled. Consequently, he thinks the term says more about those who used it than about those against whom it was used and so should be avoided. In seeking to elucidate one group of participants in the custody battle, he prefers the term 'the godly' to describe 'the hotter sort of Protestants.'[3] Much of the debate is concerned with questions as to whether 'Puritanism' constituted an ecclesiastical party or contributed to a political movement. If we are not concerned with these questions, as I am not, but rather with the degree to which Protestant commitments brought new vocational views, then it is not clear how much is gained by this change of nomenclature. 'The hotter sort of Protestant' is precisely my concern, and it is a common enough meaning of 'Puritan.' Provided we remember Russell's and similar strictures about the actual role 'Puritans' may have played in the church, we can use the term to refer to 'hotter' Protestants. I will use a variation of Basil Hall's broad typification: 'restlessly critical ... members of the Church of England who desired some modifications in church government and worship, but not ... those who removed themselves from that Church.'[4] These members thought that opponents in the Church of England still retained too many attachments to Roman ways and pressed for a more clearly Protestant practice. While this description does not and is not intended to mark out a very clearly defined group with sharp boundaries, it does point to a definite tendency among particular divines of the period. Of course, there were many whose position in such a spectrum would not be clear and others for whom it would have little relevance. But there are enough who clearly fall into this category. In this chapter I will refer to those commonly acknowledged to be Puritans, and I will include Presbyterian-oriented Elizabethan figures such as Cartwright, Travers, and Dering. After the Restoration, I will consider Nonconformists of the stripe of Baxter.

'Anglican' is also a difficult and somewhat anachronistic term. It was not known in England until 1635, and it was used to describe a reality not really known before then.[5] In addition, except for the post-Restoration Nonconformists, all the Puritans that I discuss were committed members of the Church of England and so in one sense at least were 'Anglican' themselves. In using the term 'Anglican,' I mean those who defended the existing settlement and normative practice of the church against hotter sorts of Protestants.

PERSISTING PATTERNS

There were variations in Puritan views of calling from person to person and also over time, but several features remained relatively constant. First there was a consistent distinction between a 'general calling,' which was for all and which required the fulfilment of all Christian duties, and the 'particular calling.' The latter formed part of God's order for society.[6] Indeed, at times its arrangement seemed to be seen *as* the order of society itself, for 'God – bindeth all men – to be confined within some certain state and condition of life – (and) – man should use the place and office assigned unto him –. In this manner hath God disposed the whole estate of mankind.'[7] Within this framework, the Puritans generally regarded society as having three aspects: 'a three-fold society – church, commonwealth, and family. In all there are several ranks and places. In the church, officers and private members; in the commonwealth, magistrates and people; in the family, masters and servants, parents and children, husband and wife.'[8] Even when, as among the later Puritans, callings were understood primarily in terms of economic matters (as trades, employments, and so forth), there was still little attempt to reconstruct this tripartite division.[9] Within these three aspects, God had established various social stations and had appointed men and women to carry out the duties which were requisite to their station. Society was viewed as a body or organization with each part carrying out its particular duties or functions. At times, this model tended to create an image of society which was less organic than mechanical. Analogies to clocks began to appear, and the use of military analogies was also common.[10] This viewpoint contributed to a developed understanding of the division of labour in society. So Stephen Charnock wrote, 'as there is a distinction of several creatures – so among men there are several inclinations and several abilities, as donatives from God, for the common advantage of human society – one man is qualified for one employment, another marked out by God for a different work – all men – mutually return an advantage to one another – so the variety – is a fruit of the wisdom of God for the preservation and subsistence of the world by mutual commerce.'[11] In this conception all tasks were essential and interdependent, no matter how mean or laborious they might be.[12]

This emphasis on the division of labour complemented an intense preoccupation with work and its virtues. All men were to work long, hard, diligently, and 'painfully.' Indeed, as Christopher Hill pointed out, many Puritans, including Perkins, Dod and Cleaver, Dent, Preston, Baxter, and Milton, developed something of a labour theory of value.[13] It was emphasized that, not only do we obey God's commandments in our calling; we also support and give to the commonwealth, our neighbours, our family, and, not least, ourselves.[14] Obedience and labour were focused in the particular station where God had placed each one. Each must attend to his or her own duties, not another's: 'bear your own fruit, work in your own hives, man your own oars, and make good your own standing.'[15] Others must likewise not seek to invade our duties. No idleness was allowed, and all time and effort were strictly organized to achieve the maximum service and to avoid those 'open spaces' which could be temptations to and occasions of sin. We must 'painfully employ ourselves in the works of our calling, that so we may have no leisure to entertain Satan's deception.'[16] Even recreation, when allowed, was permitted for its possible stimulus to renewed energy in a calling. Time and the use of time were strictly controlled and weighed, sometimes checked even to the minute.[17] Idleness was reprobation of the worst kind. Monks and friars were not tolerated, as they did not work for a living and did not support themselves. They were 'leeches' upon the truly godly, who were those who supported themselves, their family, the church, and the commonwealth.[18] The attitude to the poor, especially beggars, was often harsh.

This attitude was not necessarily directed to the poor generally, but almost universally a distinction was made between the two different kinds of poor who asked for alms. One group consisted of those who were too old, sick, lame, or weak, or who had too mean a living to be able to subsist: 'these are poor who, having something and taking pains, yet cannot from it make sufficient supply of their wants.' These sorts of poor were to be supported and loved even as if they were Christ.[19] The other group were those who were able-bodied and yet jobless. The Puritans did not appear able to conceive the possibility that work might be unavailable, and so this sort of poor were regarded as 'rats' and 'weasels' in the corn. They were considered lazy, dissolute, veritable 'drones' in the hive of the commonwealth. They were usually given neither sympathy nor support, but were often subjected to punishment and compulsion.

Because time and effort were so carefully husbanded, no waste was allowed. Material resources were to be arranged so that the most efficient use could be made of them. Flamboyancy in apparel, gluttony in food, and ornamentation in estate were condemned.[20] Surplus should be given to the church and the deserving poor, or else kept.[21] The whole tenor of callings was an amazingly busy one. Society was viewed as composed of men and women, all in their allotted tasks, labouring arduously throughout the full six days that God had given them. The conception of holy days in addition to the Sabbath was opposed, as it would cut into the time available for pursuing particular callings.[22] These well-known features constituted the general pattern of Puritan views of calling. However, what is perhaps of more interest is the change – the evolution – in concepts that took place within this general framework.[23] I will try to outline this evolution, beginning with the views of Elizabethan Puritans.

ELIZABETHAN TIMES

There was a certain ambiguity among the Puritans of Elizabethan times as to the exact status of a calling. Within their writings, certain historical threads were run together. There appeared traces of Luther's view of a work of faith to be pursued in the work of one's station, Calvin's view of the work of one's station as itself being a service to God, and the earlier English view of callings as the estates of society. All of these were inter-twined in some complexity and confusion.

Firstly, callings were seen as *states* of life. William Perkins said that 'a vocation or calling is a certain kind of life ordained and imposed on man by God for the common good.' It appears that Perkins did not equate calling with station or estate; rather, he meant the particular duties that God requires of us in our estate. So, he said, it is 'a certain manner or order of leading our lives in this world. For example, the life of a king is to spend his time in the governing of his subjects, and that is his calling ... In a word that particular, and honest manner of conversation whereunto every man is called, and set apart, that is (I say) his calling.'[24] However, as Perkins devel-oped his treatise he implied a somewhat different meaning. He spoke of those callings and estates of life which have no warrant from God's word as 'unlawful.' If calling were an 'honest manner ... that God requires of us,' it is difficult to see how it could be 'against the word of God.' It seems that Perkins here used calling to mean something like a 'state' or a 'manner of living' generally.[25] This was further confirmed when he related the particu-lar and the general callings: 'every particular calling must be practised in, and with the general calling of a Christian'; 'the particular calling, and prac-tice of the duties thereof, severed from the foresaid general calling, is noth-ing else but a practice of injustice and profaneness.' Here we have the 'duties' of a calling, whereas before he referred to callings as 'duties' them-selves. Perkins went on to refer to how one may 'in a good and holy man-ner use his calling.' In fact, even two callings could be entered, which seems to imply that Perkins was thinking of occupations rather than 'manners of life.'[26] Perkins fused two different ideas of calling. He saw calling as honest, faithful labour *in* a God-given state; but he also saw it *as* that state, or the work of that state itself, which work must hence be rendered honest. There appeared to be a fusion of the English Reformation idea of calling as estates with the Lutheran, and semi-Calvinian, idea of calling as godly duty.

A similar concatenation of ideas appears when we consider the teaching that each must abide in his or her calling. Perkins said clearly: 'let every man continue in that calling wherein he was called unto Christ; that is, wherein he walked and lived when it pleased God ... to call him unto the profession of Christian religion.' He reinforced this view in sundry places by saying that God 'First – ordaineth the calling itself and secondly he imposeth it on the man called.' People were bound to their calling not only in the sense that they must keep the same one but also in the further sense that all work must be done within the bounds of the calling: 'Whatsoever is not done within the compass of a calling is not of faith'; 'a man must first have some warrant and Word of God to assure him of his calling, before he can do it in faith.'[27] Certain exceptions were made for some activities which fell outside a particular calling. Recreation was allowed as long as it was edifying, and different duties were allowed on the Sabbath. Apart from these situations, however, everyone was required to be hard at work.[28]

The thrust of this teaching was at one level quite conservative. People had to continue in whatever they were doing when they became Christians. God had given them their task, and they must remain in it and accomplish all their works solely within its bounds. However, in this case as well there was another side, for one could choose a vocation: 'we are to choose honest and lawful callings to work in'; 'every man must choose a fit calling.' Perkins could easily square this view with the idea that God had chosen people's callings and chosen people for them, for when people choose their calling rightly then they know that God has already chosen them.[29] What is more difficult to square with the idea of choosing one's calling was the view that each must abide in the calling that he or she was already in. This might be easier in the case of children, who were not yet in a calling, but even here it was at least implied that they didn't necessarily follow in the family tradition. However, Perkins considered not only children but also the choice of 'men of years,' and he believed that one of the circumstances which could enter into the choice of a calling was 'affection.' So Perkins advised the Christian that 'he must search what mind he hath to any calling, and in what calling he desireth most of all to glorify God.'[30] What you desire could be a factor in your choice of calling.

On the one hand, he was saying that each should abide in his or her calling, much in the manner of those who had gone before him in England. Yet, on the other hand, he also introduced the voluntarism with respect to callings that had been hinted at by Calvin. Perkins developed the notion even further when he sought to answer the question: 'Whether a man may lawfully and with good conscience use Pollicie in the affaires of this life.' The meaning of 'Pollicie' in this instance was that of planning, making a wise choice; that is, not just following a regular, given path, but comparing options, weighing them, and making decisions. In this context the question itself is revealing, for the presumed questioner obviously had doubts about the practice of 'pollicie,' and was caught between a traditional world of clear, ascriptive paths and a newer pluralist world of greater flexibility and openness. Perkins was far short of commending a masterless man, for he said, 'All actions of policie, must be such as pertain to our calling, and be within the limits and bonds thereof.' The policy must not be 'that which I commonly called the policie of Machiavel.' But, provided these conditions were met, it was permissible to inquire 'into our selves, whether the work in hand be agreeable to the calling of the doer.' Perkins was quite open to right 'pollicie' and responsibility in the manifold choices of a profession.[31] Overall, he had a moderate position. Each must abide but can, within limits, choose. His view was not completely that of a static system of callings but was one which had developed an openness to human gifts and inclinations. This ambiguity continued in the view of the equality of callings.

All callings were ordained by God. God's special providence, 'which is the watch of the great world,' allotted 'to every man his motion and calling.' The end of all these callings was to glorify God, to sustain the commonwealth, and to 'tend to the happy and good estate ... of all men everywhere.' The implication of these remarks was that all callings were of equal importance. So 'the action of a sheepherd in keeping sheep ... is as good work before God, as is the action of a judge in giving sentence, or of a magistrate in ruling, or a minister in preaching.'[32] However, Perkins also said things in tension with this emphasis on the equality of callings. He spoke of 'the most *weighty* callings in the family, church or commonwealth.' These 'weighty' callings appeared to be those that were 'the essence and foundation of any society, without which the society cannot be: as in a family, the calling of a master and the calling of a servant, the calling of a husband and wife, of parents and children; and in the commonwealth the calling of a magistrate and subjects; and in the church the calling of the minister and the people.' As for the other callings, they 'serve *only* for the good, happy and quiet estate of a society. And these be of sundry sorts ... as the calling of an husbandman, of a merchant, etc. ... a physician ... the surgeon ... a soldier, the lawyer, etc.'[33] This distinction was a functional one, but another classification was also made consisting of those who were 'fit for sundry callings.' These fortunate people 'must make choice of the best.' 'If we are to seek after the best gifts ... we must seek for the best callings.' The ones who had the ability to be so flexible were mainly 'young students in the universities': 'They have liberty to be either schoolmasters, physicians or lawyers, or ministers of the word of God.'[34] A form of status differentiation had appeared within which the young who were able to go to university were now able to make some choice of 'better' callings.

Election and salvation occasionally became related to callings. This view is something on which Weber had placed great stress, but it is one that is not found in any figures before these Puritans. Perkins said, 'if thou would-est have signs and tokens of thy election and salvation, thou must fetch them from the constant practice of thy two callings jointly together.' He was not saying that works contribute towards salvation, a view anathema to any Calvinist, but rather that they may be a sign. Further, the 'signs' of the calling were not worldly successes, in the sense of fame or riches, but rather they were the diligent performances of work. It should also be noted that Perkins made few comments like this. It was certainly not a major theme in his writings.[35]

The earlier Puritans were emphatic that riches themselves must not be the goal of callings. Indeed, 'Covetousness is a notorious vice whereby all men, almost, apply their callings and the works thereof to the gathering of wealth and riches. This is one of the head and master sins of the world ...' 'Now when in the works of our calling we intend only to get wealth, we do, as it were, set bars on heaven's gates.' Riches themselves were seen as neutral, so that poverty was certainly not advocated. The greatest emphasis was on the diligent preservation of an estate. For this we may 'desire and seek for goods necessary.'[36] Perkins also gave advice on how to use riches, and how one should give alms. Giving should be directed to 'First, the maintenance of our own good estate and conditions ... Second the good of others, specially family ... thirdly the relief of the poor ... fourthly, the maintenance of the commonwealth.' This does not appear to be an order of priority, for it is difficult to imagine Perkins putting the church only in fourth position when he usually put it first on any such list. Nevertheless, it is a trifle disconcerting to read, 'First, the maintenance of our own good estate,' under the category of 'giving'![37] The overall situation was that, while the Puritans condemned seeking abundance and suggested certain conditions when one must forsake wealth, it was possible to follow their teachings without diminishing one's estate, provided that one eschewed the 'love ... of riches.'

A great deal of weight was placed on the fact that a calling was labour. When Perkins said, 'labour in a calling is as precious as Gold or Silver' he was not being purely metaphorical. He went on to say that 'our people' have a common saying that 'Occupation is as good as land, because land may be lost, but skill and labour in good occupation is profitable to the end because it will help at a need when land and all things fail.'[38] The link of labour and profitability was stressed often. This emphasis on labour, and on restraint, shows a sense of how difficult life could be. God 'imposeth [the calling] – on men.' He will 'bind men to their callings'; each must 'bear public callings.' Roger Fenton spoke of God's 'intolerable ordinance' which 'hath bound us to travail.' Their language evokes images of bondage, burden, and pain. While the earlier Puritans certainly emphasized the dignity of labour, they did not downplay its penal quality.[39] Labour was seen both as God given and as a source of value. But it was also a burden and, perhaps, a cross. Anyone who followed all the Puritans' proffered guidance needed to be prepared for a life of constant and earnest toil, repressing desire for fashion, riches, comfort, and, often, rest.

These earlier views of calling were not precisely defined and delineated ideas but were rather the uneasy ravelling of several strands. Calling was an estate, but also the work of an estate, but also a godly duty which one followed in the work of an estate. People must stay in their callings, but they could have preferences and choose among them. All estates were equal but some were better than others. God's choice of some to salvation was also manifested as a duty to be followed. It appears that the Puritans were drawing unconsciously on several different sources as they tried to relate to changing social orderings. They drew on an earlier English view of callings as God-given estates which were sites for duty, and also on the Lutheran view of calling as a manner of life to be lived in such estates. They took the traditional view of abiding in one's station, but they also sought to help those who could choose employments and not just accept a given status. They saw all callings as equal in the sight of God, but also thought that, as social roles, some callings were better than others. They saw labour as a service to God in a calling but also as a source of wealth as good as land or treasure. They could not seek riches, but they had to make enough to maintain their estate. They took the Calvinist notion of effectual calling and then hinted at it also as a duty to God.[40] They were people aware that society had developed some openness and that the purely traditional advice to 'abide in your callings' was not quite sufficient to meet the situation. There was a consequent tension between a relatively static and a more flexible view of the degree of individuality – judgment – allowed in the human duty to God.[41]

THE EARLY SEVENTEENTH CENTURY

While many of the motifs of Elizabethan Puritanism continued after the turn of the century, certain new elements appeared. First, between the turn of the century and the Civil War, callings were understood more in the sense of employments. The words 'trade,' 'employment,' 'occupation,' 'calling,' and 'vocation' became interchangeable.[42] A calling, originally understood as the particular duties required by God of man in a station, was now becoming objectified within the social order. Its duties became the honest duties performed by everybody in such an occupation. The normative guidelines for work tended to flow less and less from the particular commands of God and more and more from the particular duties and roles which were current in the society. The particular locus of this objectification, as an *employment*, should also be noted. Whereas the English Reformers had tended to objectify the calling in terms of one's estate or station, the emphasis in the early seventeenth century was much more on one's *activity*. Although the word 'estate' still occurred frequently, it usually referred not to a calling but rather to the social *basis* for one. The thrust was less on accepting a place in society and more on choosing and pursuing a useful trade.[43] One manifestation of this objectification was the use of the term 'ordinary' to describe callings. There could be 'special' or 'spiritual' callings such as the ministry or an extraordinary command of God. In contrast to these, the 'particular' callings were seen as mundane and as part of the general social arrangements. One was an 'ordinary' tradesman, filling the place appointed in God's providence, doing an ordinary task, albeit diligently and piously.[44]

Along with this growing identification of callings with the existing division of labour, there developed a greater voluntarism of callings. In the earlier Puritans, despite some ambivalence, the dominant view was that one either took the station which had been ascribed by one's family or society, or else continued to serve in the calling that one was in when one became a Christian. But now a Christian was urged, 'always be you tied to some labor and business.' The tone almost appeared to suggest *any* calling. Children could choose their callings. The idea of a determinate calling was downplayed. The concern now was rather at least to do *something*.[45] This element of voluntarism found an echo in the contingency noted by Thomas Scott. Greatly concerned with an anti-papist foreign policy, he envisaged a situation where there was no calling and yet maintained 'that necessity supplies the place of an ordinary calling and warrants the undertaking of any action for the avoiding of a certain mischief.' Here the notion of calling had been so situated in the given structure of the society that it could no longer supply guidance for action in abnormal circumstances. A doctrine of action under necessity now had to fill the gap it left.[46]

Another area where there was innovation concerned the attitude towards riches. Admonitions to beware of ambition and riches were still preponderant. Samuel Hieron counselled, 'should I strive to lade myself with this thick clay, still plotting to set my nest on high, when all that I have or can have is in a moment turned into vanity?' However, the emphasis on the preservation of one's estate was also strong: 'liberality must not devour herself – our property in them must not be altered,' and there was more openness to acquiring riches.[47]

Riches also lost something of their neutrality and became something of a positive good. So Robert Bolton said, 'true Christians – love riches, honour, knowledge and the like, not that they might – domineer in the world – but – give the more enlargement to God's glory, and furthermore to good causes, – perform more good works – and more honorable service to the majesty of heaven.'[48] Not only was there more openness to riches, but Christians were taught to seek them, within limits. Paul Bayne sought to show how true faith and a mind at peace with God led to 'lawful prospering' and 'Christian gaining'; he maintained that the 'true way of thriving' was 'walking in the way of God's commandments.' John Trapp admonished his readers 'to exceed and excel others – to be their crafts masters, to bear away the bell from all that are of the same trade or profession.' William Scott advised a 'Holy Avarice' so that the Christian 'by every man with whom he shall trade, he may benefit his mind [i.e., business acumen] something.' Richard Rogers wanted a 'godly thrift.'[49] Not only was the honest pursuit of prosperity allowed, but frequently it was expected that such a pursuit would be successful. 'Note, then, that walking in our calling, by the blessing of God, is beneficial unto us. Labour is painful, but God doth sweeten it with the gain it bringeth: "The diligent hand maketh rich."' 'In earthly things we will take the occasion of our gain, redeeming it with loss of pleasure.'[50] Here the riches to be expected have almost been paid for by the loss of pleasure involved, a feature not wholly to be discounted despite the more frequent admonitions that we owe all our blessings to God. If diligence as a calling often, though not always, leads to prosperity, then poverty might be a result of sin. Such a view appeared and, hence, the poor 'must not therefore disenable the godly course, to which they owe all that blessing they have, but blame their own ungodliness, when they reap that correction which themselves have sowed.'[51] There was certainly no one-to-one correlation of sin and poverty, any more than there was of godliness and riches.[52] Nevertheless, there was an implicit idea that the two pairings could not be wholly unconnected.

Despite these innovations, most of the Puritan writing of the first half of the seventeenth century continued the same motifs that were present in the preceding decades. It was still often held that all people must have callings, that they must stay in the same calling, and that they must confine their works to the bounds of their calling. Many of the writings are indistinguishable from those of the Elizabethan era.[53] The strength of the new developments – of the identification of calling and employment, of the evolving voluntarism of callings, and of the openness to the pursuit of riches – should not be exaggerated. These views were not universal. However, they were present, and were present in a way that they had not been in previous years. Where these shoots really flowered, together with some further adaptations, was in the latter half of the seventeenth century.

THE POST-RESTORATION PERIOD

The objectification of the calling which had taken place in the earlier part of the century developed later to such a point that a separation between religion and calling began to take place. In some instances the calling became less a command of God and more an allowance from Him. 'As if God had said "I am not an hard master, I do not grudge the time to look after thy calling, and to get an estate – I might have reserved six days for myself and allowed thee but one, but I have given thee six days for the work of the calling, and have taken but one day for my own service."' No longer only an allowance, the calling has appeared here as something *apart from* the direct service of God. Along these lines Thomas Watson also advised that 'A Christian must not only mind heaven, but his calling.' John Owen played off spirituality and the work of the calling against one another. He feared lest he should be thought 'too severe' for urging that 'men's thoughts of spiritual things should exceed them that are employed about their lawful callings.'[54] Indeed the term 'secular' now made an appearance in the description of particular callings. Watson said, 'you have done all your secular work on the six days, you should now cease from the labor of your calling, and dedicate the seventh day to the Lord.'[55]

A manifestation of this secularization was a cleavage which developed between the general and particular callings. Earlier the particular had been a facet of and something *within* the general calling. Richard Sibbes had described 'our particular calling wherein we are to express the graces of our Christian calling,' while John Knewstub viewed it as 'a more particular duty' of the general.[56] But now the two callings could be seen as existing alongside one another. For William Gurnall, one of the manifestations of 'the power of holiness' was that 'the Christian's particular calling doth not encroach upon his general. – The world is of an encroaching nature, hard it is to converse with it – so will our worldly employments jostle with our heavenly.' John Flavel urged, 'Be not so intent upon your particular callings, as to make them interfere with your general calling.' Timothy Cruso, a schoolmate of Daniel Defoe who had his surname borrowed for posterity, cautioned: 'let *religion* be the *main business* and employment of your lives.' 'Consider that your *General Calling* as Christians, is of more concern, than your *particular Vocation* as Men. Let Spiritual things have the constant precedency to *Temporal*.'[57]

As can be seen from these examples, callings were understood primarily as being employments and trades in, and often *of*, the world. Richard Steele gave advice not to 'accumulate two or three callings.'[58] Since callings were now not so much a particular aspect of spiritual works as something alongside them, there was a question as to whether Christians must have them. Matthew Henry thought we might 'have much to do or little to do in the world.' John Owen envisaged 'some who have neither necessity nor occasion to be engaged much in the duties of any special calling,' and maintained that 'they who are wise will be at home as much as they can.'[59] However, the dominant view was still that each person should have a particular calling.[60] Nevertheless, despite this continuity, at least one important change had taken place. In this later period, the admonition that each should have a calling did not mean that each had and must perform the particular Christian duties appropriate to his or her station. Nor did it mean that each should (primarily) have a particular 'manner of life,' including being husband or wife. Rather it had come to mean that each Christian must *have a job or trade* and labour long and hard at it. The particular jobs which Christians had to take were ascriptively determined. They were matters of choice and, consequently, lengthy advice was proffered on how to choose a calling. What was occasional and implicit earlier was now common and quite explicit. God's aims for human lives now became manifest not in the traditional patterns of the family, nor in the situation of one's conversion, nor, necessarily, in some inward vocation. Rather, they appeared 'in the various inclinations and conditions – the several abilities of men. Some are inspired with a particular genius for one art, some for another; every man hath a distinct talent.'[61] This relation to talent meant that callings could appear less equal. This was true not only in terms of their contribution to the commonwealth but also occasionally in terms of the worth of those who pursued them; for 'some men's spirits are fitted for handicrafts and hard manual labours, to which men of a higher spirit and delicate breeding will not condescend.' The best callings seldom appeared to involve working with one's hands. Luther's glorification of the *Beruf* of the peasant and the workshop now appeared to be nearing the end of its road.[62]

If callings were seen as jobs, and some jobs were better than others, then some sprightly soul might want to change jobs. This was certainly allowable. Matthew Poole took great pains to avoid a too-literal interpretation of the text on which the more traditional view had leaned for support, the Apostle Paul's injunction to 'abide in the calling in which you were called' (1 Cor. 7:20). 'They too far strain this text who interpret it into an obligation upon all men, not to alter that particular way or course of life and trading to which they were educated, or in which they formally had been engaged.' Such a change is of 'great moment,' but it may be taken provided there is 'just advice and deliberation.'[63] Such a change was allowed because the world and occupations were seen to be so changeable. In fact they were mobile: 'For look as the *Flower-de-luce* in the compass turns now this way, then that way, and never ceases moving till it settle to the north-point; just so it is with our settlements in this world. A child is now designed for this, then for that – How strangely are things wheeled about by providence.'[64] The providence by which people once understood their place in society to be fixed was now seen to be something that wheels them about. In such a mobile society, it was not only the force of necessity which led to a change of calling. The idea of upward social mobility also appeared. Christians were urged to get on in the world, to 'thrive': 'Industry and diligence is the way to thrive and grow rich in the world.' In this pursuit Christian graces will produce success; 'He that will be a rich must be a painful Christian'; 'The true way to prosperity is to commend our affairs to God by prayer'; 'submission and humility is the true way to exaltation.'[65] To be a Christian also helps in getting on.

The riches which were so acquired were of great value in the Christian life: 'Yea, riches with a blessing are so far from being a hindrance to grace, that they are an ornament to it – A rich wise man is more conspicuous; an estate may adorn virtue – A wise man that is rich hath an advantage to discover himself which others have not.' According to Thomas Manton's commentary on James 1:10, 'the rich, in that he is made low: because as the flower of the grass he shall pass away.' This would have been a golden opportunity to digress on any faults which might be found with riches and with rich men, but he did not develop this theme. George Swinnock echoed Manton: 'Godliness is profitable in prosperity: it giveth a spiritual right to temporal good things.' Richard Baxter advised, 'We should choose a gainful calling rather than another' for, if we do not, we 'cross one of the ends of our calling and are not good stewards.' Thomas Goodwin went so far as to say that man's 'reasonable soul,' which distinguished him from the beasts, was manifested in his ability 'to rise to higher objects – to put a valuation upon honours, riches and the like.'[66] The desire was not for great wealth but for a kind of security. As Richard Steele put it: 'Many a man hath gone to heaven out of a palace, and very many out of a cottage; but the middle state is the safest.'[67] As godliness often leads to riches, then poverty must often be caused by idleness and a dissolute life. John Flavel thought that this might not always be so, for 'God sometimes disappoints the most diligent men in their lawful callings.' However his 'sometimes' reveals that generally the diligent Christian could be expected to prosper, and riches could be seen as God's blessing.[68]

This sanguine view of riches had a reciprocal effect on the understanding of more spiritual pursuits. One result was an abundance of commercial metaphor in soteriological writing. George Swinnock spoke of 'this great landlord of the world [who] must needs deserve and expect a considerable rent of honour and service, somewhat suitable to the vast charge he hath been at.' Flavel compared the soul before God with the situation of the man on pins because a lawsuit is threatening the credentials of the deed to his estate: 'When your title is cleared, your hearts are eased; yea, not only eased but overjoyed.'[69] This understanding went beyond metaphor and became analogy. One result was a quite commercial understanding of redemption. More emphasis was given to the place of works in salvation. Even Richard Baxter at this point is perhaps better described as an Amyraldian rather than a true Calvinist.[70] Edward Bury advised, 'When others only wish for heaven, do thou work for it.' This was a position on the efficacy of good works in salvation which, while a minority one even in the late seventeenth century, was a view heretofore considered an abomination by the Calvinist tradition, and the principal alternative to it.[71]

When callings became understood as occupations, the original emphasis that one had to do a specific, divinely appointed task now appeared as a concern to do one's own *job* and no other. In short, one must *mind one's own business*. Richard Steele wrote, 'let [a man] be never so active out of his sphere, he will be at a great loss, if he do not keep his own vineyard, mind his own business.'[72] What we do out of our place 'is not acceptable to God'; 'we put ourselves from under God's protection.' 'God is not in that place or enterprise,' and 'it is dangerous.' Not only must we mind our own business but others had to mind theirs: 'we shall never be charged for not doing another's work'; 'it is not our sin that we do not supply another's negligence, by doing that which belongs not to our place – God requires no more than faithfulness in our place.' Indeed, 'there is poor comfort in suffering for doing that which was not the work of our place and calling – no comfort or countenance from God can be expected in [that] suffering.'[73] Thomas Scott's notion of 'necessity' had little place here. An individualism now gave content to the social mechanism. If I succeed or fail in my work it is my business. If you succeed or fail it is your business. You cannot come running to me for help, for it is 'dangerous' for me to supply your negligence; it is out of the place where God has set you and me. The former vision of the interdependent division of labour among people working in a godly fashion in their several estates and duties now became the interrelation of independent people working out their own salvation and prosperity.

Almost paradoxically, a further feature of the separation of spirituality and calling, besides the acceptance of the current social mores, was an increased otherworldliness. 'What though our outward man perish – that is our bodies and the outward state and condition of the whole man – care not – Thy relation unto ... Christ [is] of such a transcendent value in comparison to this other, as this should have no weight with thee to be regarded.' It is in this context that John Owen urged Christians to be at home in prayer as much as they could and maintained that they should be on spiritual guard, for 'other thoughts – about men's secular concernments – will frequently make an inroad on the way to heaven, to disturb the passengers and wayfaring men.'[74] This trend should be seen not as a contradiction of the secularized view of worldly employment but as its supplement. As the particular calling became more natural, the spiritual focus became concentrated in specifically pious duties. This concentration of religion in piety then reinforced the independence of worldly employment. Such employment was still a Christian duty but now much more in a derivative sense. A disjunction between creation and redemption was made, and the calling partook of God's creation *rather* than His redemption.[75] C. John Sommerville suggests that 'Labor could be regulated by religion, but it was no longer part of religion.'[76] This led to less normative control by religion on the affairs of the world. It was stressed that the creation was common to all and had its own dynamic. This natural world needed little additional advice from Christianity, apart from commands to be honest in pursuing trades and employments. Consequently, the calling in the natural sphere embraced the more general notions of mobility, thriving, riches, and success. These employments were not completely out on their own, however, for it was still God who required service in the world. The majority of godly preachers continued to urge their flocks to labour beyond the churchyard. The concentrated religious energy and asceticism which had urged Christians to live in the world, to labour there long and earnestly, to shun all idleness, and to eradicate all waste still permeated their ethics. In the unfolding of Puritanism, Christians were driven to labour painfully in the world while the limits on and guides to their conduct gradually dwindled and were absorbed into the general maxims of a thriving age. A developing race of earnest, trading, thriving, mobile Christian individuals was one end result.

CONCLUSIONS

Puritanism at large stressed that Christianity involved a distinct focus on work in the world: that vocations were a part of God's order and were to be used to serve God and to support oneself, one's family, and the commonwealth. This stress led to an increasingly mechanistic view of society and a deep awareness of, and support for, a society-wide division of labour. It also produced a continual emphasis on labour and the husbanding of time, with, on the other hand, a downgrading of recreation, a sharp criticism of idleness, and a growing suspicion of any poor but the weak and the lame. Particularly in the earlier Puritans these views were marked by ambiguity and tensions. The views of Luther and Calvin, which had previously been understood in England in terms of abiding and being dutiful in one's estate, were being combined with an openness towards new developments in the social structure. This latter attitude manifested itself in an individualism which sat uneasily with traditional views. The resulting doctrine was one which stressed individual responsibility in economic affairs but limited itself to recommending quiet labour in one's estate with a strong emphasis on being able to *preserve* that estate. Over time, however, the content of particular callings came less from God's word which challenged social patterns and more from social patterns which themselves revealed God's will. As society became more individualist, voluntarist, and secular, the content of Puritan callings kept pace. Business ethics were formed by moralizing and emphasizing the honest, diligent pursuit of practices lawful and current in the society. However, the strong belief that each should have a calling and should work diligently and efficiently in that calling meant that Christians were still pushed out firmly into the world to make their place in it.

5

Stability, Order, and Calling: The Anglicans

There was a large measure of agreement among Elizabethan Anglicans on matters related to vocations. Those who referred to callings treated them as God-given duties, though comparatively fewer Anglicans than Puritans gave much attention to these specific duties. Judging from the number of discussions, and the frequency with which the word itself was used, it appears that the question of callings was of less concern to the Anglican than the Puritan divines.[1] Some, such as John Norden, Matthew Sutcliffe, and Bishop John Woolton, were careful to make a distinction between general and particular callings. Most, however, did not.[2]

Bishop James Pilkington and others sometimes treated a vocation as an 'occupation,' but they were in the minority.[3] The dominant understanding of calling was a conflation of degree, estate, office, and duty. John Norden offered a prayer along these lines 'for God's direction in our callings':

O God of gods, O Father Great,
Thou guide of all degrees:
The high and low look up to thee
Attendant on their knees.
We have our being and our food,
Our wisdom and our skill,
Our high estate, all honour eke,
And callings at thy will.[4]

Similarly, Richard Hooker criticized the Puritan Walter Travers for having 'the bonds of an ordinary calling ... drawn like a purse.' Travers was more inclined to an occupational view, whereas for Hooker, a calling included all the duties that God required.[5] Like most Anglicans, he treated callings as social position and ascriptive duty rather than occupation and employment. This association of calling and degree set Elizabethan Anglicans in opposition to social mobility. The Puritans had been ambiguous on this point, but Anglicans spoke with one voice. People must maintain their degree, be content in their estate, be quiet, and not change their position. Thomas Floyd maintained that 'It is our duty therefore to abide content and firm in the good and commendable kind of life, that we have chosen from the beginning.' The Archbishop of York, Edwin Sandys, wanted his flock 'to be mild and quiet, like sheep ... Therefore let every man be content with his own estate. For God hath ordained distinct estates; and by his providence men are placed in them.'[6] The Bishop of Salisbury, John Jewel, echoed the biblical injunction to 'Study to be quiet and meddle with your own business' and invoked the common analogy of the body where 'every part hath his several office': 'But if the arm would take in hand that is the duty of the leg ... [this] breeds disorder in the whole body.' His hearers had to 'seek to do that' which 'to them belongeth.' John Bernade complained that 'There is seldom found any one that is constant with his calling, but thinks an other in happier case than himself.' From this 'groweth too often changing of our trade of life.' He advised, 'Let us not rudely push into other men's offices, but ... content ourselves with our calling ... not ... aspiring to that place and degree whereunto we cannot aspire.' The stress was on quietness, contentment, abiding, and obeying. The doubts about social mobility that affected Puritan moralists seemed to leave the Anglicans untroubled.[7]

This attitude towards changing a calling also meant that ambition and covetousness were severely criticized. The moralists advised their listeners not to seek after riches. Bishop Jewel cautioned, 'If riches abound we must not set our heart on them, but rather be careful for the life to come ... for the desire of money is the root of all evil ...' This attitude was not carelessness towards the world, but an admonition not to be *too* careful, for God 'doth not forbid honest and moderate forecast and provision; as if it were not lawful for Christians to deal in matters appertaining to the good estate of this life ... only we may be not overcareful.'[8] These directions to a modest manner of life did not mean that riches *per se* were viewed negatively. There were a variety of attitudes. Some, like Richard Hooker, believed that riches were a blessing because they gave opportunities. The Bishop of Winchester, Thomas Cooper, pointed out that 'Job was of great wealth and possessions, and yet we read not that he was ever blamed for covetousness.' He drew the conclusion that 'It is the poverty and humbleness of Spirit and

Minde, it is not the poverty and baseness of outward estate and condition, unto the which Christ imputeth God's blessings.'⁹ Others were not so sanguine and emphasized that the godly were often poor and that riches brought dangers in their wake. Norden maintained that it might 'please God to pull us down from prosperity to adversity, from ability and wealth to disability and poverty (as many times the most godly are by the hand of God, in love).' He found that 'The greatest impediment or let is the abundance of worldly things, as riches ...'¹⁰ However, such a critical attitude was unusual. The most common recommendation was to accept but not to seek after riches. One should flee covetousness and ambition, and live a quiet, modest life. Those born rich should not flee their estate; those born poor should accept that condition. The dominant theme was that God had ordered the degrees and callings so that none should question or change their lot.¹¹

There was variation in attitudes to the poor. At times they could be critical. Jewel postulated a partial link between poverty and idleness – 'Beggary falleth upon him [the idle] and gnaweth his bones' – but he distinguished between types of poor. He referred not to those who were 'sick, or weak, or impotent, and cannot work' but to those who were 'idle and froward, and will not work.' Similarly, Sandys wanted 'good order and wise provision' so that 'the impotent might be so relieved that they should not need to beg, and such as are able might be forced in the sweat of their brows to eat their own bread.' This was close to Norden's and Archbishop John Whitgift's praise of the Poor Laws.¹² Other writers abjured criticism of the poor and advised their flocks to give alms liberally. They did not bother to distinguish between types of poor. Edmund Grindal, when Archbishop of York, ruled that 'if any person of ability ... refuse to give reasonably towards the relief of the poor, or shall wilfully discourage other ... the church wardens and sworn men shall present him to the ordinary ... that reformation may be made.' Thomas Rogers maintained that those who opposed this view were Anabaptists and 'hypocritical sectaries, who are bountiful only to those who side with them.'¹³ Rogers was unfair, since there was a spread of opinions among the Anglicans, but he did have a point insofar as the Anglicans placed comparatively greater stress on giving alms and devoted less of their attention to the possible sins and vices of the poor.

There was a strong Anglican work ethic, usually manifested in condemnation of idleness. The purpose of work was to serve one's neighbours and the commonwealth. Bishop Sandys pointed out that 'Moses ... when he saw an Israelite in danger ... slew the enemy of God.' He drew the moral that

'All Christians are our neighbours, which do need our help. To suffer such to perish for want of help is to be guilty of their blood.' But each should do his or her own work. Jewel advised, 'meddle with your own business'; and Bernade counselled, 'let us not rudely push into other men's offices, but ... content ourselves with our calling ...'

This emphasis on doing one's own duty was not individualistic but was again shaped by a view of a providentially provided social order. Each had a debt to his or her neighbour which could be properly discharged only by service in a given place. Within this place each was to be industrious.[14] Jewel's pupil Adam Hill believed that 'the righteous are industrious.' Sandys maintained that 'Our Saviour could in no wise abide idleness' and that 'work ... is ever as needful for men as meat.' He allowed some rest, but 'he which laboureth not is altogether as unworthy to rest as to eat.' His view was summed up as, 'Rest, but rest *a little*' (Sandys's emphasis).[15] Pilkington did not exempt the gentleman: 'Read the scriptures through, and thou shalt not find where gentlemen be allowed to waste their money upon vain pastimes.' Jewel thought that 'idleness is the mother of all mischief.' He became uncharacteristically shrill at the thought: 'What is the cause of diseases ... of the body? ... idleness ... Whereof rise mutterings in cities against magistrates? Whereof rise rebellion in kingdoms against princes? ... idleness.' This stress on work did not necessarily imply manual labour. Jewel's workers included kings, counsellors, bishops (!), and so on, who did not 'use such painful labours of the bodies.' He compared these to the master of a ship – 'his labour surpasseth all the rest.'[16] But while there was a strong view of work, the Anglicans' emphases tended to differ from the Puritans' in two respects – in the Anglican stress on spirituality and in the Puritan stress on rationality.

The Puritans placed much more stress on economy and efficiency in the use of work and time. It is true that one of the most reformed of bishops, James Pilkington, said that the Lord would judge whoever 'durst misspend or waste one farthing ... unthriftily upon things not necessary.'[17] But this was a rare sentiment. Generally his colleagues showed little concern for such efficiency and instead emphasized the importance of spirituality. Even while stressing the importance of labour in a calling, they placed it lower in the rank of Christian duties. In the division between nature and grace, callings fell into the realm of nature. Hooker distinguished callings from 'religion,' and held that 'no works [can be] performed equal to the exercise of religion.' The works which gave the most satisfaction were 'prayers, fasts, and alms deeds.' He advised that 'we must ... never over charge our spirits with multiplicitie of worldly businesses, but ... set aside all worldly occasions.' Hooker's archbishop, John Whitgift, similarly believed that 'merchandise, husbandry, and the handicrafts be heavenly and spiritual, though not in the same degree.' These and 'going to the plough ... only pertain to the body and to this life ...' One should work hard and work in a calling, certainly, but for Elizabethan Anglicans, religion was usually something else again.[18]

THE EARLY SEVENTEENTH CENTURY

Early-seventeenth-century Anglicans generally had some idea of vocation, but few had well-developed ideas. Bishop Robert Sanderson of Lincoln wrote a treatise on the subject; but while he and Lancelot Andrewes were careful to distinguish general and particular callings, they were unusual in doing so.[19] Although it is dangerous to base an argument on silence or, in this case, muted tones, it does appear that, as earlier, callings were less important to Anglicans than to their Puritan contemporaries.[20]

As with the Puritans, there was ambiguity as to what a calling actually was. Jeremy Taylor understood it to be a way of life. William Willymat understood it as a 'station' or 'place' in life, as did Robert Sibthorpe and Robert Harris. Sanderson criticized the view of calling as trade and maintained that Paul 'here taketh the word [calling] in a much wider extent, as including not only such special courses of life as refer to employment, but even all outward personal states and conditions of men whatsoever ... as we may say, a man is called to marriage or to a single life, called to riches or poverty, and the like.' Sanderson limited his own discussion to 'business,' 'office,' 'employment,' and 'profession' – 'a special, settled way of life' – but he noted that this was only part of what a calling included.[21] Many others considered callings as 'trades' and 'employments.' Consequently, descriptions of callings as 'lawful,' 'ordinary,' 'worldly,' 'natural,' and even 'secular' increased.[22] In all these cases, both in the minority view of 'estates' and in the majority view of 'trades,' callings were very much located in the order of society itself rather than in any divine order for that society. Sanderson wrote: 'The Christian Calling doth not at all prejudice, much less overthrow, it rather establisheth and strengtheneth, those interests, that arise from natural relations, or from voluntary contracts, either domestical or civil, betwixt man and man.'[23] Even with an understanding of callings as trades, the emphasis was still that each must have a calling. This admonition included not only the lower classes but also 'idle gallants.' But such gentlemen did not have to stoop to anything 'labouring,' 'manual,' or 'mechanic.'

They might study law or divinity, or they might even travel in order to broaden their minds, provided that they did not waste their days in idleness.[24]

Coupled with the necessity of a calling was a stress on work. Anglicans had little to learn from Puritans on this account. Idleness was always to be censured. Henry Hammond criticized those who would 'be clothed, and not labour,' those for whom 'duty is too mechanical a thing, the shop or the plough ... are things too vile, too sordid for them to stoop to.' He concluded that 'heaven will be had without such solicitors.' Sanderson thought that the idle should 'be soundly spurred up, and whipped on end' – 'These would be well fettered and side-hankled.'[25] Despite numerous strong exhortations to work, there was a difference of tone compared to the Puritans. There was still comparatively little stress on rationalizing work. One manifestation of this was a widespread suspicion of enclosure. Again, there were exceptions. An admirer of William Perkins, Thomas Fuller, defended enclosures and urged landlords to 'drive' their tenants. He must get them to labour for a 'surplusage of estate,' and put 'some metal in [their] industry.'[26] But there was no widespread emphasis on the strict use of time, efficient use of resources, and economy of effort.

These statements on rationality need to be qualified in one particular respect. There was a rationality of piety, characteristic of the monk rather than the administrator. Jeremy Taylor hoarded up the 'few minutes,' 'the trifling hours.' John Hales warned, 'Take heed, every vanity, every superfluity, every penny thou has mispent ... shall cry out to thee,' but his concern was with what had been used selfishly which could have been given to the poor. There was little concern for strict husbandry per se. George Herbert advised his 'Country Parson' not to 'labour anxiously' as 'they overdo it, to the loss of their quiet, and health ... thinking that their own labour is the cause of their thriving, as if it were in their own hands to thrive, or not to thrive.' Given the strict regimen that Herbert suggested, which called for the parson to serve as the local constable, physician, and lawyer, in addition to performing specifically ecclesiastical and pious duties, this advice had a certain irony. However, Herbert's suspicion of too great a sense of humour (his parson, being 'generally sad,' may 'sometimes refresh himself, as knowing that nature will not bear everlasting droopings') was nowhere more evident. He thought that parsons could do all their tasks without undue anxiety.[27]

This focusing of rationality into piety illustrates the persistence of the division between nature and grace that had been prevalent in Elizabethan Anglicanism. John Donne preserved a medieval distinction between the *vita activa* and the *vita contemplativa* and had as his personal motto '*Per Rachel ho servito, & non per Lea*,' 'I serve as Rachel did and not as Leah,' that is, in a contemplative rather than an active life.[28] John Cosin described callings as 'worldly'; Henry Hammond described them as 'secular'; Jeremy Taylor often opposed 'callings' and 'religion.' He emphasized that one must have a good calling but must leave 'spaces' for more spiritual pursuits. Taylor understood a calling as something which served the body, 'and by the body it serves the soul, as by the soul it serves God.' Bishop Cosin contrasted callings with the 'spiritual' and 'heavenly' duties of the Sabbath. God had given six days 'to serve ourselves' and only one 'to serve God.' The work of the six days was only 'allowed,' 'permitted,' and 'not grudged' by God. George Herbert spoke of 'Nature serving Grace,' and distinguished the calling from 'Divine Duties.' John Hales supported the idea of a calling but felt that in it one must make 'space enough for the practice of Godliness.' A calling, though usually required, was a lesser service, and godliness needed to be infused into it by the interpolation of pious duties.[29]

Attitudes towards riches were varied. For some, riches were a blessing.[30] However, the dominant note was the need to flee covetousness and the great snares, temptations, and dangers that attended wealth. Joseph Hall spoke of 'vain and perishing' riches and 'the deceitfulness of riches.' He held that 'he that multiplies riches multiplies cares.' Some even gave a negative cast to riches themselves, as distinct merely from the perils of covetousness. Thomas Jackson maintained that God hated 'affluence, or abundance of things designed.' He sometimes depicted riches as 'a hinderance to true faith.' Owen Feltham believed that it was rare to see a rich man religious, but this too was a minority view.[31] More common was the opinion that riches were acceptable, but must be used with great care and unselfishness. As Donne put it, 'Though riches be not in themselves ill, we are to be abstinent from an overstudious heaping of them, because naturally they are mingled with ... danger ...'[32]

A similar range of views pertained to the poor. There was much support for the Poor Laws. And many divines still pointed to a contrast between two types of poor, sometimes in harsh terms. Sanderson called the able-bodied 'idle and untoward' whom 'it is alms to whip.' Hammond found such beggars 'savage,' 'barbarous,' and 'unchristian.' Some even thought that poverty always bore a relation to sin, but this was rare.[33] Whatever the particular distinctions they may have made between types of poor, and the relations they postulated between certain types of poverty and idleness, the Anglican divines always urged their flocks to care for the *worthy* poor.

Such poor had a claim and were owed a debt. John Hales wrote: 'In debt, I say, thou art for all thou hast; and wilt thou know who are thy creditors? even every man that needs thee. The hungry man begs at thy gate, he is thy creditor, thou art in debt to him for his dinner: the naked man in the streets, he is thy creditor; thou art in debt to him for his garment: the poor oppressed prisoner, he is thy creditor, thou art in debt to him for his redemption.'[34]

Nicholas Ferrar, on his deathbed, lamented that 'It would have been but a suitable return for me to have given all I had, and not to have scattered a few crumbs of alms here and there.'[35] These were some of the strongest sentiments, for the preservation of one's estate was also a strong motif. Nevertheless, many divines echoed Herbert's view that 'religion always sides with poverty.'[36]

Social mobility was frowned upon. Sanderson thought that one could choose a calling, but only by inquiring about what God wanted. One must 'submit' to God in the choice. A soldier might be promoted to lieutenant or, not surprisingly, a priest might be appointed a bishop. The government might outlaw a particular manufacture in which one was involved, and that would require change. Similar 'weighty circumstances' could push one into a new calling. However, the called one was passive, the changes were not to be seized upon but were ascriptive, determined, circumstantial.[37] Sanderson did allow for 'inclination' in choices of a calling, but they ran a poor third to 'gifts' and 'education.' He cautioned against 'ambition' and urged every-one to be 'content' in 'a settled course of life.' Hall gave similar warnings of the dangers of ambition, for 'an ambitious man is the greatest enemy to himself of any in the world besides.' 'It is better for me to live ... in a con-tented want than to desire anything else.' There were 'secret virtues and happiness in poverty.'[38] As Lancelot Andrewes warned: 'in what state or condition soever a man is placed in any nation, be he king or subject, this commands him most strictly therein to abide with God; every man to con-tent himself with his present portion whether it be of sovereignty or of inferior state under subjection.'[39] The notion of remaining in one's station remained strong. As Burgess notes, to believe otherwise 'was having ideas above one's station.'[40]

THE POST-RESTORATION PERIOD

Most post-Restoration Anglican divines had a view of calling, though the Cambridge Platonists ignored the matter.[41] It was common for a distinc-tion to be made between a general calling and a particular calling, though some neglected to make it. There was continuing difference as to what a calling was: it was described variously as an 'office,' 'station,' 'profession,' 'employment,' or 'trade,' and sometimes as several of these by the same author.[42] In all these instances, however, the calling was understood as something *within* society. Isaac Barrow spoke of 'high' and 'low' vocations, and Archbishop John Tillotson considered 'ordinary,' 'honest,' and 'lawful' vocations.[43] In general it was emphasized that everyone should avoid idleness, work hard, have a calling, and be industrious in it, though this too was rare among the Platonists.[44]

Almost invariably, a calling was seen as something apart from specifically religious duties. Robert South was one of the few to overcome this dualism. He included calling under the category of 'religion' and wrote: 'God, who has ordained both society and order, accounts himself so much served by each man's diligent pursuit, though of the meanest trade, that his stepping out of the bounds of it to some other work (as he presumes) more excellent, is but a bold and thankless presumption ... For God requires no man to be praying or reading when the exigence of his profession calls him to his hammer or his needle; nor commands anyone from his shop to go hear a sermon in the church, much less to preach one in the pulpit.'[45]

Usually the formulations were more other-worldly. Mark Frank opposed callings, as 'secular,' to piety, as 'religious.' Calling related to the body, 'religion' to the soul and to heaven. Barrow opposed industry in a calling to 'devotion,' while Tillotson opposed calling to 'religion.' For Richard Allestree a calling was 'worldly,' whereas spiritual things were 'heavenly.'[46] Within this piety there was a stress on rationality, for, as South noted, 'Christianity ... is of a thriving, aspiring nature.' Frank advised his hearers to be careful for every farthing in their giving, while Isaac Barrow urged that alms should be used in the 'most prudent way.'[47]

Many were now inclined to systematize worldly activities as well. Barrow found that 'all nature is continually busy and active ... heaven and earth do work in incessant motion; every living thing is employed in progging [*sic*] for its sustenance; the blessed spirits are always on the wing ... God himself is ever watchful, and ever busy ...' He concluded 'that industry is needful in every condition and station, in every calling and way of life.' South compared the conscience to a 'steward,' 'cashier,' or 'accountant' who requires a strict account of actions and time.[48]

Rationalized work complemented a more accepting view of riches. Richard Allestree and Thomas Traherne thought riches to be good. Frank maintained that one could have honour, riches, and faith together, and he urged the wealthy to be careful in their alms giving lest they impoverish their estates. More divines now voiced the opinion that diligence and industry should lead to riches. Barrow reckoned that giving to the poor was one way to thrive. He held that 'there is no good thing which a man naturally desireth, or reasonably can wish for, which is not in express terms proposed as a reward, or a result of piety.' The 'pious man' was promised 'success and prosperity in his designs,' together with 'comfortable enjoying [of] the fruits of his industry.' Those who had no calling were 'leeches' and 'idle gents' and would soon lose their estates. Tillotson found religion 'a sure way of thriving.'⁴⁹ There was, however, a moderating effect on this acclaim of wealth. Barrow maintained that riches were poor when compared to true wealth. Traherne equivocated and found riches to be poor things. Bishop William Beveridge was riper and described riches as 'trash,' while South found the rich 'sly' and 'sanctimonious.' He preached a sermon entitled 'Prosperity Ever Dangerous to Virtue' and declared that 'Prosperity is but a bad nurse to virtue; a nurse which is like to starve it in its infancy, and to spoil it in its growth.'⁵⁰ There was a tension between these views. Some tended to emphasize the dangers of wealth, but latitudinarians more often tended to emphasize its usefulness and acceptability.

Attitudes towards the poor showed a similar duality. While almost everyone recommended giving to the poor, some were perfunctory in their admonitions and often combined them with a hostility to beggars which seemed to convey a negative attitude towards the poor generally. Although Robert South pointed out that there were two kinds of poor, such a distinction was rare. Even so, he maintained that beggars were usually proud, wilful, and bad, and he criticized sturdy beggars. Indeed, he maintained that poverty was often the root of sin. He found that 'a man may be poor ... but yet abound in sin and vice; and experience shows, that there is not a more unsanctified, wretched and profane sort of men under heaven than beggars commonly are.' They were 'swearers, railers, idle, useless drones, and an intolerable burden to society ... what pride lurks under their rags, like a snake under leaves.' The conclusion of his tirade was unusually blunt – 'In a word, poverty is usually the effect of sin.'⁵¹

There was, however, another side to this coin. Barrow also maintained that 'this poor creature whom thou seest is a man, and a Christian, thine equal, whoever thou art, in nature, and thy peer in condition.' He considered that poverty was not always a fault and, even, that Christ lived on earth 'as a beggar and a vagrant, who died as a malefactor.' Hence he counselled liberal giving – 'he stints it not to his own family or relations; to his friends or neighbours ... to those of his own sect and opinion ... but scatters it indifferently and unconfinedly toward all men that need it; toward mere strangers ...'[52] Sometimes it is difficult to tell what Barrow and South believed about the rich and the poor, but with others there was no such ambiguity. Poverty was accepted as an estate, the rich owed to the poor, no distinction was offered between types of poverty, and giving had to be open hearted and to everyone.[53]

There was still caution about staying in one's calling, unless it be to serve God better. One should not care for riches, should not desire more, and should be content with sufficient for the preservation of one's estate. Similar sentiments were expressed by South and Bishop Edward Stillingfleet. Allestree cautioned against covetousness and preached a 'Contentedness ... with that condition, whatever it is, that God has placed us in ... cheerfully welcoming whatsoever God sends.' He found that 'the ambitious man is always disliking his present conditions.' Traherne, too, maintained that the condition one was in was that which was best.[54] However, Traherne also thought that it was inherent in man to search after riches; he praised prudence and felt that virtue would enable one to increase an estate. Tillotson advised that religious virtues were apt to lead to prosperity. 'As to our estates, Religion is likewise a mighty advantage to men in that respect ...' Isaac Barrow also thought that religion was a drive to industry and that industry was a sure way to 'success,' 'preferment,' and 'thriving.' He praised the merchant who 'is industrious who continueth intent and active in driving on his trade for acquiring wealth.'[55] Among latitudinarian Anglicans there is appearing, for the first time, a general acceptance of the pursuit of wealth, with the encouragement that piety would help one in such a pursuit.

There were also ambiguities concerning individualism. Isaac Barrow urged people not to meddle in another's business, but also criticized property – 'Inequality and private interest in things ... were the by-blows of our fall ... it begot these engrossings and enclosures of things; it forged those two small pestilent words, *Meum* and *Tuum*, which have engendered so much strife among men, and created so much mischief in the world.'[56] Robert South maintained that one must stay within the bounds of one's calling, as did Thomas Tenison. He compared men to 'wheels' in the society, urged them not to be anxious about their own benefit, and maintained that 'wicked men are so strangely out in calculating their own interest.' However, Tenison, together with Stillingfleet, Gabriel Towerson, Bishop John Pearson, and Bishop Gilbert Burnet, retained a healthy respect for the virtues of private property and showed little interest in stating what the limits on personal acquisition were. He disagreed with

Barrow and wrote: 'For does not society consist in due distinction of propriety amongst men, and in their peaceable and secure enjoying of that of which they are proprietors? Do not all public bodies bear upon the great basis of *meum* and *tuum* between particular persons, and upon the provision it makes to protect those persons in their respective titles to what they possess.'[57]

VARIATIONS WITHIN ANGLICANISM

Elizabethan Anglicans were cohesive in their views of vocation. This is surprising given their variations on some other matters, although perhaps in their times an overrriding concern with order is understandable. After the turn of the century a wider range of opinions appeared, although these were generally idiosyncratic variations overlaying a broad consensus. It was only in post-Restoration times that more patterned variations emerged. Some divines maintained the opinions held earlier in the century and tended to be more other-worldly. They had a greater interest in strictly pious duties, were suspicious of wealth and ambition, had a relatively benign attitude to the poor, and were anxious that all should stay in their calling. However, latitudinarians were more open to mobility and riches than were their fellows, and their views were coming to be little different from those of the Nonconformists.

The pre-Restoration Anglicans had generally considered the old order to be a revelation of God's will; its ranks and degrees reflected a divine order.[58] People were to be submissive and to lead quiet, harmonious lives. They were to abide in their calling, accept their lot, shun the desire to improve their station, care for the poor whom *God* had put in the society, and work patiently and diligently in the manner and the place that their forebears had. The motifs of nature and grace protected the social order from strong reforming impulses. The commands of religion were not directed primarily to social relations, except for commands to obedience and charity; instead they were confined to a 'spiritual' or even 'ghostly' realm.[59] Certain elements of this scheme continued in the latter half of the seventeenth century, but the continuity took an unusual turn. If society reflected the will of God, then as society changed, the content given to the will of God would also, surreptitiously, change. The latitudinarians appealed continually to 'common sense,' to the 'prudent' man, to the opinions held by sane people everywhere. If people everywhere, or a significant proportion of them, were becoming more individualistic, then latitudinarians would baptize their efforts.[60] They may not have heralded a new order, but they quickly came to terms with one that was already there. The existing society remained a norm to be followed: what is was the guide to what should be.[61] The Anglicans could baptize stability or baptize change, depending on whether they believed either one to be a fundamental pattern of the existing order.

6

Politics, Necessity, and Calling: Barth, Brunner, Levellers, and True Levellers

INTRODUCTION: ABIDING WITHIN ONE'S CALLING

The political and intellectual upheaval of the English Civil War reshaped many meanings, as different vocabularies fused, adapted, or resisted change. New political movements such as the Levellers and Diggers appeared, and in these movements older ideas, including that of calling, were partially retained but radically reworked. The notion of calling was by this time largely an economic and sociological one, or rather, as in the Puritan and Anglican divines, a theological notion put to economic and sociological use. However, it also had a long history as a more directly political conception. There had already been a fair degree of overlap in these uses, but it was in the revolutionary debates in and around London that a substantial fusion really took place. In this setting, the assumptions inherent in the idea of natural rights and freedoms began to penetrate the conceptions and vocabulary of calling. I will not try to cover all of these interpenetrations but will merely endeavour to outline the fate of the concept of calling as it was drawn into them.

Until the time of the Civil War, the doctrine of calling did not appear to add anything specific to the discussion of political duties. All that had happened was that those who worked with such a doctrine expressed their views of the task of the magistrate, the ruler, and the subject in terms of their callings. In actual substance the views offered were much the same as the views of those who used the vocabularies of 'degree,' 'estate,' 'office,' or 'duty.' The basic conception was that people had social stations or callings and carried out the functions required by their particular role. However, beyond the question of what particular type of roles were described as callings there is an additional, implicit, political meaning, since by its very nature a view of calling betrayed a particular understanding about, and attitude towards, existing political and social structures and roles, and the social division of labour.

We have already noted the conservatism of the teaching to 'abide in your calling,' a conception which lent divine legitimacy to the existing degrees of rank and status. This was a conception in which the existing order was itself the expression of the divine command. However, there was a conservative feature of the concept of calling which went beyond any particular conservative use to which it might be put. For even beyond the question of whether one might change a calling was the question of what it actually means to be *within* a calling. One might change callings but still be required to be *in* one. And if one was in a calling then there was another form of submission required – the teaching that each must 'abide in his calling,' not in the sense of not changing it for a different one, but in the sense that *one must not go beyond a calling or go outside of it.* This teaching required one to do a *specific* task and no other; it required activity to be focused *in one place*, regardless of whether one might be allowed, or able, to change the particular place. One could not meddle with another's affairs but must mind only one's own business and duty. The range of allowable action was limited to one's function as a particular type of member of the body. This teaching took different forms at different times: in the earlier Anglicans and Puritans it meant that one must fulfil one's *own* duty; in the later Puritans and latitudinarians it meant that one should look after one's own trade and welfare without being too much troubled about how well one's neighbour was doing. However, in both these instances, part of the pattern was the same – to keep to oneself, one's own work, one's own affairs.

This conservatism is brought out, perhaps unwittingly, in the writings of the modern theologians Karl Barth and Emil Brunner on the subject of vocation. Brunner wrote that 'The idea of the Calling and of the Call is unintelligible apart from that of Divine Providence ... God ... says to me here and now: "Act, where you are, as you are."'[1] In view of this acceptance of Providence, 'The idea of the Calling characterizes the concrete time and place, the sphere and the content of action ... as God-given and therefore ... "right."'[2] Hence, for Brunner, 'you do not need to search for your sphere of service ... Since we are called, here and now, our "sphere of labour" and our duties are appointed to us. Our service consists in the fulfilment of "the duties of our state."'[3]

Because of this strict focusing of responsibility, Brunner was critical of those who saw reform of life as a *principle* (Brunner's emphasis). By a 'principle' he appeared to envisage something static or fixed – a rule or a law – in contrast to the more existential demands of a Calling. He described the person bound to this principle thus: 'His whole life is spent in this unceasing endeavour to alter conditions, the personal meaning of life is forgotten ... [this] ... produces a way of life which ignores real life ... It is the modern form of fanaticism.' In contrast to the strenuous reformer Brunner posited a Lutheran view of calling with a 'thankful acceptance of the place, at which I am now set, from the hands of Providence as the sphere of my life ... at the same time it keeps the door open for me *to undertake such reforming work when it is the duty appointed to me in my particular office*'[4] (emphasis added). This last statement uncovers the core of what it means to abide *within*, as distinct from just *remaining* in, one's calling. One might reform, change, criticize, show mercy, seek justice, and fight oppression, but only within the bounds of one's particular office and no other. The sphere of one's responsibilities was bounded by one's particular place in the social order and this place was a result of divine providence.[5]

Karl Barth, Jacques Ellul, and, more recently, Miroslav Volf have taken a more critical view of this identification of calling with a place in the social order. Barth said that when Luther speaks 'of the obedience to be rendered at it, he does so on the assumption of a well-known order of superiority and subordination which is established and obtains for all higher and lower stations, to which man must adjust himself, and according to the equally well-known conditions of which he has to perform this work as the work which God has prescribed.' In so speaking about Luther, he also clarified the assumptions inherent in Brunner's view of the calling. Barth went to the root of the matter when he asked: 'What about the superiority of the divine calling over all other prescribed stipulations of the human sphere of operation? Is not its freedom forfeited again if it must coincide *ipso facto* with the well-known limits of a human station and vocation? Does this not again bind man's obedience to a law which is different from the calling itself, except that now this is the law of the world and its historical and transitory order instead of that of the cloister? Ought not the divine calling and man's obedience necessarily entail the transformation and new definition and form of the sphere of operation?'[6]

Barth sought to show that almost every view of calling before his own had taken the existing division of labour in the society for granted and so subjected any divine imperative of calling to that division.[7] However, even Barth himself echoed Brunner's theme that 'faithfulness in vocation must exclude any intention of radically reforming life.'[8] The ambivalence was more apparent than real, for we are attempting to force Barth to speak on a distinction that he himself did not wish to allow. Nevertheless, although this is only one aspect of Barth's intended discussion, it does illustrate the constricting implications of the doctrine of calling when it is portrayed in terms of a given social order.[9]

Bishop Robert Sanderson was well aware of this. He was open to the possibility of changing one's calling, provided certain conditions were met, but he was equally clear about what a calling, and being in a calling, implied. He maintained that the Apostle Paul, in his injunction to 'Abide in your callings,' was writing to the Corinthians who 'interpret their calling to the Christian Faith as an exemption from the duties of all other callings, as if their spiritual freedom in Christ had cancelled *ipso facto* all former obligations, whether of nature or civility.' Paul, according to Sanderson, asserted the continuing bonds to the 'further and more universal extent to all outward states and conditions of life.' What this meant was that 'The Christian Calling doth not at all prejudice, much less overthrow, it rather establisheth and strengtheneth, those interests that arise from natural relations ...' Sanderson's general rule was that, abiding in the station where 'God has placed him,' a man had to 'contain himself within the bounds thereof, and cheerfully and contentedly undergo the duties that belong thereto.'[10]

The teaching that a person was to stay in the same calling in which he or she was called was comparatively rare after the Restoration. However, the teaching that one had to stay *within* a calling continued at least until late in the seventeenth century. This teaching on the limits of one's duty took a variety of forms beyond the individualism of the Nonconformists and the divine social order of the earlier Anglicans. One form was the frequent criticism of 'mechanic preachers.' Bishop Joseph Hall complained of preaching by cobblers, tailors, felt-makers, 'and such like trash.' In June 1641, when the Commons summoned various lay preachers to answer for themselves, one critic declaimed, 'God ... doth furnish our Church plentifully with learned men' and does not need 'such as you preach the gospel'; 'I tell you I am angry with you, my very purse [*sic*] feels it, it is your enticing to conventicles and private meetings that makes men and women to neglect their callings and trades two or three days a week to follow your own heels.' Not only had the 'mechanics' drawn people out of their calling, they had gone out of their own.[11] For a man unordained, a man of trades, and more especially for a woman – for there were some – to take up preaching was a violation of the law of calling, even if the cobbler returned to his cobbling the very next day, or even within the hour.

One of the most significant implications of this aspect of calling concerned politics. If all had to attend to their own business, then who was to attend to affairs of state? The answer was, of course, those who had such a calling. But, then, what political activity was allowed within such a framework? It is the answers to this question, and the transmutations of the notion of calling that these answers involved, that we shall now investigate.

CALLING AND POLITICS: MEDDLE WITH YOUR OWN BUSINESS

The teaching that staying in one's own calling required abstention from political activities reached back at least to the reign of Henry VIII. It arose in a gradual integration of a newer doctrine of calling with an older medieval view of the estates of society. The exact dimensions of this integration are hard to define. However, in the official and semi-official propaganda against the rebellions of 1549, the expression reached some clarity. John Cheke, a professor at Cambridge and a former tutor of Prince Edward, directed his pen against Ket's rebellion in Norfolk. His was one of the more sympathetic responses, but he drew on the doctrine of calling to put the rebels firmly in their place. Cheke advised them to search the Scriptures where 'we learn not only to fear [God] truthfully, but also to obey our king faithfully and to serve in our own vocation.'[12] He inquired, 'Is this your true duty ... to leave your duties ... go back on your promises ... to disobey your betters ... ?';[13] for 'God's word teacheth us no man should take in hand any office but he is called of God like Aaron.' 'The thing ye take is not your right, it is another man's own ...'[14] The substance of what Cheke said was commonplace, but by introducing the idea of calling he said that obedience in a calling meant that those without a specific political office must refrain from political activity. This might seem obvious in the context of a full-scale rebellion, but it had far wider implications.

The Bishop of Winchester, John Ponet, also considered the political implications of the doctrine of calling when he was exiled in Strasbourg in 1556. However, being on the receiving end of Mary's persecution, rather than of a rebellion, he turned Cheke's view on its head. In his *Short Treatise of Politike Power*, he admitted that usually 'every commonwealth [is] kept and maintained in good order by obedience,' but he questioned what might happen in unusual circumstances.[15] What happens to the body 'if the sinews be too much racked and stretched out, or too much shrinked together, it breedeth wonderful pains and deformities in man's body.' In the same way, 'If Obedience be too much or too little in a commonwealth, it causeth much evil and disorder.'[16] In this situation Ponet considered that vocations provided limits on magistrates as well as on the people. In fact, he maintained that the people's vocations required that they restrain the magistrate:

'For too much [obedience] maketh the governors to forget their vocation, and to usurp upon their subjects; too little breedeth a licentious liberty, and maketh the people to forget their duties. And so both ways the commonwealth groweth out of order ...'[17]

Ponet was highly unusual in such an interpretation of calling, as indeed he was striking in his views on obedience. But it is significant that he used the doctrine of calling to teach that the people have political responsibilities: the calling now embraced an idea of citizenship. As Cheke's work was reprinted in 1641 and Ponet's work was reprinted in 1642, their disagreement was, in a way, refought in the Civil War. Until then, however, it was the doctrine of Cheke that held sway.

In 1583 Bishop John Jewel offered the common advice to 'study to be quiet and meddle with your own business.'[18] He employed the familiar imagery of the body and drew the direct political consequence that each had to 'seek to do that to them belongeth ... but ... when every private man will govern, and the subject take in hand to rule the prince, all must needs come to rack and ruin.' He warned his readers to beware of the perils of such governorship, for the labours of princes, magistrates and counsellors 'are greater than all the labours of the body.'[19] The same theme was echoed in Richard Hooker's vision of 'everyman ... left to the freedom of his own mind ...'; it 'shaketh universally the fabric of government, tendeth to anarchy and mere confusion, dissolveth families, dissipateth colleges, corporations, armies, overthroweth kingdoms, churches and whatsoever is now through the providence of God by authority and power upheld.'[20]

In 1604 the Anglican preacher William Willymat offered his advice on loyalty and obedience under the heading 'Private men may not intermeddle or take upon them the office of the magistrates without a lawful calling.'[21] He distinguished 'three several kinds of people' of whom 'there is none but they appertain and belong to one of those three.' The kinds consisted of 'first Emperors, Kings and Princes within their several empires, kingdoms and jurisdictions; secondly subordinate or subalternal magistrates who have and hold their commissions and authority from the first; and thirdly private subjects which are to be ruled and governed by the second and first sorts of men.' These latter had 'no public charge or office' and they had to restrict themselves 'to attend upon only each of them his own private business according as his own place, function, and calling requireth.'[22] They were 'private [men] or common subject[s] without any lawful calling to any authority or office: this last kind of men may not intrude themselves without any lawful calling into any matter of action or office that of right belongeth to the lawful magistrate.' Such persons were to observe 'moderation' in 'public affairs,' 'namely that they are not of their own motion without any calling to busy themselves in public affairs, nor intermeddle with the government nor reformation of them ... nor attempt any public thing.' Though Willymat did allow one to point out injustices to a magistrate, the attitude of those in the third set of callings had to be essentially passive, since 'If they espy any fault in the common policy that needeth any amendment, they must not stir at all therein, nor take to themselves authority to redress it, or once uncalled to put out their helping hand, having in that respect their hands bound behind them.'[23]

Willymat's view made explicit something which seems to have been implicit all along: in treating calling as office or duty, he had conflated the calling of God with an institutional calling, such as that given to the magistrate or minister. To do something without a calling was confused with doing something without a commission from instituted authority. This was a not uncommon view and occurred among Puritans as well. Willymat offered this conclusion: 'in few words, this fixed duty of a loyal subject, it is, that private men may not attempt any public Magistrate's office without a lawful commission, or calling, neither to reform anything amiss, nor to do any good in the commonwealth ...'[24] This was also a persistent theme in the series of sermons offered at Paul's Cross. In 1626 Robert Harris pronounced, 'Happy that state, wherein the Cobbler meddles with his last, the Tradesman with his shop, the Student with his book, the Counsellor with State, the Prince with the Sceptre, and each creature live[s] in his own element.'[25] The basic outlines of this teaching are not particularly noteworthy. They reflected a simple and commonplace view of the chain of being. Shakespeare's famous words summarize it well:

Oh, when degree is shak'd
Which is the ladder of all high designs,
The enterprise is sick. How could communities,
Degrees in schools and brotherhoods in cities,
Peaceful Commerce from dividable shore,
The primogenitive and due of birth,
Prerogative of ages, crowns, sceptres, laurels,
But by degree stand in authentic place?
Take but degree away, untune that string,
And hark, what discord follows.[26]

What the notion of calling added to this picture was the caution against 'meddling'; that all had 'their hands tied behind them.' This went far beyond mere opposition to self-aggrandizement or the upsetting of degree; it meant that one could not even 'reform anything amiss' or 'do any good in the commonweal ...'

In this brief survey, we have taken just a few examples to illustrate the continuity of the view that a calling required political passivity from those without a specific political calling. The Puritans sometimes honoured this in the breach, of course, for their ministers could claim that their diatribes against a corrupt court and wayward magistrates were really only theological teaching or pastoral ministry; or else, for those with a Presbyterian bent, that the minister's calling involved such political statements. In any case, by the time of the Civil War, the doctrine was well established.

CALLINGS CHALLENGED: JOHN GOODWIN AND THE LEVELLERS

In the period of the Civil War, these views became for the first time a matter of controversy. When William Thomason defended the role of Parliament he told the people that it was no business of theirs to be 'reformers,' they should be only 'informers':

It is not fit for you to trouble yourselves and them [the MPs] in this kind, because of your different constitutions ... It is well if you have enough wisdom to steer you right in your private and mechanical affairs, which is your proper station or calling, and you may do well to consider, whether you do well to neglect that business God hath set you about, to meddle with that you have no calling unto ... let it be your trades and callings, and to keep yourselves within your limits, and to the conscionable exercise of your proper employments, and not to intrude into what you understand not; if you will needs be active in reformation, let it be in the reformation of yourselves.[27]

Here Thomason confused trade, office, duty, and commission, all with the intent of keeping people from political activity.

The Puritan leader Robert Greville, Lord Brook, used the ammunition of the calling against the bishops themselves. He maintained that the bishops could not have civil roles: 'I answer confidently, and I hope truly, that these two offices, or Callings, did not under the Lawe meet in one, except in some *extraordinary* cases.'[28] Even the apocalyptic sermon of Thomas Case (1598–1682) to the House of Commons showed the restraining effects of the calling. His declaration that 'Reformation must be universal,' his exhortation to 'Reform all places, all persons and callings. Reform the benches of judgement, the inferior magistrates ... the Church ... Reform the universities

... cities ... countries ... inferior schools of learning ... the Sabbath ... the ordinances ... etc.,' despite its evident zeal, still took the social division of labour, duty, and responsibility for granted.[29] 'As you would have the Parliament to reform above; so do your reform below ... reform your families, reform yourselves.'[30] Any reformation had to take place *in situ*; the MPs themselves could heed such a cry only because they already *had* political callings. At heart Case's rallying cry did not contradict Thomason's admonition that 'if you will needs be active in Reformation, let it be in the reformation of yourselves.'[31] In 1643 the ringing tones of 'The Solemn League and Covenant' were couched in the framework of a reformation *within* the structure of callings. There was the repeated formula 'That we shall sincerely, really and constantly, through the grace of God, endeavour in our several places and callings, the preservation of the reformed religion ...'[32] This type of refrain opened sections I, II, and III.[33] The Covenant sought for a reformation of each *in* his or her place and calling.

In 1648 the Parliament still held to the same view. As a response to John Lilburne's tract *The Mournful Cries of Many Thousand Poor Tradesmen*, the Commons authorized the official response: 'A Declaration of Some Proceedings of Lt.-Colonel John Lilburne.' Apart from the not-uncommon political excuse that economic problems were due to an 'unseasonable seed time in 1646, and the unkindly Spring following,' the Commons told Lilburne that in any case he had no business raising a fuss. In response to Lilburne's lament that his many sufferings had caused a diminution in his estate, his antagonist tartly replied, 'if you had used as much diligence since in your own callings, as you have done in those you less understand, and had let out the current of your thoughts, which have been misimployed about Politiques, to the Oeconomy of your families, the account of loss had not run so high ...'[34] 'In the mean time, till care can be taken for prevention of beggary, increase not their number by the addition of yourselves, neglect not your callings, forbear your clandestine Constitutions.'[35]

The Presbyterian divine Edward Gee made similar observations. He defined 'usurpation' as 'an intrusion into the seat of authority without any lawful right, title, or calling.'[36] Here Gee brought together the language of rights with that of callings and public commissions. He asserted that 'a calling from the people' was 'necessary and essential to a humanely constituted magistracy.'[37] Marchamount Nedham criticized Gee on this very point in his *The Case of the Commonwealth of England Stated*. Nedham's reply showed that he understood a call to be some sort of popular political consent or commission. He maintained that 'if only a call from the people constitute a lawful magistracy, then there hath very rarely ever been any lawful magistracy in the world' for 'most princes came into the seat of authority not only without a call but absolutely against the wills of the people ...' In any case, how could one have such a call in a state 'divided by civil war'?[38]

A similar type of conflation, reflecting the same ambivalence towards callings, occurred in the work of John Goodwin. In Goodwin's *Right and Might Well Met*, a defence of Pride's Purge published in January 1649, there was a broad statement concerning breaking out of the limits of one's calling.[39] Goodwin, who later became Cromwell's chaplain, was an Arminian and, after being ejected from his vicarage by Parliament, was the pastor of one of the most influential Independent congregations in London, one which included many of the more important merchants and Independent political figures.[40] Goodwin was generally a left-leaning figure, joining the Levellers to argue with Ireton and Nye at Whitehall. Back in 1645, William Walwyn had some very nice things to say about him: 'a faithful servant of God and sincere lover of his country ... a man ... that values neither life nor livelihood, could he therewith, or with loss thereof, purchase a peaceable liberty to his Country, or a just Parliamentary government.'[41] Later, however, Goodwin seemed convinced that the purged Commons represented about the limit of the political change he would like to see, and he parted company with, and henceforth criticized, the Levellers.[42]

At the time that he was beginning to distance himself from the Levellers, Goodwin took up the question of callings. He centred his argument on this point because: 'The first born of the strength of those who condemn the said act [Pride's Purge] ... lieth in this: that the Actors had no sufficient authority to do what they did therein, but acted out of their sphere, and so became transgressors of that law which commandeth every man to keep order and within the compass of his calling.'[43] In opposing this 'first born,' Goodwin offered two arguments, though he appeared to think that they were the same argument. His first argument was that the Army did have such a calling:

Nor did they stretch themselves beyond the line of their callings, to act therein as they did. Their calling and commission was, to act in the capacity of soldiers for the peace, liberties and safety of the Kingdom. What doth this import, but a calling to prevent, or suppress by force, all such persons and designs, whose faces were set to disturb or destroy them? ... and consequently ... they have, and hold a calling, to proceed against them as they did ...

If the calling which the Parliament itself had to levy forces against the King ... was warrantable and good, then was the calling of the Army to act as they did in the business under debate, warrantable and good also ...[44]

The other argument that Goodwin offered was that, in cases of necessity, one could violate the law of callings: 'callings were made for men, and not men for callings ... if the law of callings at any time opposeth, or lieth cross to the necessary conveniences of men ... it suffereth a total eclipse of the binding power of it.'[45]

The basis for both arguments was one of necessity: Goodwin gave analogies to the doctor whose patient was unable to give consent and to the 'inferior mariner' when the master of the ship was drunk. He concluded from these examples that 'Yea many of the laws of God themselves, think it no disparagement unto them, to give place to their elder sister, the law of necessity ... So that whatsoever is necessary, is somewhat more than lawful ... Yea, the truth is that the law of necessity ... cannot ... be denied to be one of the laws of the land, being the law of nature ...'[46] He also spoke of the 'law of nature and necessity' and 'sovereign necessity' and held that the 'necessities of men call more effectually than men themselves.'[47]

Apart from this equivocation as to whether the law of callings was abrogated by necessity or only reconstituted on a firmer foundation, Goodwin had another ambiguity: this concerned the nature of a calling. In the quotations we have just considered, Goodwin used at least four meanings of 'calling': the station in society in which one was placed by God; the duty to act in a certain circumstance; the right to act in such a circumstance; and, finally, what he referred to occasionally as a 'formal call,' a 'commission' from the people or the parliament. Apart from his conscious distinction between a 'formal' and an 'informal' call, Goodwin did not appear to notice any difference among these conceptions. In his statement that 'the call of the Army to act as they did ... [is] ... as authentic, clear and full as that of the Parliament,' all these meanings were fused together.

Goodwin's views were similar to those of the Levellers. Up to 1646, the Levellers had generally understood callings in terms of estates and trades.[48] They emphasized that all must labour at a calling and that none should move out of a calling.[49] The only exceptions to this trend were in the specific context of Lilburne's tracts against the bishops in 1637 and 1639, when he was at pains to show that their calling was from the devil. In these works he denied the possibility of an 'inward calling' and maintained that only an outward 'commissioning' constituted a true call.[50] After 1646 the understanding of calling as trade continued, but different usages began to creep in.[51] The notion of calling as general duty began to win out over the understanding of calling as estate and place. As with Goodwin, the Levellers were not clear as to whether they had found a new basis for callings or were breaking the law of callings. In 1648 John Wildman emphasized that necessity gave a call: 'If our duty bind us when we see our neighbour's house on fire, to waive all formes, ceremonies or complements, and forthwith (not waiting for order or leave) to attempt the quenching thereof without further scruple, as thereunto called of God, we say if we be so obliged and called in the case of a particular, then much more are we obliged and called, when we behold the great Mansion House of this Commonwealth, and of this Army ... on fire.'[52] Walwyn expressed a similar sentiment: 'but the same necessity and public safety that justifieth the Parliament against the King, will also justify the Army against them.'[53]

Wildman summarized this position in the same way that Goodwin had: 'look for no other call; for the voice of necessity is the call of God.'[54] Reflecting on all this in the *Manifestation* of April 1649, Lilburne put the same case in a different form and in a more subdued tone:

'Tis a very great unhappiness as we well know, to be always struggling and striving in the world ... So that if we should consult only with our own selves, and regard only our own ease, We should never interpose as we have done, in behalf of the Commonwealth ... but since a Common Duty ... requires of us an increase of care and circumspection, which if it produces not so good a settlement as ought to be, yet certainly it will prevent its being so bad as otherwise it would be, if we should all only mind our particular callings and imployments.[55]

Lilburne was expressing the same sentiment as he had a year earlier in *The Mournful Cries of Many Thousand Poor Tradesmen*; but now he was expressing it as the necessity of moving out of one's calling. *Walwyn's Wiles*, published in the same month as the *Manifestation*, accused Walwyn of attempting to draw people out of their callings.[56] Walwyn's reply was ambiguous: he told of one Samuel How, 'a Cobler by trade, and a contented man in that calling,' who had been allowed to preach in his accuser's church. But, he asked, 'Who ever heard me speak either in behalf of butchers and coblers, as to places of government? I profess, I know not where, nor when.' Even this was distinctly two-sided, though, for Walwyn went on to say that 'though for their callings, I make no difference between them and myself; for the callings are honest, and mine can but be so!'[57] This ambiguity, if intended, seemed to reflect a man who was unwilling to admit that people could or should go out of their calling, but who also wanted to keep from denying such a position. If the subtlety was unconscious, it would appear that Walwyn himself couldn't really articulate his position. Humphrey Brooke muddied the waters still further in his hasty attempt to defend his friend. He contended that Walwyn's 'only end' was 'that the

Commonwealth might be so settled, that men might with comfort and alacrity set themselves about their particular callings and employments.'[58]

The views of the Levellers in the period between 1647 and 1649 were the same as those of Goodwin. For them, calling was a term which conflated trade, estate, right, and duty. Necessity was the basis of political action, but they were uncertain as to whether necessity was really the fundamental basis of callings or whether, on the contrary, it allowed one to break out of a calling. Their ambiguity appeared to result from a confusion between duties which were grounded in the particular estates and structures of society and those which were naturally rooted, which transcended any particular social forms. They wanted to hold on to the doctrine of calling, but they also wanted to modify its form so that it allowed political responsibility and required political action from those who at present had no political office.

CALLINGS REJECTED: THE DIGGERS

As with the Levellers, Digger views on calling evolved. There is a marked difference between the language of *The Law of Freedom in a Platform* and that of earlier Digger pamphlets. The earlier writings work with a conventional view, but in *The Law of Freedom*, Gerrard Winstanley appeared to reject the notion of calling altogether.

In October 1648, Winstanley had advised his readers to 'follow your course of trading in Righteousness as Reason requires.'[59] In March of the following year, in the anonymous pamphlet *More Light Shining in Buckinghamshire*, he complained that 'thousands that would, and desire to live in a lawful Calling, lawfully, are of all people most oppressed.' Those who did the oppressing, the gentlemen and the rich, 'do live altogether out of God's way, and in Rebellion to his law.' The first reason for this lawbreaking was that such people 'live without a Calling, and so are idle, being Vagabonds ... and so but Vermin in a Commonwealth, and by their own law, ought to be put in a house of Correction, and to be made work.'[60] Even allowing for the rhetorical effects which the turning of the doctrine of calling against the rich and the gentle doubtless was designed to achieve, it appears that here we have a view not dissimilar to that common in the rest of English society. Two months later, in a further anonymous pamphlet, Winstanley echoed the same theme and criticized 'Lawyers ... Judges ... and other monopolies over all sorts and trades ... they striving rather to uphold their own theft and deceit, than admitting any just composure and agreement of the people.' Such people have a 'needless Calling.'[61]

In June, Winstanley returned to the theme of a reformation of every man in his place – 'And this we count is our duty, to endeavour to the uttermost, every man in his place (according to the National Covenant which the Parliament set forth) a reformation, to preserve the people's liberties.'[62] The same theme recurs in his play on the 'Solemn League and Covenant' in his *Watch-Word to the City of London and the Army*, published in August. He repeated that 'we ... endeavour a reformation in our place and calling'; 'everyone in his several place and calling should endeavour the peace, safety and freedom of England ...'; 'we endeavour a reformation in our place and calling according to the Word of God.'[63] It is hard to know whether Winstanley was fooling himself in this refrain or merely trying to fool his audience. If there was anything he was *not* seeking it was a reformation of each only in his or her place and calling. Even allowing for his idiosyncratic reading of the document, it appears that he wished to abolish the system of places and callings – the traditional social structure – inherent in the National Covenant once and for all.[64] *More Light Shining in Buckinghamshire* had found even *An Agreement of the People* 'too low and too shallow to free us at all.'[65]

By January of 1650, Winstanley obviously had acquired a jaundiced view of callings. In a passage reminiscent of Shakespeare's Falstaff, he complained that 'Surely this power [of] the laws ... is the burden of the creation ... for though it pretend justice, yet the judges and law officers buy and sell justice for money, and wipes their mouths like Solomon's whore and says "It is my calling," and are never troubled at it.'[66] *The Fire in the Bush* contained similar sentiments. Winstanley maintained that it was one of the consequences of the Fall that mankind lived 'upon riches, honours, pleasures, ministers, lawyers, armies, wife, children, ordinances, customs, and all outward forms of Worship ... yea upon anything without [i.e., outside] them.'[67] The inclusion of riches and honours seems obvious, but that of wife and children is peculiar. Winstanley was clearly disgruntled with every aspect of the existing social order and, given his explicit repudiation of 'community of women,' couldn't be bothered here with making distinctions.[68] In any case, he was at pains to point out that the Scriptures were written by 'shepherds, husbandmen, fishermen and such inferior men of the world' and that it was only the fallen elder brother who demanded to be acknowledged as above his fellows in degree.[69]

It was in Winstanley's *magnum opus*, *The Law of Freedom in a Platform*, that his rejection of callings was most clear. This was manifested in two ways; in the structure of the argument and in the vocabulary in which it was couched. In the whole of the *Law of Freedom*, there is no mention of the term 'calling' or any variation of it. This in itself is not remarkable, as several other of the Digger pamphlets did not mention it either. However, in the case of the *Law of Freedom* the absence is more noteworthy. For, as we have already noted, the notion of calling, albeit in a modified form, had been a part of the Digger conceptual structure and vocabulary. Furthermore, there were in the *Law of Freedom* instances where the notion of calling would be quite fitting but was nevertheless still absent. There was criticism of the system of titles and honours, of the work of lawyers, of idleness and unemployment. There were various suggestions on how to improve trades.[70] The term 'calling' was used for at least some of these conceptions in earlier Digger writings, but not now. This fact is even more striking when we consider Winstanley's new society. He describes diversities of trades and discusses the roles of the master of a family, an overseer, a peacemaker, a soldier, an elder, a taskmaster, an executioner, a judge, husbandry, 'mineral employment,' and so forth.[71] It is hard to think of any other mid-century discussion covering such a range of tasks which would not employ the notion of calling. Its absence in Winstanley's later work is conspicuous.

If we consider the thrust of what he was advocating, one reason for such an absence becomes clear. Winstanley wanted a new society: he wanted new roles, new tasks, new offices. In a sense he wanted new 'callings,' and so he would not put up with the old ones. He had already pointed out, in 1649, that in his new society 'no one shall lay claim to any creature and say, "This is mine, and that is yours, This is my work, that is yours"; but everyone shall put their hands to till the earth and bring up cattle ...'[72] Winstanley wanted not only new relations of property but also of labour. No one would be able to say, 'This is my work.' This meant in traditional terms that no one could say, 'This is my calling.' Apparently it had taken Winstanley some time to see that a new society meant the *abolition* of callings. But at length, the realization that 'extreme necessity calls for the great work of restoration ...' won out over the remnants of the previous model.[73] A new society had no use for the immanentized callings of the old. Social restructuring could be based on the understanding that the existing social structure itself stems from the direct hand of divine providence. If one believed that a social order not only contained but was itself an expression of corruption and concupiscence, then one could no longer consider its estates as the necessary *loci* and *foci* of Christian, or any other, responsibilities. 'True levelling' required the levelling of callings.

CALLING AS ABSTRACT RIGHT

Among the Diggers the term 'calling' was used in an economic and social rather than in a directly political sense. In this regard their conceptions were different from those to be found in Goodwin, Nedham, and the Levellers. However, despite this asymmetry, the fate of the calling in Winstanley's work provides an insight into the work of others and even into the nature of a calling itself. The fact that the Diggers eventually abandoned the concept of calling tends to confirm my earlier conclusions from the work of Barth and Brunner. While the notion of calling then current in England might have allowed for reformation *within* estates and offices, and might even have changed the particular duties of these offices, it still immanentized the divine calling in the existing social order and hence was not in a position radically to criticize or change that order.

The example of the Diggers shows, in turn, the conservative implications of a retention of a doctrine of calling. John Goodwin and the Levellers wanted to change understandings of calling with respect to the political responsibility allowed to and required from particular estates, stations, and trades. Apart from this they were relatively uncritical of the notion and took great pains to distance themselves from the 'True Levellers,' the Diggers. As Lilburne said, 'This conceit of levelling of property and magistracy ... would, if practised, destroy ... any industry in the world and raze the very foundation of ... subsistence ... who will take pains for that which when he hath gotten it is not his own, but must equally be shared in by every lazy, simple dronish sot? ... The ancient encouragement to men that were to defend their country was this: that they were to hazard their persons for that which was their own, to wit, their own wives, their own children, their own estates.'[74]

It is true that they thought, as Walwyn said, that God 'regards neither fine clothes, nor gold rings, nor stately houses, nor abundance of wealth, nor dignities, and titles of honour, nor any man's birth or calling ...'[75] However, here the opposition was based on the fact that the distinction was one not of virtue but of privilege. While it is true that they did not want a change that would be only 'Notionall, Nominall, Circumstantiall,'[76] yet they 'never had it in [their] thoughts to Level men's estates, it being the utmost of [their] aim that the Commonwealth be reduced to such a pass that every man with as much security as may be enjoy his propriety.'[77] As for 'Orders and Dignities, We think them ... requisite for the maintenance of the Magistracy and Government.'[78] What the Levellers objected to was not the division of dignities, estates, and callings, but who was allowed to fill such places and offices. They demanded 'that virtue, though in poor men, should be more regarded.'[79] While it is probably true that the vehemence of their statements on the levelling of estates and callings was strongly conditioned by a need to distance themselves from people who were regarded as 'beyond the pale,' their sentiments showed a marked consistency. The social and economic order was accepted, and callings had to be preserved. The incumbents might be changed, but the structure remained.[80]

Where the Levellers did differ from exponents of older doctrines of calling was in expanding the range of people who had political callings, or, perhaps, the range of callings that included political rights and obligations. They were unsure whether the reason for this expansion was that 'necessity provides a calling' or that 'necessity ... needs no calling.' Despite this confusion, Goodwin and the Levellers did infuse the notion of calling with new content. In each case, the basic appeal was to raw necessity. But this necessity had somehow to be tied to a notion of order, degree, and calling – necessity was therefore the basis either of social obligation or of its overthrow. The fact that two such radically different positions were conflated as one argument is an indication of the difficulty of applying an immanentized view of calling to a novel situation. What came out of this brew was an attempt to extend the notion of the duties of citizens – their calling – to include political responsibilities. God's command to all in their estate now included the duty, and the complementary right, to succour the commonwealth in an hour of necessity. It became, in J.G.A. Pocock's terms, a 'mode of civic consciousness.'[81] The distinction of the calling of ruler and subject was blurred and undercut; other callings now had political responsibilities. Exactly how many other callings had such responsibilities was not clear. Goodwin's argument of a calling from necessity applied only to the army; that of the Levellers was specifically related only to them and their supporters. Their arguments could, in principle, be extended across the population, but it is not clear whether they themselves intended to do so. The case of the franchise could be indicative of their views in this, but is one of the most debated aspects of the Leveller program.

Whatever the extent of the franchise and the breadth of civic responsibility, Goodwin and the Levellers radically altered the sense of calling. By asserting the political rights of callings and grounding them upon necessity, they removed the calling from its capture by a predetermined set of socially defined responsibilities. The immanentization of the calling which began in Luther and Calvin, and which was clear in early-sixteenth-century England, drew its power from the express command of God. When the calling was abstracted once again from the society, it reappeared not as an explicit, inscripturated, and inward divine call but as duty and obligation founded upon necessity. This necessity could in principle be further grounded in divine providence, but its origin in the will of the Creator would still be relatively tenuous. God's inward call and textual command might impose clear standards, but the need to act in the unknown, and apparently contingent, web of history made very different demands. A Christian could act on a calling, but the secularist could join in action based upon necessity. The grounds of obligation had become natural, and the duties of a calling had now become natural law and natural right. It became possible to speak of callings without speaking of God, or indeed of any caller whatsoever. The calling was now abstract right and duty.

7

Economics and Calling: John Locke's Duality

One of the few political theorists to have been studied in relation to vocation is John Locke. Indeed, in his compelling reconstruction of Locke's thought, John Dunn argues that a concept of calling lies at the heart of his work.[1] While accepting, as I do, that C.B. Macpherson correctly demonstrated the 'possessive individualism' of Locke's positions, Dunn argues against Macpherson's view that Locke was intent on justifying unlimited appropriation and accumulation in a market society. Dunn maintains that it was in fact Locke's religion that provided the 'coherence' of his mind.[2] Views similar to Dunn's, at least on this latter point, have become common.[3]

Locke certainly regarded theology as 'one science ... incomparably above all the rest,' 'the knowledge of Him being the chief end of all our thought.'[4] His theology emphasized concern for a future estate, 'Heaven being our great business and interest ... the chiefest place in our thoughts.' Hope for and fear about an afterlife permeated all of Locke's life, perhaps accounting for his 'uneasiness.' He lived under a God who had 'rewards and punishments of infinite weight and duration in another life.'[5] However, the afterlife was not the only concern, for 'the next thing to happiness in the other world is a quiet prosperous passage through this ... these two are everybody's business.' Such 'prosperous passage' and 'comfortable hopes' involved one firstly in working in the 'particular calling' of a trade or profession and also in something else, for 'those ... [with] plentiful fortunes are excused from ... a particular calling ... yet ... are under an obligation of doing something.'[6]

Dunn points out that Locke's idea of the calling involved at least two aspects.[7] One is the 'particular calling' which embraced the diligently industrious pursuit of a particular profession or trade. The other, the 'general calling,' is preparation for a future life, often through study and prayer. If a man of wealth does not have a particular calling, he is nevertheless bound to do something worthwhile as a service to God. Locke's 'calling' was intensely individualistic. Men were directly responsible to God in their callings, and hence they were not to interfere with one another's work. Consequently, any who failed in their calling could expect little sympathy, for that calling was their personal, God-given duty. Its requirements were differentiated according to social station, but it was at heart an individual pursuit of salvation and of heaven. One was responsible to God for one's own actions. In this respect Locke relates calling and the foundation of society. Men enter into society 'that by mutual assistance, and joint force, they may secure unto each other their proprieties ... leaving ... to every man the care of his own eternal happiness, the attainment whereof can neither be facilitated by another man's industry, nor can the loss of it turn to another man's prejudice.'[8] Society gives security which allows each to seek, and work for, heaven.

It is this individualism and this privacy of responsibility which, according to Dunn, give rise to the features of Locke's possessive individualism that Macpherson has rightly emphasized. When the focus of life and existence has been so privatized, the integrity of private property comes to the fore; hence Locke's obsession with what Laslett describes as 'secure and quiet possession.'[9] Dunn seeks to reinforce this position by showing parallels between Locke's views and those of various Puritans. He concludes, somewhat ironically, that if Locke's views were related to this 'complex of notions' then Macpherson 'must at times do him a certain injustice.'

Certainly there was in Puritanism a strong strain of property-oriented individualism. It is also clear that this stress on the preservation of property could be coupled with a marked antipathy to the accumulation, or attempted accumulation, of property. We have noted that strictures on accumulation had broken down in later Puritanism, but even in Puritanism's earlier phases, when the desire for riches and advancement was usually sharply curtailed, the stress on *preservation* was strong. A conception of calling, with its great stress on working out one's own salvation in fear and trembling, often led to a great preoccupation with the preservation of individual property, even when divorced from any justification for increasing one's estate.

Hence, it is certainly plausible that if Locke placed stress on a calling, his individualism could be explained, or partly explained, by his vision of the individual striving all alone and responsible before the face of God. This is the type of explanation that Dunn attempts. However, in the light of the complex developments in doctrines of calling, it is not enough to relate Locke to a purported traditional view; rather, it must be asked what elements of what earlier views he actually manifested. While Dunn intends only to give a brief outline in order to highlight certain features and notes that the calling was really a set of concepts employed by many different persons over a considerable period of time, he still leaves certain developments unrepresented and tends to present the calling only in its purest theological form.[10] As the calling was a 'complex of notions,' it is a little troublesome that Dunn describes the idea as if it were a fairly consistent doctrine, as though Puritan, or any other, views of the relation of economic activity to the activity of the calling were relatively constant over time. Relating Locke's ideas to the notion of calling produces as many questions as answers if his *specific* understanding of calling is not discussed. In expressing his views, Locke shared much of the phrasing but little of the content and intent of the divines of the preceding century.

LOCKE AND CALLING

In speaking of calling, Dunn said that 'It was not what was done (unless this directly damaged other people) but why it was done that mattered.'[11] But, as we have tried to illustrate earlier, the focus of calling could shift onto, in Dunn's terms, *what* it was that was done. This latter appeared to be the more important feature for Locke. Weber remarked of Puritan ethics that 'Labour must be ... performed as if it were an absolute end in itself, a calling.' This, too, drew little sympathy from Locke, for although 'the gentleman is bound to do something,' and 'We ought to look on it as a mark of goodness in God that he has put our earthly life under a necessity of labour ...,' yet 'Labour for labour's sake is against nature.'[12] In fact one of the most striking features of Locke's understanding of calling was the variety of elements that entered into it. He had conceptions akin to various Puritan and latitudinarian views and also appeared to draw on guides for the conduct and carriage of gentlemen. To this mixture he added distinctive features of his own.

Locke made the common distinction between a particular calling – the tasks that God had given one because of one's particular social situation – and a general calling – the duties of all, regardless of position, consisting largely of prayer, study, and other pious activities.[13] Locke conceived of this distinction in such a way that the general calling was understood as specifically religious. Indeed, he occasionally used the terms 'religion' and 'general calling' synonymously: 'a man [must] understand fully the business of his particular calling in the commonwealth, and of religion, which is his calling as he is a man in the world ...'[14] With the focus of religion falling in the general calling, the particular calling became, for Locke, a much more *natural* activity. Indeed, he sometimes polarized the particular calling and religion itself: 'Besides his particular calling for the support of this life, every one has a concern in a future life, which he is bound to look after. This engages his thoughts in religion ...'[15] So for Locke the particular calling became 'ordinary' and a matter of 'lower concernment' – 'which is by no means to have the first place in our studies.'[16] This calling now became very much, although not exclusively, a matter of this life rather than the next.[17] The conception of religion was then of something concerned with a future life in heaven with no concerns below but the spiritual duties that would aid the attainment of heaven. Hence, 'The only business of the church is the salvation of souls,' which business was a matter of no concern to the commonwealth.[18] Locke distinguished 'Civil Society, or the State' and 'Religious Society, or the Church' thus: 'The end of civil society is civil peace and prosperity, or the preservation of the society and every member thereof ... but beyond the concernments of this life, this society hath nothing to do at all.'[19] Our own familiarity with, or stereotyping of, religion of this kind should not keep us from realizing what an unusual sort of statement this was in seventeenth-century England, where religion was commonly understood as a much more encompassing form of existence.

The particular calling, for Locke, did not embrace all the duties that God had given by virtue of a particular station in society. Rather it focused on work and generally functioned as another word for employment or trade. Locke referred to 'profane callings' and to Peter King's 'calling' as an MP.[20] As with most post-Restoration figures, this calling was not located in God's order for society but in the society itself. It formed 'the ties of civil society and government ...'[21] Along with this understanding of the particular calling came the view that one could choose a calling according to 'convenience' – 'what course he likes best.' Locke wrote a long footnote on the Apostle Paul's injunction to 'Let every man abide in the same calling wherein he was called' in order to demonstrate to his readers that 'it is certain it was lawful for them as well as others to change, where it was lawful for them to change without being Christians.' His paraphrase of the text read, 'Christianity gives not any one any new privilege to change the state or put off the obligations of civil life which he was in before.'[22] Because of this objectification of the calling and his contention that God added no new social obligations to the Christian to remain in his condition, Locke even appeared quite open to the fact that some people might not have any particular calling at all.[23] Everybody had to do something, but it need not be a calling.

However, this understanding of particular callings as employments became confused a little when Locke discussed the calling of a gentleman, a prime concern in his educational writings.[24] For Locke, a gentleman's calling consisted of having 'the Knowledge of a man of Business, a Carriage suitable to his Rank, and to be Eminent and Useful in his Country, according to his station ...' as well as being properly concerned with 'the service of his country and ... moral and political knowledge ...' This calling hence meant not a job – hardly surprising, if one was writing of gentlemen – but the whole range of duties specific to a station.[25] Even here, however, Locke was not quite consistent and occasionally wrote of a gentleman's calling in terms of his specific *office* in the commonwealth as distinct from the requirements of his particular social position.[26] In considering the duties of a gentleman, Locke also advised on the matter of recreation. He suggested to Clark that he have his 'son learn a trade, a handicrafts trade ...' and maintained that this was, in an amateur fashion, quite befitting 'a gentleman's calling.' Dunn also pointed out that Locke suggested three hours of manual work for gentlemen and scholars.[27] While this was, in 1688, still an unusual position, it was by no means unique and had been advocated fifty years earlier by Thomas Morrice and Ben Jonson's friend Edmund Bolton.[28] In 1655 the Duchess of Newcastle thought 'it were better to see a gentleman hew down trees, or dig in the bowels of the earth amongst minerals, than painting or pencilling.'[29] Where Locke did provide something new was in relating such labour directly to a calling. Apart from handiworks, he suggested trades more generally, accounting being one of his favourites.

Locke's individualism also pervaded his view of calling, both general and particular. While he did say that callings were to be of use to one's fellow men, nevertheless the individual emphasis predominated.[30] In terms of salvation he placed great stress on the fact that nobody else could help, that it was each person's own responsibility and lonely struggle.[31] In terms of trades, he emphasized one's unconcern over the affairs and fate of another: 'every man may consider what suits his own convenience and follow what course he likes best. No man complains of the ill management of his neighbour's affairs ...'[32]

The general pattern of Locke's understanding of calling was very similar to one common among post-Restoration divines, especially the latitudinarians.[33] This similarity showed in his tendency to separate religion and particular callings; to see particular callings, though God given, as matters of lower concern; to understand particular callings as trades and employments; to envisage the possibility of changing callings and of having no calling at all; and in the individualism which pervaded his conception both of salvation and of economic conduct. However, Locke's views did differ from these other understandings, particularly the Puritan ones, on several points. He appeared to be a little more reticent with respect to the latitude allowed in devoting time to the increase of one's estate. He devoted more attention to the calling of a gentleman, though even here he stressed the usefulness and importance of learning a trade, an emphasis common in the later Puritan writings. One marked change in tone was the fact that, for latitudinarian Locke, religious enthusiasm was no longer a virtue. In fact a gentleman's calling was a genteel profession rather than a passionate labour under the shadow of God's judgment and love, though this should not lead us to underestimate Locke's passion for salvation.

The major difference between Locke's views and the Puritan discussions of calling came in his conception of work, labour, and economics. The Puritans, even the later ones, would invariably discuss labour under the rubric of calling, and calling under the rubric of sanctification. They certainly stressed that callings were socially useful, but their principal concern was with the place of callings in the economy of salvation. However, when Locke dealt with work, he was concerned with it as far more than a service to God. Locke thought of labour as more than either an end in itself or a sign of God's call. For Locke labour was that by which men appropriated property; it put a distinction between the common and the particular. Labour was also the source of nearly all values, the particular form of value he emphasized being that of usefulness. Both Dunn and Macpherson have noted Locke's taste for commercial metaphor. Gerald Cragg pointed out that he regarded 'virtue' as the 'best purchase' or the 'best bargain' and that he tended to analyse even Jesus' actions in prudential terms.[34] It would seem strange, then, if we related Locke's zeal for property protection purely and solely to religious motives. It would be doubly strange in view of the fact that Locke was, among his many accomplishments, an important economist. His economic knowledge, his concern for money as capital, as a means of driving trade, building up national power, and contributing to the benefit of the whole commonwealth, his glorification of the mechanic as a contributor to civilization, all show that he was as interested in the consequences of work and the usefulness of its products, both corporately and individually, as in the sanctifying aspects of work itself. In order to highlight this range of Locke's views we need to say something about seventeenth-century economic thought.

TWO TYPES OF ECONOMICS

The seventeenth century had two apparently irreconcilable approaches to economic conduct. These can be loosely categorized as the 'moral' and the 'technical' approaches. These categories are based not on particular conclusions reached on particular questions but on differing conceptions of the proper mode of argument about economic matters. The 'moral' stream was congruent with the strictures on usury, self-seeking, and oppression that had been the dominant emphasis in the sixteenth century. In 1611 Roger Fenton, a Protestant divine, wrote *A Treatise of Usury*, which relied heavily on Beza, Calvin, Zwingli, Erasmus, and Oecolampadius. He castigated usurers and condemned arguments based on necessity because 'necessity is lawless.'[35] Similar concerns pervaded the anonymous *Usury Arraigned and Condemned* (1625).[36] The puritanically inclined John Blaxton, in his *The English Usurer* (1634), buttressed his argument with references to the Anglicans Sandys and Jewel and to Puritans such as Downame ('the hammer of usurers'), Preston, Dod, Bolton, Perkins, and Northbrooke.[37] This type of argument continued into the Civil War period in the work of the prosecutor of King Charles I, John Cook, and William Potter, but after the Restoration it was in decline.[38]

After the Restoration, economic arguments became more distinctly technical. This was not because previous moral arguments were secularized or transformed. Rather, another relatively long-standing tradition, the 'technical' one, came to dominate the field. This tradition had earlier antecedents, but if we restrict the discussion to the seventeenth century, the first example is the work of the Mint-master, Gerard de Malynes. In his *The Canker of England's Commonwealth* (1601), he developed arguments on inequality of trade and the use of money that were technical in nature and had little connection to an understanding of calling or of 'moral' economics generally.[39] His overriding concern was stimulation of trade. Twenty-odd years later, Thomas Mun and Edward Misselden criticized Malynes's writings; but, despite their differences, all three shared a common concern for more technical arguments. Neither the morality of usury, the intrinsic worth of labour, the nature of oppression, nor the virtue of charity were of much concern to them. They were interested in what money policies would increase trade.[40] Indeed, Misselden asked, 'what else makes a commonwealth, but the private wealth ...?' and 'is it not lawful for Merchants to seek their *Privatum Commodum* in the exercise of their calling?'[41] The same themes occurred in *The Defence of Trade* (1615) by Sir Dudley Digges, a member of the East India Company, while Sir Thomas Culpeper remarked that he would 'leave proofs of the unlawfulness of usury to divines' and would concern himself only with the economic effects of higher and lower interest rates.[42] This tradition continued throughout the mid-century turmoil, and after the Restoration it was the dominant form of discussion of economic matters. Sir Josiah Child ('the most sordidly avaricious man in England'), Samuel Fortrey, Roger Coke, Thomas Manley, John Graunt, and Dudley North all managed to discuss questions of poverty, trade, money, interest, and employment with only a nod and a wink to the moral tradition.[43] Sir Thomas Dalby even lumped clergy with beggars as 'wholly unemployed.'[44]

When these two schools co-existed, what little attempt there was at communication between them met with even less success. Few people were involved in both, and the structures of the two ideologies seemed incompatible. A clear expression of this incommensurability occurred in the debates between Joseph Lee and John Moore. Each was a clergyman, and between them they wrote five separate pamphlets from 1653 to 1656 on the question of enclosures and common fields.[45] Moore began by complaining that enclosure turned husbandmen into cottagers who could no longer care for their families on the tiny plots that were all they had left. Hence he thought that enclosure was inherently oppression of the poor and was tantamount to not loving Christ. Lee conceded that not caring for the poor was a sin, but argued that since private farming yielded more than farming in common, after enclosure increased weekly contributions could be given to the poor. Anyway, men 'have liberty ... to lay down their Arable land for grass, when pasturage is more profitable than tillage,' and 'the monarch of one acre will make more profit thereof, than he that hath his chare of forty in common.' In a later pamphlet, Lee admitted that he was a participating owner in a proposed enclosure and virtually disavowed any social responsibility on the part of landlords if it interfered with economic efficiency: 'Let it be granted that our land and business lying nearer together fewer servants will be kept; are any bound to keep more servants than are needful for their business; or may they not cast how to do the same business with least labour ... Is a man bound to keep servants to pill straws or labour in vain? by what law?'[46] Indeed, Lee asserted the 'undeniable maxim, that everyone by the light of nature and reason will do that which makes for his greatest advantage' and that 'the advantage of private reasons will be to the advantage of the public.' Moore scorned this response and mimicked the enclosers: 'We shall gain by it ... we shall treble our rents. Hence those Heathenish speeches of theirs. May I not make the best of my own ... Our estates are ours, Who is Lord over us?' In reply to Lee's sceptical 'what law?' Moore replied: 'although thou are a *civil owner*, yet thou are a *Spiritual Usurper*' (emphasis in original). Joyce Appleby summarized this debate, if such it may be called, thus: 'There was no common ground for Lee and Moore to meet upon and resolve their difference. Two different codes, two different conceptions of the relation of the private to the public, two different social visions informed their values as well as their reading of the same biblical texts.'[47]

I have categorized these contending views as 'moral' and 'technical.' However, while these terms might summarize the spirit of the various writings, they are not sufficient to do justice to what was involved. Richard Baxter's 'moral' economy was quite technical in its casuistry of trade. The writings of Joseph Lee show that he was an exponent of the 'morality' of private self-interest. Perhaps the two conceptions can now better be described thus: there was one conception which saw justice, charity, and stewardship as the highest norms, to which all considerations of efficiency, gain, and growth, of the person or of the commonwealth, had to be subject. The other conception saw self-interest as the unredeemable core of economic transactions, efficiency as an incontrovertible good, the public wealth as the sum of private wealths, and the growth of trade as an unquestioned overriding goal. As these points were assumed rather than argued, the authors of the latter focused almost solely on discussions of the means by which these accepted goals could be brought about; hence their apparently 'technical' character. But as any view of economics is never purely a technical matter but always involves a conception of, and a prescription for, human behaviour, the authors who devoted themselves to questions of efficiency and trade gradually began to recommend behaviour ('a new morality') which was conducive to their goals. As their assumptions were submerged, their arguments were purportedly purely recommendations for human conduct which would help such economic goals. The conduct they suggested was predominantly of a type which was subversive of what we have previously called the 'moral economy,' whether the latter was in Anglican or Puritan garb.

This 'new morality' was marked by several features. One was a tendency to equate perceived regularities in economic behaviour and results with the law of nature. Another was that when the 'technical' economists urged the necessity of getting the poor to labour, they no longer focused on the effects on those who were themselves unemployed, but were concerned with the effect on the kingdom of losing such labour. The remedy offered for unemployment went against the grain of all previous Anglican and Puritan teaching, since many of the economists urged increased consumption – the more the better. Roger Coke, Nicholas Barbon, Dudley North, and William Petty all held the view that people had the moral obligation to spend freely in order to provide employment for the poor. Barbon even favoured the promotion of fashion by the sovereign as a means of boosting consumption. This clamour in praise of private gain was a world away from the realm of the diligent pursuit of a calling. Even a relatively commercial Puritan such as Richard Steele appeared mild and conscience-stricken compared with Barbon. But it was this economic morality that began to triumph in late-seventeenth-century England. It had no explicit ties with particular religious doctrines. Most of its advocates were merchants or those connected with trade and monetary policy who cared little for any explicit religious foundation to their work.

CALLING AND ECONOMICS

Locke was highly unusual in late-seventeenth-century economic discussions in that he wrote in *both* the 'moral' and the 'technical' streams. He wrote sophisticated treatments of interest rates while also treating work as a moral and theological category.[48] This duality shows some ambiguity in Locke's attitude towards commercialism. Had he wished to consider work merely in the terms current in mercantilism, he had enough examples close at hand, such as colleagues on the Council for Trade and Plantations when he was its secretary. His reply to Josiah Child's pamphlet on interest rates also baptized him into the world of technical argument.[49] Had Locke merely wished to justify the conduct of industrious property holders and to excoriate the irrationality and idleness of labourers, the terms of reference and arguments offered by Petty and Barbon would have supplied ready equipment.

Eli Hecksher described the mercantilists, among whom he included most economists contemporaneous with Locke, as fundamentally 'amoral ... both in their aims as also in the means for the attainment of their ends.' This amorality arose 'from their widespread indifference towards mankind, both in its capacity as a reasoning animal, and also in its attitude towards the eternal.'[50] Hecksher thought he detected a 'new set of motives' which 'no longer had anything to do with divine precepts.' In particular, he emphasized the acceptance and, indeed, praise of '*a love of gain*' (emphasis mine).[51] If these assertions are correct, then it is clear that Locke was not, *in this sense*, a mercantilist. This is not to deny that, when Locke dealt with economic questions in a technical fashion, his views were similar to those of mercantilist 'morality' – except, perhaps, for his views of a 'natural law' of money.[52] But Locke's general frame of mind and scheme of priorities also included quite different conceptions. Very few things are as clearly opposed to Locke's views as Hecksher's picture of a derogation of reasoning capacity and attitudes towards the eternal. Locke was also very suspicious of those who were given over to 'a love of gain.' He entered the 'technical' economists' realm and rules of debate, but he also employed a 'moral' framework which went beyond it. Locke's thought does not finally embrace one conception or the other. Instead there is a dualism in his approaches to economic matters.

There are several possible reasons for Locke's peculiarity, and they can all be treated on a variety of levels. In a biographical vein it may be noted that Locke was unusual among the economists in that he had a traditional classical education. However, beyond this is the fact that Locke's treatment of the idea of calling was an attempt to reconcile the Christian doctrine of the earthly and heavenly implications of vocation with the more truncated categories and norms current in economic discussions. Work for Locke was particularly a creative activity. Men impressed their personalities upon that at which they worked. He was as clearly interested in the usefulness of work and its products as he was in work itself. This view represented a further externalization of the notion of calling that we noted earlier. As Hundert said, later Puritans like Richard Baxter transformed 'a Catholic notion of good works into a theory of good work stressing the efficient results, social utility, and personal satisfaction arising from planned intense labour. Locke, raised by a Puritan father and rising in society largely by his own efforts, completed the secularisation of this conception by investing the products of creative action, defined by him as work, with the personality of the worker ... One's property was the extension of self by virtue of the injection of personality into nature through work.'[53]

In Locke's emphasis on the fruits of labour, the focus of the doctrine of calling shifted from God's elective activity to the usefulness of the tasks originally conceived of as a response to that activity. Consequently, while we must emphasize the importance of the doctrine of calling for Locke, we must not ascribe to him merely a traditional view of calling and of labour. Locke's views were certainly not theological 'polythene,' but they were equally certainly not Puritan theological armour.[54] Locke, who was innovative in so much, was innovative here as well. His notion of labour relied not only on its fruits in heaven but also on its fruits on earth. His commendations of labour owed as much to his recognition of the usefulness of practical invention as they did to his belief in the necessity of labouring for God's approval. He had a notion of calling and Christian responsibility which encouraged him to prosper through investment, to help direct the financial affairs of the kingdom and its colonies, and to retire and die a wealthy man. He had very much come to terms with the world.

Locke drew differing strands together. His *Essay* has been described as taking a *via media* between scepticism about the possibility of discerning truth and insistence on certainty;[55] his educational writings stressed judicious restraint; his conception of rationality was twofold; his view of work combined elements from theology and from mercantilism; his suggestions for the gentlemen were multifaceted; his religious friends lay among the latitudinarians;[56] his apologetics in *The Reasonableness of Christianity* were an attempt to find a denominator on which all could agree; his state of nature was a reconciliation of logical, historical, and anthropological perspectives.[57] Indeed, Locke's conviction that Christianity was 'the most modest and peaceable religion that ever was' seemed to move him towards a theoretical enterprise that could properly reconcile all things.

The Locke who emerges is a complex figure, weaving elements of an old order and a new order into a radical program, yet still with uneasy theoretical tensions. He saw work itself as a calling, as obedience to God; but he spoke of it principally as the creator of wealth. Locke was obsessed with 'comfortable hopes of a future life when this is ended' and equally concerned with 'a quiet, prosperous passage through this life.'[58] His view of human conduct drew on both these sources and differing elements of his view of calling, labour, and property, and can be traced back to either of them. Locke sought to hold together his comfort in heaven and earth; consequently, neither heaven nor earth alone is enough to understand him.

8

Calling and the Shaping of the Modern World

PROTESTANTISM AND CALLING

The history of calling has no simple line of evolution. There were several paths, and in the Levellers, the Diggers, and to some degree in Locke there were idiosyncratic variations. However, developments in the Reformation, combined with the differences between Anglicans and Puritans, shed light on the general relation between vocation and Protestantism.

In the Reformation there was a distinct change in concepts of work. The views of Luther, Calvin, and other Protestants were markedly different from those of earlier and contemporary Catholics. For Augustine and Thomas Aquinas work was divinely mandated and important. But it was still tied to a lesser kind of life. Anyone who sought for the highest Christian obedience would aspire to a contemplative life, and such a life was the only true vocation. With Luther there came a different world. The workshop was a sphere of the highest Christian service. Those who forsook the work of their place were abdicating their primary Christian duty. While Tauler and Eckhart had, in passing, said similar things, Luther made it the central point of his vision of service. Calvin developed the same theme but with a new emphasis on useful activity rather than social station. Whereas Augustine's and Aquinas's hearers were to serve in the world when necessary, Luther's followers were driven out to serve in the world, and Calvin's followers were unshackled to transform the world.

Similar changes occurred in England, where Protestant views were also in sharp contrast not only to those of more traditional Catholics but also to those of their fellow humanists. While the latter were also committed to types of reform, they had no commitment to callings parallel to that of the evangelicals. The active life that they commended was one of learning, counselling, and politics, and they retained a preference for rest and the contemplative life. For the Protestants all work had the same spiritual value and was epitomized in shoes, dishes, and ploughs – preaching and cobbling were spiritual equals.

If we regard Puritans as stronger Protestants, after the accession of Elizabeth a similar pattern appears. There was a correlation between an emphasis on calling and strong Protestant views. Certainly there were common themes among Anglicans and Puritans. Both groups condemned idleness and placed great and continued stress on the importance, virtues, and fruits of hard work. In this sense, as Greaves notes, there was no distinctive Puritan 'work ethic.'[1] However, there was a Puritan ethic of rationality in work in that, before the Restoration, the Puritans showed far more concern for systematizing and organizing labour and work time. Another matter in which there was a large measure of agreement was in attitudes to the poor. Both groups distinguished two types of poor, called for charity towards the helpless poor, and excoriated the able-bodied, who were thought to be idle and forsaking their divine duty.

The two most notable differences between Anglican and Puritan views of calling were, firstly, that Anglicanism was consistently more conservative.[2] Many Anglicans adopted views akin to those of the Puritans – such as the conception of calling as trade, the notion that one could change a calling, the more open attitude to thriving, the greater emphasis on individualism, and the urge to rationalize work habits. But in each of these cases the Anglicans accepted a view which had been advocated by Puritans of an earlier period. The Puritans consistently adopted views or, in the case of changing a calling, became open to them, before the Anglicans did. In these instances, the Anglican view was more reflective of the hierarchical orders of the society of the sixteenth century. There was a large measure of continuity with previous views and a more traditional understanding of the social order. The Puritans, on the other hand, were the first of the divines to advocate views which later became current in society.

The second notable difference was that the earlier Anglicans conceived of callings as something additional to the specifically religious and pious duties which were the central Christian concern. The earlier Puritans had a more integrated view and understood callings themselves as a fundamental part of religion. For them a calling was not a work of the body to provide a necessary basis for spiritual duties; rather, it was in itself an act of the highest piety and obedience which was immediately heavenly as well as earthly. One aspect of this difference was that the Anglicans focused on rationalizing acts of piety, while the Puritans extended their asceticism to the whole world, particularly the world of work.[3] David Little has pointed out that the Anglicans accepted the existing order of church and commonwealth as a structural embodiment of the will of God. The Puritans, however, believed that God's word, in creation as well as in the Bible, required a particular form of response, a 'striving' to create an order in which 'everything must be tested anew.' He described this as a 'conflict between a *pattern of conformation* and a *pattern of reformation*.'[4] In the arena of vocation this meant that Puritans stressed work and activity while Anglicans stressed status and acceptance. When the Puritan view was extended into social affairs, the economic bond took on a contractual rather than an ascriptive basis. The pattern of work had to be reformed and subjected to a religious rigour whose model was the church. The rational, time-focused world of the monk now set the pattern for all Christians' lives. Work became a discipline.

There was one area in which later Puritans took over a particular aspect of Anglicanism. This was the separation of calling from religion.[5] After the Restoration it was the previous Anglican view that became dominant. The Puritan impulse appears to have been weakened sufficiently that it no longer maintained its distinctive sanctification of work. The result was not that previous work discipline diminished but that the restraints inherent in Christianity no longer played a significant role in conditioning the realities of economic life. Whereas the Anglicans began with a view of spirituality as something that existed above natural life and suffused it with grace, the Puritans had located that gracious activity within the life of work itself and, hence, began to transform work into disciplined vocation. They re-ordered the nature, purpose, and priorities of labouring. When secularizing tendencies, not to mention wars and revolutions, wore them down, the Nonconformists retreated to a place outside the world, or to times taken apart for piety in the workshop. They kept their worldly callings, but now the world itself dictated what was expected in those callings. Puritanism decayed as certain of its virtues triumphed. It could ride, or help create, the waves of new economic attitudes, but at the same time other tides pulled them and shifted the position of the ground beneath. The resulting vector shows similarities to what Max Weber described as the 'spirit of capitalism,' an economic asceticism becoming increasingly devoid of religious heart.

MORE VARIATIONS ON A THEME FROM MAX WEBER

This study suggests that there was a correlation between Protestantism and the new view of everyday work as religious vocation, and the rationalizing of work.[6] Weber was correct in seeing this relation, and it shows some brilliance on his part to have discerned it. However, there were ways in which he was incorrect in his interpretation of sources. Weber stressed not only the new doctrine of vocation but also purported Calvinist doubts over predestination and election, which in turn led to ascetic, restless work habits driven by an attempt to reassure an uncertain soul. There are four problems with this latter claim. The first is that Calvinism was not a monopoly of the Puritans in England: it was long widespread, perhaps even dominant, among other Anglicans.[7] Second, a doctrine of predestination was not a monopoly of Calvinism, or even of Protestantism. It was common currency in sixteenth-century theology and was shared by Tridentine apologists, Anglican bishops, and Puritan agitators.[8] Third, some of Weber's supposedly 'Calvinist' sources, such as his major one, Richard Baxter, were by no means strict predestinarians.[9] Fourth, and perhaps most important, there is not much indication that early Protestants, Calvinists, or Puritans were unusually troubled in their sense of salvation and God's grace. Most were quite secure in their assurance.[10]

Weber was also unclear concerning the inner dynamic of Protestantism, in particular the degree to which the 'Protestant ethic' could better be portrayed as a *corruption* of Protestantism. He accepted that it was necessary to see how 'Protestant asceticism was in turn influenced ... by the totality of social conditions, especially economic.' He also wrote of a 'gradual modification' of the doctrines of Calvin and maintained that 'Calvin's theology must be distinguished from Calvinism.'[11] But still the relation is vague. This is a not-unimportant point, for it was precisely on this question that R.H. Tawney departed from Weber. Tawney maintained that it was a deterioration of Calvinism that produced the 'Protestant ethic.'[12] Tawney's point is reinforced by the fact that the most self-interested or 'rational' views of economic life in seventeenth-century England were, as appears in the study of Locke, present not in Puritan or latitudinarian divines, but in relatively secular writers on the more technical aspects of economics. A set of social views triumphed, and they were ones that Puritans had adopted sooner than Anglicans. But the more self-interested aspects of these new views were not specific to Puritanism and, indeed, Puritanism was much more reticent than some other sectors in the society in advocating them. Puritanism, then, appears not as the principal dynamic in their development but as *less resistant* to them than Anglicanism.[13]

In this respect, the picture of post-Restoration times that emerges from this discussion is similar to one which Tawney portrayed fifty years ago – Puritanism as a weaker link in Christian resistance to the development of a self-interested economic culture and, to mix the metaphor, a fertile ground for the growth of such a culture. There are a variety of possible reasons for this link; however, a theology that emphasized a calling, taught the equality of callings, and elevated and advocated everyday work as a direct service to God was, in the nature of the case, likely to attract those seeking economic change and advancement through work. It could be argued that the analysis may be drawn further as the doctrine of calling itself might stem from an earlier such convergence of concerns and so might, in a Marxist sense, be a type of ideology. With respect to individualism, which Tawney emphasized, there may be some truth to this claim, as it seems plausible that an emphasis on the individual pursuit of salvation makes more sense when the possibility of an individual life becomes more apparent.[14] But, in the case of work itself, the argument is less plausible. The doctrine's roots were in the very different world of the Bible and, in the earliest days of the English Reformation, it was stressed most strongly by those who were most critical of anything resembling self-seeking and who were, in their views of social relations and of stewardship, in some senses the most medieval in outlook. Similarly, Luther, the fountainhead of Reformation views of calling, was scandalized by suggestions of changing station or getting wealth. In Luther, the doctrine of calling was an integral part of theology, stemming directly from the believer's immediate relation to God, the rejection of any mediating function by a priest, and the opposition to the supposed higher vocation of a select spiritual élite. Differing views of calling mirrored differing theologies of Catholic and Protestant. Since this study has been restricted to ideas and has not dealt with other aspects of history, it says nothing about what historical effect the new doctrine of vocation may have had. However, it is clear that the idea of calling, a distinctive and major feature of these centuries, arose specifically among the Reformers, was integrated with the doctrines of the Reformation, and remained a particular focus of the more zealous Protestants. There was indeed a distinctively Protestant ethic, though it was not quite Weber's.

OUR INHERITANCE

Apart from questions of individualism, or economic action, or rationality, or zeal for reconstruction, or any other of the possible correlations, causalities, or affinities swirling in the eddies of Weber's thesis, we should also pause to consider the spiritual realities and effects of the Protestant calling.[15] It is something that has affected and shaped moderns whether or not we believe in callings or in any other kind of spiritual discipline. As

Charles Taylor says: 'there was something peculiar about Calvinists, and ... Puritans ...' They 'generated one of the central ideas of modern culture,' *the affirmation of ordinary life* (emphasis added).[16] Luther declared that God and the angels smile when a man changes a diaper; Tyndale equated washing dishes with the preaching of the word; Perkins proclaimed that wiping shoes was sanctified and holy.[17] As Milton put it:

> To know
> That which before us lies in daily life
> Is the prime wisdom.[18]

This wisdom has its costs – ones that often seem to outweigh its gifts. But we cannot understand ourselves or our world without it. So we do well to remember from what and from whom we have inherited it.

> When Adam thus to Eve: 'Fair consort, the hour
> Of night, and all things now retired to rest,
> Mind us of like repose; since God hath set
> Labour and rest, as day and night to men
> Successive, and the timely dew of sleep
> Now falling with soft slumbrous weight inclines
> Our eyelids; other creatures all day long
> Rove idle, unemployed, and less need rest;
> Man hath his daily work of body or mind
> Appointed, which declares his dignity,
> And the regard of Heaven on all his ways ...'[19]

Notes

1 Introduction: The Importance of a Calling

1 Weber's writings on this topic were originally a series of journal articles in the *Archiv für Sozialwissenschaft* in 1904–5. I shall refer to the Talcott Parsons edition, *The Protestant Ethic and the Spirit of Capitalism.*

2 Homans's quotation is on the dust-jacket of Samuelsson's *Religion and Economic Action.* The excellent review of this work by E.S. Morgan in the *William and Mary Quarterly* is still one of the best and most succinct statements of the Weber thesis in existence.

3 The literature on the Weber thesis is voluminous, so that it is best to give a bibliography of bibliographies. See, for example, Green, *Protestantism, Capitalism and the Social Sciences*; Kitch, *Capitalism and the Reformation*; Eisenstadt, ed., *The Protestant Ethic and Modernization*; Nelson, 'Weber's Protestant Ethic: Its Origins, Wanderings and Foreseeable Futures.' Good recent surveys are Poggi, *Calvinism and the Capitalist Spirit: Max Weber's Protestant Ethic*; Goldman, *Max Weber and Thomas Mann: Calling and the Shaping of the Self*, 18–51; and Lehmann and Roth, eds., *Weber's Protestant Ethic: Origins, Evidences, Contexts.* See also Gordon Marshall, *In Search of the Spirit of Capitalism*; and Lehmann, 'Ascetic Protestantism and Economic Rationalism: Max Weber Revisited after Two Generations.' One of the best studies is still Little, *Religion, Order and Law.*

4 Weber, *Religion of China*; *Sociology of Religion*; *General Economic History.*

5 See Nelson, 'Weber's Protestant Ethic,' 71 ff.

6 Ibid., 72.

7 Hancock, *Calvin and the Foundations of Modern Politics*, 228.

8 Weber, *Protestant Ethic*, 77–8. Miroslav Volf raises the point that the Protestant's calling was not in fact "'labour ... performed as ... an absolute end in itself"

... but a means to glorify God'; see his *Work in the Spirit: Toward a Theology of Work*, 227.

9 Sombart, *Der Moderne Kapitalismus*; Weber, *Theory of Social and Economic Organization*, 147.

10 Weber, *Protestant Ethic*, 17, 19, 21, 200. For Weber's distinction between modern and pre-modern capitalism, see his *General Economic History*, part 4.

11 Weber, *Protestant Ethic*, 51.

12 Ibid., 117.

13 Weber, *Sociology of Religion*, 182.

14 Weber, *Protestant Ethic*, 172.

15 Weber, *Sociology of Religion*, 220; see also his *Religion of China*.

16 Weber, *Protestant Ethic*, 157. In an otherwise illuminating discussion of Weber, Thomas Pangle in his *Spirit of Modern Republicanism* still tends to conflate Weber's treatment of the 'Protestant ethic' and the 'spirit of capitalism'; see 16–22.

17 Weber is often misunderstood on this point by critics whose arguments are thus decidedly off the mark. Kurt Samuelsson, for example, offers a wealth of examples whose purpose is to show that Calvin and Calvinists thought that 'wealth as an end in itself was odious.' Samuelsson, *Religion and Economic Action*, 31.

18 Weber, *Protestant Ethic*, 91.

19 Ibid., 183.

20 See Nelson, 'Weber's Protestant Ethic,' 75. Malcolm H. Mackinnon's 'Part I: Calvinism and the Infallible Assurance of Grace' and 'Part II: Weber's Exploration of Calvinism' still overemphasize the theological rather than the psychological focus of Weber's analysis of Calvinism. See Oakes, 'The Thing That Would Not Die.'

21 Weber, 'Anti-critical Last Word on the Spirit of Capitalism,' 1114, 1115, 1124.

22 Skinner, *Foundations of Modern Political Thought*, see especially 1: 215, 225; Todd, *Christian Humanism and the Puritan Social Order*.

23 Collinson, *Godly People: Essays on English Protestantism and Puritanism*, 548.

24 See Morrill, *Nature of the English Revolution*; R.C. Richardson, *Debate on the English Revolution Revisited*.

25 Macpherson, *Political Theory of Possessive Individualism*.

26 Dunn, *Political Thought of John Locke*.

27 See also Ashcraft, *Revolutionary Politics and Locke's 'Two Treatises of Government'*; Tully, *Discourse on Property: John Locke and His Adversaries*.

28 See Barth, 'Vocation'; Brunner, *Divine Imperative*, 200–8; Ellul, 'Work and Calling'; Volf, *Work in the Spirit*. See also Meilander, *Friendship: A Study in Theological Ethics*, 87–8; Hardy, *Fabric of This World*, ch. 2; Adams, 'Vocation'; Redekop, 'Mennonites, Creation and Work'; Schuurman, 'Reformed Vocation

under Assault'; P. Marshall, 'Vocation, Work and Rest' and 'Work and Vocation: Some Historical Reflections.'

29 The comments made by David Zaret on this matter are pertinent. See his 'Use and Abuse of Textual Data.' See also Von Greyer, 'Biographical Evidence on Predestination, Covenant, and Special Providence.'

30 I have attempted to cover Protestant Reformers, Catholic humanists, Puritans, Anglicans, and Nonconformists. I also sought to look at Recusants, Baptists and other separatists, and Quakers and fringe sects, but there was too little vocational writing in the works I saw to provide material for, or justify, any safe or interesting conclusions. The same can be said for political figures and theorists such as King James I, Hobbes, Harrington, and Filmer. In general, callings were not one of their concerns. I would not want to make too much of this even by way of a negative conclusion. The texts are also silent on specific vocations of women, and the authors usually only had males in mind. I have tried to use inclusive language except where it would be too obviously anachronistic, as, for example, in the book title.

2 Freedom, Necessity, and Calling

1 See Schmidt, 'klesis' in Kittel, ed., *Theological Dictionary of the New Testament*; Weber, *Protestant Ethic and the Spirit of Capitalism*, 204ff; Scharmann, Mensching, Lau, Freytag, Nordmann, and Fichtner, 'Beruf,' in Mohr, ed., *Die Religion in Geschichte und Gegenwart.*

2 Schmidt, 'klesis.'

3 For studies of *klesis* see Weber, *Protestant Ethic*; Schmidt, 'klesis'; Holl, 'Die Geschichte des Worts "Beruf,"' in his *Gesammelte Aufsätze zur Kirchengeschichte*; Scharmann et al., 'Beruf.'

4 See Beardslee, *Human Achievement and Divine Vocation in the Message of Paul*; Schmidt, 'klesis'; Barth, 'Vocation,' 600–7. Holl appears to be erroneous on this point, cf Holl, 'Die Geschichte des Worts "Beruf,"' 190.

5 This view is contrary to Arendt, *Human Condition*, 290. See Agnell, *Work, Toil and Sustenance: An Examination of Views of Work in the New Testament*; Engnell, 'Some Biblical Attitudes to Work. 1. Work in the Old Testament'; Gartner, 'Some Biblical Attitudes to Work. 2. Work in the New Testament.'

6 Genesis 4:17, 20, 21, 22; 9:20; 10:9; 11:3.

7 See also Isaiah 11:1–7; Hosea 2:18–23.

8 Matthew 7:24; 9:34; 10:10; 13:3, 30; Luke 10:7; 15:8, 11; John 4:35.

9 Cf 2 Thessalonians 3:6. See also A. Richardson, *Biblical Doctrine of Work*; Gryglewicz, 'La valeur du travail manuel dans la terminologie grècque de la bible'; Sevenster, *Paul and Seneca*, 211ff.

10 Cf 1 Corinthians 4:12; 15:10; 16:16; Ephesians 4:28; Romans 16:12; Galatians 4:11; Philippians 2:16; Colossians 1:29; 1 Thessalonians 5:12.

11 Ephesians 4:17–32, esp. v. 28; 2 Corinthians 11:9; 12:13; 2 Thessalonians 3:8; 1 Thessalonians 4:9–12; Acts 20:35. Paul's statements appear to contradict Arendt's view that he recommended labour only 'as a good means to keep out of trouble,' cf Arendt, *Human Condition*, 289.

12 2 Thessalonians 3:10; See also Matthew 9:34; 10:10; Luke 10:7.

13 On the attitude of those actually engaged in the work, see Geoghegan, *The Attitude toward Labour in Early Christianity and Ancient Culture*, 48–58.

14 Xenophon, *Oeconomicus*, IV:2, 3; Mossé, *Ancient World at Work*, 25. See also Jacard, *Histoire sociale du travail*, 66–75.

15 Aristotle, *Politics*, 1329a, 1–2.

16 Isocrates, *Areopagitica*, 26.

17 Cicero, *De officiis*, I:42, 150; Mossé, *Ancient World at Work*, 25.

18 Xenophon, *Oeconomicus*, IV:15; Aristotle, *Politics*, 1318b, 1; Cicero, *De officiis*, I: 42. See also Burford, *Craftsmen in Greek and Roman Society*, esp. 29–30 on Cicero's attitude to farmers; Geoghegan, *Attitude toward Labour*, 37–8.

19 Arendt, *Human Condition*, 290.

20 Westerman, 'Between Slavery and Freedom.' See also Kaiser, *Theology of Work*, 32ff.

21 Aristotle, *Nichomachaean Ethics* I:5; Aristotle, *Eudaemonian Ethics* 1215a, 35f; Aristotle, *Politics* 1337b, 5; Arendt, *Human Condition*, 302; Schlaifer, 'Greek Theories of Slavery from Homer to Aristotle'; Finley, 'Between Slavery and Freedom,' in his *Economy and Society in Ancient Greece*, 116–32.

22 Aristotle, *Politics* 1256a, 30f. Aristotle equated *skole* and *aergia*, leisure and laziness. Cf Arendt, *Human Condition*, 323–4.

23 Hesiod, *Works and Days* 1, 383–617.

24 See Pieper, *Leisure: The Basis of Culture*, 20–1.

25 Edelstein, *Meaning of Stoicism*, 74–8.

26 Seneca, *Epistolae* 31, 4–5; 44, 1–4; Seneca, *De brevitate vitae* 15, 3. See also *Epistolae* 13, 20, 28, 88, 89; Sevenster, *Paul and Seneca*, 215.

27 Grant, *Early Christianity and Society*, ch. 4: 66–95; Lightfoot, ed., *Apostolic Fathers*, 487–511 ('Ad Diognetus').

28 Lightfoot, ed., *Apostolic Fathers*, 487–511.

29 Augustine, *De civitate dei*, I, 29; XI, 25; Deane, *Political and Social Ideas of St. Augustine*, 44, 108ff.

30 Butler, *Western Mysticism*, 157–65; Arendt, *Human Condition*, 13, 15, 304, 376–7; Augustine, 'Sermon,' CLXIX, 17; Augustine, *De civitate dei*, XI, 16; XIX, 1, 2, 19; Augustine, *Expositio in Psalmos*, 69, 7; Augustine, *In Ioann. Evangel.*, 6, 25–6; Augustine, *Tract in Ioann.*, CXXIV, 5.

31 Cf O'Brien, *Essay on Medieval Economic Thinking*, 129; Killeen, *Philosophy of Labour According to Thomas Aquinas*.

32 Thomas Aquinas, *Summa theologiae*, ii. 2. 179; ii. 2. 181. 104; ii. 2. 182. 1, 2; Thomas Aquinas, *Expositio in Psalmos*, 45. 3; Thomas Aquinas, *Summa contra gentiles*, iii. 135; Arendt, *Human Condition*, 290, 303–4, 377.

33 Rolle, *Amending of Life* (1434), 4, 6; Haines, 'Church, Society and Politics in the Early Fifteenth Century as Viewed from an English Pulpit,' 154. See also Parker, *Rich and the Poor* (1493); Betson, *Here Beginneth a Treatise to Dispose Men to Be Virtuously Occupied in Their Mind and Prayers* (1500). Walter Hilton, 'Epistle on the Mixed Life,' speaks of three lives, the third being a mixed life which combines the active and contemplative.

34 Christopher Holdsworth in his 'The Blessing of Work: The Cistercian View' points out the high view of work among the Cistercians and maintains that this was different from the other 'attitudes prevailing' in monastic circles in the twelfth century (68). He also says that this emphasis prefigured Weber's Protestant ethic. However, while there may be a greater stress on work, this is not the key point at issue. The question is whether the work is itself a Christian *vocation*.

35 Beton, *A Right Profitable Treatise* (1500), fol. cii.

36 Owst, *Literature and Pulpit in Medieval England*, 554, 556, 565; Rolle, *Amending of Life*, 2ff.

37 See Owst, *Literature and Pulpit*, 568–9.

38 Ibid., 550–1.

39 Eckhart, 'Contemplative and the Active Life.'

40 Luke 10:39–42 (Jerusalem Bible).

41 He does not, however, draw out the feminist implications of the text.

42 Eckhart, 'Contemplative and the Active Life,' 195.

43 Ibid.

44 Ibid., 197.

45 Ibid.

46 Ibid., 195.

47 Johann Tauler, 'Vocation,' in his *Oeuvres Complètes*, 3:458 (the translation in the quotations is mine). Compare vol. 4; 126–47 on vocation as conformity to Christ. See also Scharmann et al., 'Beruf,' 1077.

48 Tauler, 'Vocation,' 456.

49 Ibid., 457, 460. There are indications that Wyclif held a similar view.

50 Barth, 'Vocation,' 601. See also Lau, 'Beruf III, Christentum und Beruf,' in Scharmann et al., 'Beruf,' 1078; Holl, 'Die Geschichte des Worts "Beruf,"' 199ff. *The New Catholic Encyclopedia* lists only 'clerical' and 'supernatural' life as categories of 'vocation,' see 735–8.

51 What is true for the German is true for those languages where there is now a word with this sense. The Dutch *beroep*; English *calling, vocation*; Danish *kald*; and Swedish *kallelse* have this sense only after Luther's innovation. Before Luther they had generally meant a specifically spiritual call. See Weber, *Protestant Ethic*; Holl, 'Die Geschichte des Worts "Beruf"'; Scharman et al., 'Beruf'; Schmidt, 'klesis.'

52 Weber, *Protestant Ethic*, 207, 210.

53 See Althaus, *Ethics of Martin Luther*, 36ff. See also *Luther's Works*, 14:15; 13:369; 46:246.

54 See Cranz, *Essay on the Development of Luther's Thought on Justice, Law and Society*, 156; Althaus, *Ethics of Martin Luther*, 37; *Luther's Works*, 7:190; 51:348–52.

55 Cranz, *Essay*, 157.

56 Ibid.

57 Wingren, *Luther on Vocation*, 64; Althaus, *Ethics of Martin Luther*, 39; Holl, 'Die Geschichte des Worts "Beruf,"' 217–18. See also Wingren, 'Concept of Vocation – Its Basis and Its Problems.'

58 Althaus, *Ethics of Martin Luther*, 101; *Luther's Works*, 31:360.

59 Althaus, *Ethics of Martin Luther*, 101. This contradicts the views of Troeltsch, *Social Teachings of the Christian Churches*, 2:555ff.

60 Althaus, *Ethics of Martin Luther*, 102–3; *Luther's Works*, 45:258–9.

61 Althaus, *Ethics of Martin Luther*, 102–3.

62 Wingren, 'Concept of Vocation,' 70–6, 125, 203–4.

63 Ibid., 178. This is said with respect to 1 Corinthians 7:20.

64 Calvin, *Commentary on the First Epistle to the Corinthians*, 150–5.

65 Calvin, *Institutes of the Christian Religion*, 2. 10. 6. See also *Institutes*, 3. 4. 6.

66 This does not appear to be the case for ministers, cf Calvin, *Institutes*, 4. 3. 10–16.

67 Calvin, 'Contre la Secte des Libertines,' in *Corpus Reformatorum Calvani Opera*, 7:211–12; Harkness, *John Calvin: The Man and His Ethics*, 212.

68 Calvin, *Commentary on First Corinthians*, 153–5 (on vv 20, 24 of ch. 7). See also Bouwsma, *John Calvin: A Sixteenth-Century Portrait*.

69 Troeltsch, *Social Teachings*, 611.

70 Calvin, *Institutes*, 1. 17 and 3. 1. 1.

71 Calvin, 'Contre la Secte des Libertines,' 248.

72 Little, *Religion, Order and Law*, 60.

73 Biéler, *Social Humanism of John Calvin*, 17–18.

74 Cf James, 'Effect of the Religious Changes of the Sixteenth and Seventeenth Centuries in Economic Theory and Development,' 44.

75 Miegge, *I Talenti Messi a Profitto*, 7, 112–13; Calvin, *Corpus Reformatorum Calvani Opera*, 45:567ff.

76 Calvin, *Commentaries on a Harmony of the Evangelists, Matthew, Mark and Luke*, commentary on Luke 10:38.
77 Calvin, *Institutes*, 1. 16. 3.
78 Calvin, *Commentaries*, commentary on Luke 10:7.
79 Calvin, *Commentary on Philippians*, 252. See Tonkin, *Church and the Secular Order in Reformation Thought*, 115.
80 See Tonkin, *Church and the Secular Order*, 128, and Little, 'New Order of John Calvin,' in his *Religion, Order and Law*, 33–80.

3 Reform, Estate, and Calling

1 To classify ideas of vocation in Reformation England I have described the views of three groups, each of which consists of people of similar opinions. These groups are the 'More circle,' the 'earliest reformers,' and the 'Commonwealth Party.' I have taken the 'More circle' as representative of Catholic humanist views, and the other two groups as showing aspects of the impact of Protestantism in England. The earliest reformers, Tyndale and Frith, wrote and preached in much the same period as the More group, in the 1520s and 1530s, while the 'Commonwealth Party' flourished around 1550. Nearly all the terms that one could use to classify figures in Reformation England are fraught with difficulty. See Haigh, 'Introduction,' 1–17, and 'The Recent Historiography of the English Reformation,' 19–33, in Haigh, ed., *English Reformation Revised*; O'Day, *Debate on the English Reformation*; and Lake and Dowling, eds, *Protestantism and the National Church in Sixteenth Century England*. I believe that the use of 'humanist' for the 'More circle' and the use of 'Protestant' (or 'evangelical') for the 'earliest reformers' and the 'Commonwealth Party' point to important characteristics of identifiable groups. It should be added, of course, that most of the Protestants were also 'humanist' in their education and much of their outlook. However, they had additional 'Protestant' characteristics not shared by the 'More circle.'
2 Lupset, 'Treatise of Charity' (1533), in *Life and Works of Thomas Lupset*, 212.
3 Ibid., 212–13.
4 Ibid., 215.
5 'the body hath his proper virtues, and the soul likewise ... The virtues of the body be, as to fast, to watch, to go on pilgrimage, to travail with hand and foot for to help their neighbours, to distribute ... alms deeds, to build up churches ...' Ibid., 221.
6 On criticism of covetousness, see ibid., 248.
7 Of these goods, 'We must have a certain slight regard to our body, and a slighter regard to the world, but care we may not for either of these two ... Only our

soul is the thing to be cared for ... our spirit and mind only hath things, that truly be called goods ...' Lupset, 'An Exhortation to Young Men,' *Life and Works of Thomas Lupset,* 258. See also 'A Treatise of Dying Well' (1534), in *Life and Works of Thomas Lupset,* 270–1.

8 Starkey, *Dialogue between Pole and Lupset* (1538), 23.
9 Ibid., 24.
10 Ibid., 25.
11 Ibid., 25–6.
12 Ibid., 24–7.
13 More, *Utopia,* vol. 4 in *Yale Edition of the Complete Works of St. Thomas More,* 127–9.
14 Ibid., 135.
15 Ibid., 225–7.
16 Cf ibid., 125–35; Starkey, *Dialogue,* 77–81, 89–91, 142–5. Elyot is an exception, being enamoured of riding, hunting, and hawking.
17 Hogrefe, *The Sir Thomas More Circle,* 46, 130–1, 137–9.
18 'Introduction' to Sylvester, ed., *St. Thomas More: Action and Contemplation,* 14.
19 On More's early spirituality see Marc'hadour, 'Thomas More's Spirituality,' in Sylvester, ed., *St. Thomas More;* on his later spirituality see Martz, 'Thomas More: The Tower Works,' in Sylvester, ed., *St. Thomas More.* See also Marc'hadour, 'Saint Thomas More'; and '*Obediens usque ad Mortem:* A Key to St. Thomas More.'
20 On Starkey and reform, see Jones, *Tudor Commonwealth,* 107, 110, 124, 163, 195–6. On Rastell, see Jones, *Tudor Commonwealth,* 47–8; Hogrefe, *Sir Thomas More Circle,* 118. On Heywood, see Jones, *Tudor Commonwealth,* 47–8, 91–2; Hogrefe, *Sir Thomas More Circle,* 283–8.
21 Jones, *Tudor Commonwealth,* 68.
22 Tyndale, 'Parable of the Wicked Mammon' (1527), in *Doctrinal Treatises and Portions of Holy Scripture,* 97.
23 Ibid., 98.
24 Ibid., 102.
25 Ibid., 100, 101.
26 Ibid., 100–1, 102.
27 In Cranmer's writings and the prescribed homilies of the 1540s, 'calling' meant social degree and estate. These works emphasized abiding in one's condition. See Cranmer, 'A Sermon on Rebellion,' in *Works,* 2:191–5; Cheke, *Hurt of Sedition* (1549), 2–5; Preston, *Primer, or Book of Private Prayer* (1553), 5:336–70; Cranmer, ed., 'Certain Sermons' (assembled under the general editorship of Cranmer, first published in 1547 and used through Elizabethan times).

28 See Tyndale, *Works of Tyndale and Frith*; Frith, 'Disputation of Purgatory,' in *Works of John Frith*, 81–203.

29 See Frith, 'A Mirror, or Glass, to Know Thyself,' in *Works of John Frith*, 271–2.

30 Ibid., 271.

31 Ibid., 275–6. The story of St Silvanus was also used by Odo of Cheriton in the early thirteenth century: see Holdsworth, 'Blessing of Work: The Cistercian View.'

32 On Frith's theology and his originality, see Wright, 'Introduction' to *Works of John Frith*; Clebsch, *England's Earliest Protestants, 1520–1535*, 134ff.

33 Clebsch, *England's Earliest Protestants*; Frith, 'A Mirror,' 271–2.

34 The earliest sixteenth-century use that I have found of the word 'calling' to mean estate is in Cranmer's 1539 Bible where 1 Cor. 7:20 reads 'in the same calling in which he was called.'

35 Crowley, *Voice of the Last Trumpet ... Calling All Estates of Men to the Right Path of Their Vocation* (1549).

36 Ibid., 1.

37 Crowley, 'One and Thirty Epigrams,' in *Select Writings of Robert Crowley*, 40–1. See also 58ff, 66ff.

38 Cowper, ed., introduction to Crowley, *Select Writings*, x.

39 Crowley, *Select Writings*, 4.

40 Ibid., 88–9.

41 Ibid., 112; Crowley, *Way to Wealth: Wherein Is Taught a Remedy for Sedition* (1550), 6, 27.

42 Lever, *Sermons* (1550), 29, 50. On stewardship, see 106–7.

43 Latimer, 'A Sermon of the Lord's Prayer,' 339. See also 340ff and C.M. Gray, *Hugh Latimer and the Sixteenth Century*, 26–39; Latimer, 'Sermon of the Plough' (1548), 'Inflation of Prices and Decay of Standards' (1549), and 'A Cure for Violence and Corruption' (1549), in Chandos, *In God's Name*. (The titles are Chandos's.)

44 On Hooper, see Opie, 'Anglicizing of John Hooper.' On Becon, see Bailey, *Thomas Becon*; Hughes, *Theology of the English Reformers*, 80ff. On Bradford, see H.C. White, *Tudor Books of Private Devotion*, 166ff.

45 Crowley, *Select Writings*, 37; Latimer 'Sermon of the Lord's Prayer,' 346; Latimer, *Works*, 1:359.

46 Becon, 'Catechism,' in *Works*, 1:398. Less common were Becon's views on thrift, see 1:398–401.

47 See Becon, *Works*, 1:25, 336, 604–16; 2:386–7, 398–401; Hooper, *Works*, 1:450ff; Hutchinson, *Works*, 6–7; Lever, *Sermons*, 28–33, 48–51, 92–5.

48 Becon, *Works*, 1:36, 608, 616.

49 Hooper, *Works*, 1:456; Hutchinson, *Works*, 6; Latimer, *Works*, 2:23. For Crowley see *Voice of the Last Trumpet*; for Lever see *Sermons*, 109–10.

50 Protestants were criticized frequently for promoting unease and rebellion. See
Stephen Gardiner, *Obedience in Church and State: Three Political Tracts by
Stephen Gardiner; De Vera Obedienta* (1535); *Letters*, letter no. 119, 274; Jones,
Tudor Commonwealth, 74–5; L.B. Smith, *Tudor Prelates and Politics*, 99,
103–4, 242–3.

51 Tawney, *Religion and the Rise of Capitalism*, 121; Allen, *History of Political
Thought in the Sixteenth Century*, 142; Zeeveld, *Foundations of Tudor Policy*,
172–3, 196; L.B. Smith, *Tudor Prelates*, 126; Jones, *Tudor Commonwealth*, 10,
64, 80–3, 101, 125, 131, 192, 214.

52 Though Becon allowed for some voluntarism; see *Works*, 1:608.

53 Skinner, *Foundations of Modern Political Thought*, 1:225. See also Yost,
'William Tyndale and the Renaissance Humanist Origins of the *Via Media*';
O'Malley, 'Erasmus and Luther: Continuity and Discontinuity as a Key to
Their Conflict.' Skinner emphasizes the humanist-educated background of these
reformers, especially Latimer, Lever, and Becon (223ff). This is the case for most
Protestants; however, in itself it tells us nothing about any similarity of views on
the matter at hand. He also asserts that the humanists stressed *negotium* (217ff),
but I would maintain that they stressed it more as a necessary foundation for
otium. This position was not very different from that of Thomas Aquinas.

54 Margo Todd's *Christian Humanism and the Puritan Social Order* seeks to abolish 'the old myth' that there was a distinctly Puritan social theory. In doing this
she discusses far more than matters of work and calling, and on these other matters I would not presume to comment. She refers frequently to a 'Protestant
Ethic' and considers the Puritans and, *a fortiori*, the earlier reformers 'as only
one component, if a vocal one, of an important tradition of social activism and
progressivism which had existed among Catholics as well as Protestants since
the beginning of the century' (8). For her, 'the conditioning influence in the
sixteenth and seventeenth centuries was Christian humanism' (16–17). 'The
tradition of More and Erasmus ... was continued in the generation of the commonwealth men ...' (40). In attempting to show this she convincingly demon-
strates Lupset's, Starkey's, More's, and others' critique of idleness, their calling
people to labour diligently, their praise for the *vita activa*, and their desire for
social reform. While what she says is accurate, these views are not novel (except
perhaps for their stress on politics and learning) and are little different from
medieval conceptions. They do not contain the new and distinctive elements
which came in with Protestantism, were manifest in the Commonwealth men,
and continued into Puritanism.

Richard M. Douglas maintains that humanists and Protestants used two different vocabularies. The former relied on classical treatises on ethics, pedagogy,
and medicine. The latter relied on Scripture. The humanists also stressed 'life-

style,' *genus vitae*, which was dependent on inborn aptitude, whereas the Protestants stressed *vocatio*, which was according to divine command. The former believed in 'choice' (*eligere*), whereas the latter believed in being 'called' (*vocari*), being chosen. See Douglas's 'Talent and Vocation in Humanist and Protestant Thought.'

55 This lack of differentiation led Skinner to overlook some distinctive aspects of the two movements. While he agreed that 'Most ... of the humanists were more concerned to offer their advice to Princes and other "governors,"' yet he held that the 'most radical ... insisted on the need for the whole body of citizens to acquire and practise the virtues as a precondition of attaining a well ordered commonwealth' (*Foundations of Modern Political Thought*, 229). However, it is clear that the 'most radical' were in fact the Protestants whom Skinner, in this instance, considered together in one category with their unreformed fellows. It was those not of Protestant persuasion who concentrated their advice on the prince and his counsellors.

56 Todd uses the term 'calling' to refer to humanist teaching on work, but her sources do not. Cf Todd, *Christian Humanism*, 123, 200.

57 See Pocock, *Machiavellian Moment: Florentine Political Thought and the Atlantic Republican Tradition*, 338ff.

4 Work, Rationality, and Calling

1 Miller and Johnson, eds, *The Puritans*, 1:7.
2 See Todd, *Christian Humanism and the Puritan Social Order*, 2.
3 Russell, *Causes of the English Civil War*, 84–5.
4 B. Hall, 'Puritanism: The Problem of Definition,' 290. See also Lamont, 'Puritanism as History and Historiography: Some Further Thoughts,' 133–40; Lake, *Moderate Puritans and the Elizabethan Church*; 'Puritan Identities'; and 'Calvinism and the English Church, 1570–1635'; Collinson, 'A Comment: Concerning the Name Puritan'; P. White, 'The Rise of Arminianism Reconsidered'; Sasek, *Images of English Puritanism: A Collection of Contemporary Sources, 1589–1646*; Underdown, *Revel, Riot and Rebellion: Popular Politics and Culture in England, 1603–1660*, 40ff; Greaves, *Society and Religion in Elizabethan England*, 3–14.
5 Russell, *Causes of the English Civil War*, 84.
6 Knewstub, *Lectures upon the Twentieth Chapter of Exodus* (1578), sixth lecture; Sibbes, *Works*, 4:66–7; Sibbes, *Beams of Divine Light* (1639), 184.
7 Perkins, 'Epistle Dedicatory' of 'A Treatise of the Vocations,' in Perkins, *Works* (1603), 902–39. See also T. Scott, *Vox Populi, Vox Dei, Vox Regis*, 1; Northbrooke, *Treatise against Dicing, Dancing, Plays and Interludes* (1643), 72; Field,

Godly Exhortation (1583), fols ciii ff. See also Greaves, *Society and Religion,* 16–17.

8 Gurnall, *Christian in Complete Armour* (1655), 279; T. Taylor, *Christ's Combate and Conquest,* 150; Preston, *Life Eternal* (1631), part 1:146–50.

9 Northbrooke, *Treatise against Dicing,* 73; I. Morgan, 'New Monks?' ch. 5 of *Godly Preachers of the Elizabethan Church,* 143.

10 Prynne, *Histrio-Mastix,* 1:500; Preston, *Sermons Preached before His Majesty* (1630), 18; Gurnall, *Christian in Complete Armour;* Perkins, *Works,* 903, 919.

11 Charnock, *Discourse upon the Existence and Attributes of God* (1680), 531. See also T. Scott, *Vox Populi, Vox Dei, Vox Regis,* 21; Northbrooke, *Treatise against Dicing.*

12 Whateley, *A Bride Bush,* 9; Hieron, *All the Sermons of Samuel Hieron,* 245–7; Baxter, *Practical Works,* 11: ch. 27, and 12: ch. 27.

13 See C. Hill, 'Pottage for Freeborn Englishmen,' in his *Change and Continuity in Seventeenth Century England,* 338–50; Sibbes, *Saint's Cordial* (1637), 366; Dod and Cleaver, *Plain and Familiar Exposition of the Ninth and Tenth Chapters of Proverbs* (1612), 65–6; W. Gouge, *Of Domesticall Duties* (1626), 2; Watson, *Saint's Delight* (1657), 233.

14 Cf Perkins, *Works;* T. Scott, *Vox Populi, Vox Dei, Vox Regis.*

15 Richard Harris, 'Portents of Dissolution,' in Chandos, *In God's Name,* 224.

16 Downame, *Christian Warfare* (1604), 116.

17 Prynne, *Histrio-Mastix,* 1:302–3, 307, 947, 968; Thomas Cartwright, *First Reply to Whitgift's Answer to the Admonition,* in Whitgift, *Works,* 3:437ff; [Anon.], 'A Defence of Such Points in R. Some's Last *Treatise* as M. Penry Hath Dealt Against,' in Some, *Godly Treatise Concerning the Ministry* (1588), 154; Bayne, *Exposition of Ephesians* (nd, author died in 1617), 543; Greene, *Refutation of the Apology for Actors* (1615), 3; Watson, *Body of Practical Divinity,* 248; Dod and Cleaver, *Household Government* (1621), sig. x 3; Stubbes, *Anatomy of Abuses* (1583), 'Letter to Reader'; Hake, *Touchstone for This Time Present* (1574), fol. 132.

18 Northbrooke, *Treatise against Dicing,* 57; Perkins, *Works,* 906.

19 Prynne, *Histrio-Mastix,* 1:325, 453; Bayne, *Exposition,* 306; Perkins, 'Of Questions Concerning Temperance' in Merrill, *William Perkins, 1558–1602,* 220, 225–7.

20 John Owen appeared to be an exception to this, being frequently criticized while vice-chancellor of Oxford for going around in powdered wigs and wearing ribbons and bells. See Toon, *God's Statesman.*

21 Perkins, in Merrill, *Perkins,* 209–10; and in *Works,* 933.

22 Cartwright, *First Reply,* in Whitgift, *Works,* 3:437ff.

23 See the similar picture given by Greaves in his 'Work and Worship,' ch. 9 in

his *Society and Religion*. Despite some agreement on the general features of Puritan views, there is still widespread disagreement on particular features. See Cohen, 'Saints Zealous in Love and Labour: The Puritan Psychology of Work'; Sommerville, 'Anti-Puritan Work Ethic'; Seaver, 'Puritan Work Ethic Revisited'; Constantin, 'Puritan Ethic and the Dignity of Labour: Hierarchy versus Equality'; George and George, 'English Protestant Economic Theory: The World and Its Callings,' ch. 3 in their *Protestant Mind of the English Reformation*; Manning, 'Religion, Politics and the Godly People,' ch. 3 of Manning, ed., *Politics, Religion and the English Civil War*; Tawney, *Religion and the Rise of Capitalism*; Breen, 'Non-existent Controversy: Puritan and Anglican Attitudes on Work and Wealth, 1600–1640'; Foster, 'Wealth: The Calling, Capitalism, Commerce, and the Problem of Prosperity,' ch. 4 of his *Their Solitary Way*; C. Hill, 'William Perkins and the Poor,' in his *Puritanism and Revolution*, 212–33; C. Hill, *Society and Puritanism*; Eisen, 'Called to Order: The Role of the Puritan *Berufsmensch* in Weberian Sociology,' 203–18. Some of these treatments build their case using comparatively few primary sources. In general, there is little attention given in these works to the question of *changes* in Puritan views, which is perhaps an additional reason for their differing interpretations. Michaelson, 'Changes in the Puritan Concept of Calling or Vocation,' 315–36, gives an outline similar to the one here, but covers few primary sources.

24 Perkins, *Works*, 903. For discussions of Perkins, see C. Hill, 'William Perkins and the Poor'; and Michaelson, 'Changes in the Puritan Concept,' 315–36. Various authors tend to emphasize only one aspect of Perkins's views. See Michaelson, 'Changes,' 320, 321. George and George, in 'English Protestant Economic Theory,' 135ff, emphasize only that one must abide in the calling; Michaelson, 'Changes,' 319; H.C. White, *Social Criticism in the Popular Religious Literature in the Sixteenth Century*, 170–1, 241; Breen, 'Non-existent Controversy,' 273–87, 275; Foster, 'Wealth,' 99ff. Little, *Religion, Order and Law*, 118, and Knappen, *Tudor Puritanism*, speak of Perkins's view of calling as being only a view that a specific station, work, office, or function is God ordained. George and George, 'English Protestant Economic Theory,' 138–9, 142, emphasize that all callings are equal; Foster, 'Wealth,' 99, sees callings as flexible. H.C. White sees calling as either static or flexible, cf *Social Criticism*, 179–80, 184, 243–4. I have referred principally to Perkins's work, as he is the only Puritan author to describe callings in a systematic way. However, Perkins's views are typical of other Puritans of the period.

25 Perkins, *Works*, 904. But Perkins also says that these 'are not callings or vocations, but avocations.' On callings as employments, see Bisse, *Two Sermons Preached* (1581), sig. B 5.

26 Perkins, *Works*, 911, 919. See also Wright, *Middle-Class Culture in Elizabethan England*, 178.

27 Perkins, *Works*, 904–5; Dering, *Works* (1597); Chaderton, *Sermon on Romans 12, v. 3–8* (1584), 107–8; Greenham, *Works* (1612), 645, 676–7. See also the discussion in Knappen, *Tudor Puritanism*, 397ff.

28 Perkins, edited by Breward, *Work of William Perkins*, 513, 755; Dering, *Works*.

29 Perkins, *Works*, 913.

30 Ibid., 913; H.C. White, *Social Criticism*, 177–8.

31 Perkins, *Whole Treatise of the Cases of Conscience* (1606), 485–8.

32 Perkins, *Works*, 903, 904, 913. Compare Tyndale, *Doctrinal Treatises and Portions of Holy Scripture*, 102.

33 Perkins, *Works*, 912–13.

34 Ibid., 913–15.

35 Ibid., 912.

36 Ibid., 924–5. See also Merrill, *Perkins*, 189, 190, 195, 224; Cleaver, *Godly Form of Household Government* (1600), 61ff.

37 Merrill, *Perkins*, 190–7; Perkins, edited by Breward, *Work of William Perkins*, 311, 416–17, 474. See also his discussion of why, even if we have two coats, we need not give one away, in Merrill, *Perkins*, 209. See the discussions in Knappen, *Tudor Puritanism*, 412ff; Downame, *Christian Warfare*, 47.

38 Perkins, *Works*, 906; Merrill, *Perkins*, 209, 210, 226.

39 Perkins, *Works*, 912; George and George, 'English Protestant Economic Theory,' 131–2, 147.

40 Perkins, *Works*, 909–15.

41 C. Hill, 'Protestantism and the Rise of Capitalism,' 15–39.

42 See Bayne, *Exposition*, 475, 558; Prynne, *Histrio-Mastix*, 1:325, 873, 985; George and George, 'English Protestant Economic Theory,' 130; T. Scott, *Vox Populi, Vox Dei, Vox Regis*, 3, 4; Sibbes, *Soul's Conflict with Itself* (1637) 33; A. Jackson, *Pious Prentice* (1640), 83; Cowdrey, *Table Alphabetical* (1604), see under 'Vocation,' 'Station'; Sprint, *Propositions Tending to Prove the Necessary Use of the Christian Sabbath* (1607), 26.

43 Conceptions of calling as state or estate still occur: cf Snawsel, *Looking Glass for Married Folks* (1631), 18; W. Gouge, *God's Three Arrows* (1631), 100.

44 T. Scott, *Vox Populi, Vox Dei, Vox Regis*, 25; Northbrooke, *Treatise against Dicing*, 51; R. Rogers, *Garden of Spiritual Flowers* (1632), 103.

45 Northbrooke, *Treatise against Dicing*, 79. See also Bayne, *Exposition*, 554, 558; A. Jackson, *Pious Prentice*, 'Epistle to the Reader,' and 104–5, 114; Adams, *Works*, 2:259; Downame, *Guide to Godliness* (1622), 258–9.

46 T. Scott, *Vox Populi, Vox Dei, Vox Regis*, 25, see also 32. On necessity and calling in the Levellers see chapter 6 of this volume.

47 Hieron, 'Prayer for One Whom God Hath Enriched with Outward Things,' in
   Works (1635), selections in Emerson, *English Puritanism*, 183; Bayne, *Exposition*, 383, see also 563; Sibbes, *Soul's Conflict with Itself*; Bastwick, 'Letter to
   Mister Wyks,' in *The Letany* (1637), 17; R. Rogers, *Seven Treatises* (1603),
   579–77 (*sic*); Downame, *Plea of the Poor* (1616), 130–8; T. Taylor, *Three Treatises* (1633), 159–60. This seemed to be the view of Nehemiah Wallington, see
   Seaver, *Wallington's World*, 127–8.
48 R. Bolton, *Works* (1641), 2:141–2; Preston, *New Covenant* (1630), 178; R. Hill,
   Pathway to Prayer and Pietie (1613), 38–41.
49 Bayne, *Exposition*, 241, 551; Knappen, *Tudor Puritanism*, 414; Trapp, *Commentary on the New Testament* (1647), 531; W. Scott, *Essay of Drapery* (1635),
   'Introduction' by S.L. Thrupp, 10; R. Rogers, *Seven Treatises*, 577.
50 Bayne, *Exposition*, 381–475. See also 383, 385, 551; T. Scott, *The Projector*
   (1623), in T. Scott, *Vox Populi, Vox Dei, Vox Regis*, 6; Sparke, *Crumbs of Comfort to Groans of the Spirit* (1650, orig. 1623), sig. D3.
51 Bayne, *Exposition*, 553.
52 Cf. Richardson, *Cause of the Poor Pleaded* (1653), 14; Watson, *Plea for Alms*
   (1658), 21, 33–4.
53 On the emphasis that all must have callings, see Sibbes, *Soul's Conflict with
   Itself*; Prynne, *Histrio-Mastix*, 1:504–5; Bayne, *Exposition*, 378; Northbrooke,
   Treatise against Dicing, 54. On staying in one's calling see Bayne, *Exposition*,
   222–3; A. Jackson, *Pious Prentice*, 56. On staying within the bounds of one's
   calling see Bayne, *Exposition*, 375; Burroughs, *Rare Jewel of Christian Contentment* (1648), 217–18.
54 Watson, *Body of Practical Divinity*, 244–7; Owen, 'Grace and Duty of Being
   Spiritually Minded' (1681), in *Works*, 7:305, and also 7:302–5; Henry, *Works*,
   110, 260–1; Swinnock, 'Christian Man's Calling,' in *Works*, 1:300, 316–18;
   Steele, *Tradesman's Calling* (1684), 48, 62–3, 85; Baxter, *Christian Directory*,
   1:336. Baxter also speaks of a more integrated conception, *Saints Everlasting
   Rest* (1650).
55 Watson, *Body of Practical Divinity*, 245; see also Owen, 'Grace and Duty,'
   304.
56 Sibbes, *Soul's Conflict with Itself*, 243; Knewstub, *Lectures*, 330; Perkins, *Works*,
   903–4.
57 Gurnall, *Christian*, 435, 437; Flavel, *Works*, 4:391; Cruso, *Usefulness of Spiritual
   Wisdom* (1689), 19 (emphasis in original). See also Swinnock, 'Christian Man's
   Calling,' 305, 308.
58 Steele, *Tradesman's Calling*; Baxter, *Christian Directory*, 1:133, 4:146–7.
59 Henry, *Works*, 110; Owen, 'Grace and Duty,' 303, 305.
60 Poole, 'Matthew – Revelation,' in *Commentary on the Whole Bible* (1685),

3:560; see also Flavel, *Works*, 4:387; Gurnall, *Christian*, 435; Watson, *Body of Practical Divinity*, 247, 293, 555.

61 Charnock, *Discourse*, 531. There is also advice to stay in one's calling, cf Flavel, *Divine Conduct* (1678), 84; Goodman, *Penitent Pardoned* (1694), 86–8. R.M. Douglas regarded a concern with inclinations in vocation as typical of a humanist rather than a Protestant stress. I think this was true in the Elizabethan period but not a century later. See his 'Talent and Vocation in Humanist and Protestant Thought.'

62 Manton, *Epistle of James* (1693), 201; Flavel, *Works*, 4:388; Gurnall, *Christian*, 284, 401.

63 Poole, 'Matthew – Revelation'; Flavel, *Works*, 4:388–9. A minority still insists that one must stay in one's calling, e.g., Henry, *Abridged Commentary*, 611; Baxter, *Practical Works*, 2:ch. 41.

64 Flavel, *Works*, 4:388; Poole, 'Matthew – Revelation': 'The world is a mobile thing, and trades and particular courses of life wear out, and what will now bring in a due livelihood, possibly seven years hence will not furnish any with bread; and it is unreasonable in such a case to think that the role of Christian profession ties up a man under the changes of providence to such a course of life as he cannot, in it, in the sweat of his face, eat his bread.'

65 Flavel, *Works*, 5:32, 394; Manton, *Epistle of James*, 379. See also Henry, *Works*, 329; Steele, *Tradesman's Calling*, 52; T. Gouge, *Surest and Safest Way of Thriving* (1673), 11. Gouge's work contains commendatory prefaces by Owen and Baxter. All these references refer to more than spiritual 'exaltation.'

66 Manton, *Epistle of James*, 68; Swinnock, 'Christian Man's Calling,' 377; Baxter, *Christian Directory*, 1:450, 4:146–7. T. Goodwin, *Exposition of Ephesians* 1.1–2.10 (1681), 655. See also Swinnock, 'Christian Man's Calling,' 311, 316, 376; Watson, *Body of Practical Divinity*, 244, 246, 555–7 (on prudence and piety); Charnock, *Discourse*, 530; Flavel, *Works*, 4:387, 390; 5:174–6; Baxter, *Christian Directory*, 4:131. There are apparent exceptions to this trend, cf Baxter, *Christian Directory*, 1:133, 256, 477; 2:624–30; T. Goodwin, *Works*, 62ff; Heywood, 'Two Worlds' (1699), in *Works*, 188ff; Brooks, 'The Late Fiery Dispensation' (1670), in *Works*, 6:66ff; Steele, *Tradesman's Calling*, 52ff, 62–3, 88; Newcombe, *Autobiography* (1671), 135–6.

67 Steele, *Husbandman's Calling* (1668), 35.

68 Flavel, *Works*, 5:400–1; Steele, *Tradesman's Calling*, 88. See also 38–47, 'aim at a comfortable and plentiful possession.'

69 Swinnock, 'Christian Man's Calling,' 11; Flavel, *Works*, 5:180. See also Swinnock, 'Christian Man's Calling,' 300–7; Flavel, *Works*, 5:174–5; Watson *Body of*

Practical Divinity, 300, 555; Heywood, 'Two Worlds,', 222–3; Baxter, *Christian Directory*, 4:142.

70 See Packer, 'Doctrine of Justification in Development and Decline among the Puritans,' 18–31, 25. See also Allison, *Rise of Moralism*; Haroutunian, *Piety Versus Moralism.*

71 Baxter, *Christian Directory*, 1:285; Bury, *Husbandman's Companion* (1677), 84–5.

72 Steele, *Tradesman's Calling*, 4. He was less individualist in his *Husbandman's Calling*, cf 242.

73 Gurnall, *Christian*, 281–3, see also 279. Watson, 'Parting Counsels,' in *Body of Practical Divinity*, 141. David Zaret's study of covenantal ideas in Puritanism stresses the growing affinities with a contractual outlook, *Heavenly Contract: Ideology and Organisation in Pre-Revolutionary Puritanism*, see esp. ch. 7.

74 Goodwin, *Works*, 62; Owen, 'Grace and Duty,' 304, see also 302–6; Heywood, 'Two Worlds,' 18off; Brooks, 'Late Fiery Dispensation,' 66ff.

75 Cf Watson, *Body of Practical Divinity*, 246–67.

76 Sommerville, *Secularisation of Early Modern England: From Religious Culture to Religious Faith*, 81.

5 Stability, Order, and Calling

1 For references to calling see Hooker, *Works*, 3:532; 5:526; *Answer to a Supplication to the Privy Council* (1612), 18; Pilkington, *Works*, 465; Bernade, *The Tranquility of the Mind* (1570), 26; Sandys, *Sermons*, 52, 117, 157, 182, 194; Cooper, *Admonition to the People of England*, 157; Woolton, *Christian Manual* (1570), 10, 31, 91, 119; Norden, *Progress of Piety* (1584), 69, 81, 124, 127, 129ff, 181; *Pensive Man's Practice* (1584), fol. 28; Whitgift, *Works*, 3:437. Bancroft, *Survey of the Pretended Holy Discipline* (1593), 154; Sutcliffe, *Examination of M. Thomas Cartwright's Late Apologie* (1596), 34. Bishops Jewel, Grindal, and Usher did not use the term or an equivalent.

2 Norden, *Progress*, 169; Woolton, *Christian Manual*, 115; Sutcliffe, *Examination*, 38.

3 Pilkington, *Works*, 465; Norden, *Progress*, 69; Sandys, *Sermons*, 139; Bernade, *Tranquility*, 26.

4 Norden, *Progress*, 133; see also 118, 126, 128, 131, 134, 165; *Pensive Man's Practice*, fol. 9, fol. 46.

5 Hooker, *Answer*, 18. On calling as duty also see Hooker, *Answer*; on calling as office, see Cooper, *Admonition*, 115, 118, 157; Woolton, *Christian Manual*, 13, 81–3; on calling as degree or estate, see Pilkington, *Works*, 56, 465; Bernade, *Tranquility*, 103; Sandys, *Sermons*, 139; Woolton, *Christian Manual*, 71, 84, 115.

6 Floyd, *Picture of a Perfit Commonwealth* (1600) 241; Sandys, *Sermons*, 139.

7 Jewel, 'Exposition upon the Two Epistles of St. Paul to the Thessalonians,' *Works* (1583) 2:813–946, 864; Bernade, *Tranquility*, 23, 103. See also Sandys, *Sermons*, 136–7, 195; Cooper, *Admonition*, 157; Norden, *Pensive Man's Practice*, fols 27, 28; *Progress*, 69, 75, 80; Woolton, *Christian Manual*, 23, 40, 91, 174. See also Greaves, *Society and Religion in Elizabethan England*, 377–80.

8 Jewel, 'Exposition,' 2:1043–4; Sandys, *Sermons*, 182, 195; Cooper, *Admonition*, 132ff, 152; Woolton, *Christian Manual*, 90–1, 139; T. Rogers, *Catholic Doctrine of the Church of England* (2 parts, 1579, 1585), 352.

9 Hooker, *Works*, 2:452, 485. Cooper, *Admonition*, 134–5; see also 148, 150; Norden, *Pensive Man's Practice*, fol. 45; T. Rogers, *Catholic Doctrine*, 352–3; Pilkington, *Works*, 125.

10 Norden, *Progress*, 27–8, 141; see also 23, 69, 126–7, 185; Woolton, *Christian Manual*, 39; Cooper, *Admonition*, 147–8; Bernade, *Tranquility*, 4, 12; Pilkington, *Works*, 46–53, 125, 132–3, 151, 446, 450, 456, 465; Sandys, *Sermons*, 135.

11 Cf Norden, *Pensive Man's Practice*, fols 29, 40, 45, 46; T. Rogers, *Catholic Doctrine*, 352.

12 Jewel, 'Exposition,' 2:941; Sandys, *Sermons*, 230; Whitgift, *Works*, 1:389; Norden, *Progress*, 175–6. See also Nowell, *A Catechism*, 228; Pilkington, *Works*, 470.

13 Edmund Grindal, 'Injunctions at York for the Laity' (1571), in *Works*, 140; T. Rogers, *Catholic Doctrine*, 354–5; Woolton, *Christian Manual*, 136–7; Norden, *Progress*, 140; *Pensive Man's Practice*, fol. 40; Whitgift, *Works*, 2:389; Bullinger, *Works*, 2:61ff, 4:157, 494; Sandys, *Sermons*, 54, 107, 108, 183, 193, 230, 264ff; Pilkington, *Works*, 55, 455.

14 Sandys, *Sermons*, 109; Jewel, 'Exposition,' 2:864; Bernade, *Tranquility*, 103, 124; Norden, *Progress*, 168–9; *Pensive Man's Practice*, fol. 9.

15 Adam Hill (1593), quoted in Millar MacLure, *The Paul's Cross Sermons, 1534–1642*, 124.

16 Pilkington, *Works*, 151; Jewel, 'Exposition,' 2:941. See also Pilkington, *Works*, 152, 437; Sandys, *Sermons*, 138, 152, 182, 193; Woolton, *Christian Manual*, 10, 40; Norden, *Progress*, 28–9, 131, 175.

17 Pilkington, *Works*, 150–1.

18 Hooker, *Works*, 2:29; 3:52; Little, *Religion, Order and Law*, 150–1. Quotations within quotations are from Hooker. See also Whitgift, *Works*, 3:437; Norden, *Progress*, 30.

19 Sanderson (Bishop of Lincoln), *Works*, 3:91–144, 'Sermon in St. Paul's Church on 1 Corinthians 7. 24' (1621), 93. This sermon is reprinted in M.S. Smith, *English Sermon, Vol. I, 1550–1650*, 200. Where relevant I have also cited this edition, as it is more readily available. References to other parts of Sanderson's

corpus are from the *Works*. See also Lancelot Andrewes (Bishop of Winchester), *Works*, 6:42ff; 3:330ff.

20 For references to callings see Herbert, *Works*, 234ff; Cosin, *Works*, 1:169; J. Taylor, *Whole Works*, 2:445; *Holy Living and Holy Dying*, 1ff; Donne, edited by Gill, *Sermons of John Donne*, 253; Fuller, *Holy State and the Profane State* (1642), 2:10, 46, 85, 109ff; Willymat, *Loyal Subject's Looking Glass* (1604), 47; Sibthorpe, *Apostolike Obedience* (1627), 2, 33; H. King, *Sermon Preached at Paul's Cross* (1621), 30; J. Hall (Bishop of Exeter and Norwich), *Works*, 6:269; Hammond, *Sermons*, part 1:31.

21 J. Taylor, *Holy Living*, 1ff, 7; Willymat, *Loyal Subject's*, 47ff; Sibthorpe, *Apostolike Obedience*, 6–7; Harris, *God's Goodness and Mercy* (1622), 8; Sanderson, 'Sermon,' 207; *Works*, 3:95. Sanderson also tends to conflate calling as *becoming* a Christian with calling as the *duty of* a Christian, 'Sermon,' and *Works*, 5:661ff.

22 Cf Hales, *Works*, 3:67, 74, and 2:287; Herbert, *Works*, 244, 251, 274; Hammond, *Sermons*, 63; Andrewes, *Works*, 6:42, 287, and 3:338; Cosin, *Works*, 1:169, 185; Willymat, *Loyal Subject's*, 146; Fuller, *Holy State*, 46, 109, 119; Carleton, *Jurisdiction Regall, Episcopall, Papall* (1610) 15, 120; Crashawe, *Sermon Preached at the Cross* (1608), 171.

23 Sanderson, 'Sermon,' 204; *Works*, 3:91. See also Hales, *Works*, 2:287, and 3:67; Knox, 'Social Teachings of Archbishop John Williams,' 180ff. Sanderson also used the analogy of a clock to describe society, 'Sermon,' 212; *Works*, 3:102.

24 J. Taylor, *Holy Living*, 5. See also Andrewes, *Works*, 6:42–63; Herbert, *Works*, 244, 251, 274, 278; Sanderson, 'Sermon,' 207ff, 216; *Works*, 3:95, 107.

25 Hammond, *Sermons*, 255. 'Side-hankled' – to be reined in so tightly as to be unable to jump; the imagery throughout this section is that of a rebellious horse. Sanderson, 'Sermon,' 295; *Works*, 3:93; Herbert, *Works*, 274. On exhortations to work hard and avoid laziness see Sanderson, 'Sermon,' 213 (in criticism of monks), 224–5; *Works*, 2:184; and 3:106, 118, 119, 141; Hall, *Works*, 6:269ff; Stephen Denison, *The New Creature* (1619), quoted in MacLure, *Paul's Cross Sermons*, 141; Fuller, *Holy State*, 48; and *Collected Sermons*, 2:397, 408–9; J. Taylor, *Holy Living*, 1ff; Andrewes, *Works*, 3:389; and 6:40–1, 189, 207, 263; Cosin, *Works*, 1:166–7, 185; Donne, 'Alienation of God,' in Chandos, *In God's Name*, 271–4; and *Works*, 6:232; Herbert, *Works*, 244ff, 251; Andrewes, *Works*, 5:44ff; Feltham, *Resolves, A Duple Century* (1628), 150–2, 323.

26 Fuller, *Holy State*, 99, 100; *Collected Sermons*, 2:504ff; Hammond, *Sermons*, 292–3; Hall, *Works*, 6:271.

27 J. Taylor, *Holy Living*, 2; Hales, *Works*, 2:161. See also Herbert, *Works*, 240ff, 247, 259ff, 267; T. Jackson, *Works*, 9:252–3.

28 The quotation is from Petrarch and is based on Genesis 29:5. See Keynes, *Bibliography of Dr. John Donne*, 205–6; R.S. Jackson, *John Donne's Christian*

Vocation, 144–5. R.B. Shaw argues that Calvin's doctrine of vocation is central in the work of both George Herbert and John Donne, with Donne exploring the 'vertical' axis of destiny and Herbert exploring the 'horizontal' axis of duty. See Shaw's *Call of God: The Theme of Vocation in the Poetry of Donne and Herbert*. While I think he overstates the case, nevertheless there is a lot of truth in his description. However, there was nothing specifically Calvinist about their views. In other respects they were typical of their Anglican contemporaries.

29 Cosin, *Works*, 1:168, 185; Hammond, *Sermons*, 63; J. Taylor, *Holy Living*, 2, 4; and 'Of Christian Prudence' (1651), 484; Herbert, *Works*, 261ff; Hales, *Works*, 3:74; Andrewes, *Works*, 6:263. See also Sanderson, 'Sermon,' 241ff; and *Works*, 3:140ff. Here again, it must be said that there were variations and ambiguities in the Anglican doctrine. Herbert believed callings existed even in Eden, while Hammond emphasized that piety was not enough. The closest thing to a rejection of this dualism was the Calvinist Joseph Hall's contention that 'The homeliest service that we do in an honest calling, though it be but to plow or dig, if done in obedience, and conscience of God's Commandment, is crowned with an ample reward; whereas the best workes after their kind [pious duties] if without respect of God's injunction and glory, are loaded with curses.' But even here Hall regarded prayer and preaching as being 'the best workes after their kind.' This was not, as George and George contend, 'much the same thing' as Perkins's equation of 'washing dishes' and 'preaching' as being of equal worth in the sight of God. Hall was merely saying that good ploughing was better than bad praying. See Breen, 'The Non-existent Controversy: Puritan and Anglican Attitudes on Work and Wealth, 1600–1640,' 277–8; Hammond, *Sermons*, 255; Hall, *Works*, 1:137; George and George, *Protestant Mind of the English Reformation*, 139.

30 Ferrar, *Ferrar Papers*, 103–4; Herbert, *Works*, 275; J. Taylor, 'Of Christian Prudence,' 484. See also Fuller, *Holy State*, 46, 48, 101ff; Hammond, *Sermons*, part I:177, 202, 263, 268, 299; Hales, *Works*, 3:77ff; Knox, 'Social Teachings of Archbishop John Williams,' 180, 183; Hall, *Works*, 6:61.

31 Hall, *Works*, 7:59, 62, see also 61, 623, and 6:266, 371; T. Jackson, *Works*, 4:23; 5:334–5; and 10:349; Feltham, *Resolves* 349; Andrewes, *Works*, 2:80, 88–9; 5:3ff; and 6:255; Chillingworth, *Works*, 3:151–80; William Pierce, 'The World, the Flesh and the Devil' (1641), in Chandos, *In God's Name*, 366; Hales, *Works*, 3:64–5; and 2:159, 167ff, 179ff; 'Righteous Mammon' (1618), in Chandos, *In God's Name*, 218–22; J. Taylor, *Whole Works*, 6:556–7; Donne, *Sermons*, 2:182ff; Cosin, *Collection of Private Devotions* (1627), 52–3.

32 Cf Donne, *Sermons*, 3:51; see also Andrewes, *Works*, 6:44, 254; J. Hall, *Works*, 6:266, 371; and 7:62, 623. Hammond dissents from this view, *Sermons*, part

I:177, 202, 263, 268; perhaps also Donne, *Sermons*, 2:77ff, and Williams, in Knox, 'Social Teachings,' 180. Thomas Jackson holds that the rich are not necessarily virtuous, *Works*, 5:334–5; Herbert says that diligent labour doesn't particularly lead to thriving, *Works*, 247; Sanderson says that people may well have been able to get profits without too much work, and that work can even lead to suffering, 'Sermon,' 231, 236; and *Works*, 3:127, 133.

33 Cf Hammond, *Sermons*, part I:249; Sanderson, 'Sermon,' 217–18; *Works*, 2:185–6; and 3:108ff; Donne, *Sermons*, 2:76ff; Andrewes, *Works*, 5:63–4; Herbert, *Works*, 248ff; T. Jackson, *Works*, 10:584–90; Fuller, *Holy State*, 46.

34 John Hales, *Works*, 2:160.

35 Quoted in B.K. Gray, *History of English Philanthropy*, 54.

36 Herbert, *Works*, 197, 243ff; Andrewes, *Works*, 2:42, 51, 53; 3:290ff; 5:43ff; and 6:207, 260–2, 297; Donne, *Sermons*, 2:184; Reidy, *Bishop Lancelot Andrewes*, 197ff; Hales, 'Righteous Mammon,' 219; T. Jackson, *Works*, 4:23; 9:130–1; and 10:587–9; Feltham, *Resolves*, 60–1, 269, 410; Thorndike, *Works*, 1:54; 4:869; Fuller, *Holy State*, 48; J. Hall, *Works*, 6:268, 568; 7:43, 59, 457, 460; and 10:134, 186; Sanderson, 'Sermon,' 212; *Works*, 3:102ff; and 2:204–5; Hammond, *Sermons*, part I:43, 242–3, 248.

37 Sanderson, 'Sermon,' 205, 220–2, 239–40; *Works*, 3:93, 112–14, 138–9.

38 Ibid., 204, 207, 220, 228–30, 241; *Works*, 3:91, 95, 112, 123–6, 140. See also Herbert, *Works*, 275, 381; J. Hall, *Works*, 7:61ff, 445, 460; see also 1:246; 2:254; 6:26–8, 458–9; 7:43.

39 Andrewes, *Works*, 6:40; see also 6:255, 290; and 4:28. See also T. Jackson, *Works*, 9:251, 429, 432–3; and 10:497, 498, 586; Cosin, *Collection of Private Devotions*, 52–3; Hales, *Works*, 2:167ff, 287; and 3:64–5; J. Taylor, *Whole Works*, 10:24; Andrewes, *Works*, 5:33ff; and 6:256; Herbert, *Works*, 247; Thorndike, *Works*, 4:869; Feltham, *Resolves*, 145, 167, 171, 400, 409; Willymat, *Loyal Subject's*, A3, 47, 49, 52ff; on John Williams, see Knox, 'Social Teachings,' 180–1; H. King, *Sermon*, 30–1; Harris, *God's Goodness* 8.

40 Burgess, *Politics of the Ancient Constitution, 1603–1642*, 133.

41 Cf Wilson, *Works*, 2:352; Frank, *Works*, 2:384; Beveridge, *Works*, 5:164; and 10:155; Barrow, *Theological Works*, 4:385, 395; Tillotson, *Works*, 5:259; South, *Sermons*, 1:70ff; and 4:113; Sherlock, *Principles of Holy Christian Religion* (1673), 61; Jenny, *Sermon Preached at the Funeral* (1673), 11–12; Allestree, *Whole Duty of Man* (1657), 39ff; 231.

42 On general and particular callings, see Barrow, *Theological Works*, 3:395ff, 402, 411ff, 425; South, *Sermons*, 3:190ff; Tillotson, *Works*, 9:66ff. On calling as station, see Frank, *Works*, 2:385; Barrow, *Theological Works*, 3:411ff, 425. On calling as office or duty, see Barrow, *Theological Works*, 3:425; Traherne, *Christian Ethics*, 152ff. On calling as profession, see Frank, *Works*, 2:384;

Barrow, *Theological Works*, 3:411ff; South, *Sermons*, 3:191; and 4:113. On calling as employment or trade see Barrow, *Theological Works*, 3:401ff; Tillotson, *Works*, 5:259.

43 Barrow, *Theological Works*, 3:415; Tillotson, *Works*, 5:260. On this point, see Schlatter, *Social Ideas of Religious Leaders, 1660–1688*, 189.

44 See Beveridge, *Works*, 5:164; Wilson, *Works*, 2:352; Barrow, *Theological Works*, 3:344ff, 359, 413; Tillotson, *Works*, 5:257, 265; 9:60ff, 68ff, 107; South, *Sermons*, 3:119ff; Allestree, *Whole Duty*, 136ff, 163ff, 270ff. John Sommerville argues that Dissenters were closer to what he describes as the 'Protestant Ethic' whereas the Anglicans placed most emphasis on industry. This is not incompatible with my findings. See his 'Anti-Puritan Work Ethic,' 72, 73.

45 South, *Sermons*, 3:191. He appears to imply something a little different in 2:97. Tillotson implies something similar in *Works*, 5:260, but his usual formulation is different, see next note.

46 Frank, *Works*, 2:384, 389; Barrow, *Theological Works*, 3:393; Tillotson, *Works*, 5:256–9; 9:62, 69; Allestree, *Whole Duty*, 39. See also C. Hill, *Society and Puritanism*, 176; Traherne, *Christian Ethics*; Wilson, *Works*, 2:352; Beveridge, *Works*, 8:362ff.

47 South, *Sermons*, 3:195; Frank, *Works*, 2:384; Barrow, *Theological Works*, 1:71. See also Beveridge, *Works*, 9:352; and 6:359; Tillotson, *Works*, 8:119ff; Tenison, *Sermon Concerning Discretion in Giving Alms*, 13–14.

48 Barrow, *Theological Works*, 3:344ff, 383, 396; South, *Sermons*, 2:235; Tillotson, *Works*, 9:66ff; Sharp, *Sermon on I Timothy iv. 8* (1676), 11–18.

49 Allestree, *Whole Duty*, 51; Traherne, *Christian Ethics*, 152ff; Frank, *Works*, 2:384; Barrow, *Theological Works*, 1:178, 196–7; and 3:357–9, 371, 399, 407, 413, 416. See also South, *Sermons*, 2:233, 244; and 3:192.

50 Barrow, *Theological Works*, 1:178; 3:245; and 5:25; Traherne, *Centuries, Poems and Thanksgivings*, 1:218–19; Beveridge, *Works*, 6:358; South, *Sermons*, 1:167; and 2:89ff, 95. See also Cudworth, *Sermon before the House of Commons* (1647), 54; Whichcote, *Select Sermons*, 130–9; Compagnac, *Cambridge Platonists*, 59ff; Wilson, *Works*, 2:350–1; Beveridge, *Works*, 5:164, 178; 8:352ff; 9:185ff, 292ff, 356ff; and 10:45; South, *Sermons*, 1:165, 363; and 2:238; Allestree, *Whole Duty*, 92, 118, 132–3, 200ff.

51 South, *Sermons*, 1:68, 167, 363, 406; 2:239; and 4:162ff. See also Allestree, *Whole Duty*, 51, 118, 133ff; Tenison, *Sermon*, 13–14; Clarkson, 'The Lord the Owner of All Things,' in his *Sermons and Discourses* (1696), 304–10. South quotes the simile 'as drunk as a beggar,' *Sermons*, 4:162.

52 Barrow, *Theological Works*, 1:6, 7, 51, 53 (pp 3–96 of this volume are on giving to the poor). Sprat also recognizes that paupery may be due to external circumstances, see his *History of the Royal Society of London* (1667), 400–2.

53 Cf Beveridge, *Works*, 5:368ff; 6:343–4, 354, 361, 435–6; 7:592; 8:352, 374; 10:27, 32, 42–5; Wilson, *Works*, 2:406–8; Frank, *Works*, 2:387–92.

54 Frank, *Works*, 2:385–6; Beveridge, *Works*, 5:179; 6:360, 8:353ff; 10:45; South, *Sermons*, 1:167, 172; and 2:254; Stillingfleet, *Works* (1710), 1:63–4; Allestree, *Whole Duty*, 92–118; Traherne, *Centuries, Poems*, 218.

55 Traherne, *Centuries of Meditation*, 17ff; *Christian Ethics*, 153ff; Tillotson, *Works*, 9:66; Barrow, *Theological Works*, 1:24, 196–8; and 3:344ff, 358ff.

56 Barrow, *Theological Works*, 1:152; and 3:411; South, *Sermons*, 2:89, 95, 275; and 3:191; Tenison, *Sermon*, 13–14.

57 Schlatter, *Social Ideas*, 87, 90, 95–7, 100, 119–20.

58 Glen Burgess describes the dominant theological view as an 'order theory'; however, he does not deal with the role of vocational theory in such an order: *Politics of the Ancient Constitution*, 132–8.

59 Little, *Religion, Order and Law*, 139, 151–2. 'Ghostly' was Hooker's term.

60 Cf Schlatter, *Social Ideas*, 203. Christopher Hill remarked that 'Latitudinarian' was 'the word used to describe ex-Puritans who conformed to the restored episcopal church in 1660, or other conformists who had accepted the Cromwellian state church': *Some Intellectual Consequences of the English Revolution*, 62. I think that this is only a partial description, but to the degree that it is true, it would suggest one reason for a convergence of Puritan and latitudinarian views. For a fuller discussion of the meaning of 'latitudinarian' see John Spurr, '"Latitudinarianism" and the Restoration Church.'

61 John Spurr described the 'Restoration Church of England's *via media* between Catholic and Reformed' as 'a broad path, wide enough to accommodate those who wished to hug either side and those who yawed from one to the other,' *Restoration Church of England, 1646–1689*, 163.

6 Politics, Necessity, and Calling

1 Brunner, *Divine Imperative*, 200.

2 Ibid., 200.

3 Ibid., 208.

4 Ibid., 202–3.

5 I have highlighted only one side of Brunner's views. Elsewhere he stresses reform more strongly, see ibid., 250ff, 613–15. Yet it is clear that Brunner's discussion of calling necessarily highlights his conservative side.

6 Barth, 'Vocation,' in vol. 3, part 4, of his *Church Dogmatics*, 645.

7 Barth himself goes to the other pole and almost lifts callings beyond any historical context; but his discussion of calling is the greatest that exists in modern theology. Barth's criticism of Luther and Brunner, in 'Vocation,' 641–2, 644–5, lays

the important questions bare. But Brunner's critique of Barth's view of calling – 'that in Barth Creation comes off badly compared with Redemption' – is also to the point. How does the calling relate to history, and how does history relate to the created order? When Barth speaks of this 'transitory' order he is surely right to resist the implied baptism of specific historical circumstances; but what of the fact that we live our lives in just these specific historical situations and no other? Gustav Wingren's *Luther on Vocation* raises these points, and he develops the themes in his *Creation and Gospel*. Any intended development of a Christian view of calling must take cognizance of Barth and Brunner's mutual critiques, paying specific attention to the relation of creation and history. See also Ellul, 'Work and Calling'; Volf, *Work in the Spirit*; Meilander, *Friendship: A Study in Theological Ethics*, 87–8; Hardy, *Fabric of This World*, ch. 2; Robert M. Adams, 'Vocation'; Redekop, 'Mennonites, Creation and Work'; Schuurman, 'Reformed Vocation under Assault'; Paul Marshall, 'Vocation, Work and Rest'; 'Work and Vocation: Some Historical Reflections.'

8 Barth, 'Vocation,' 641.

9 Volf, *Work in the Spirit*, makes many of the same criticisms of Protestant, especially Lutheran, views of vocation. Instead of a view of work based on vocation, he suggests that we develop one based on (theological) charisma, and instead of one rooted in creation he suggests one driven by redemption. This 'work in the spirit' would be both pneumatological and eschatological. Volf's criticisms of the reformers are generally accurate, if overstated. However, it is not clear why he wants to polarize the discussion in the form of vocation versus gift, and creation versus eschatology. Vocation tries to answer the question of *location*, something to which gifts are relevant but not sufficient, since they focus only on a subjective pole. That someone has gifts for something is not a sufficient reason for doing it: something less fitted but more urgent may be appropriate. Similarly, creation tries to answer the question of *what* is redeemed: the eschatological focus itself cannot substitute for this. Volf needs to find means of dealing with the issues addressed by the Reformed doctrines and incorporating them in his work. The result could be the most developed and satisfactory theological treatment of work yet available.

10 Sanderson, *Works*, 3:91.

11 For these and other examples, see Manning, *English People and the English Revolution*, 40–1. William Walwyn was also criticized on the same grounds, see Price et al., *Walwyn's Wiles* (Apr. 1649), 286–317, in Haller and Davies, eds, *Leveller Tracts*, 302ff.

12 Cheke, *Hurt of Sedition* (1549), 2.

13 Ibid., 17.

14 Ibid., 5–6, 17.

15 Ponet, *Short Treatise of Politike Power* (1556), 47.
16 Ibid.
17 Ibid.
18 Jewel, *Works* (1583), 2:864.
19 Ibid.
20 Hooker, *Laws of Ecclesiastical Polity*, in *Works*, 2:362, 363.
21 Willymat, *Loyal Subject's Looking Glass* (1604).
22 Ibid.
23 Ibid., 48.
24 Ibid., 49. See also Filmer, *Quaestio Quodlibetica* (1653), 137–8; *Patriarcha*, in *Patriarcha and other Political Works*, 97.
25 Harris, *God's Goodness and Mercy*, sermon given at Paul's Cross (1626), 8.
26 Ulysses speaking in Shakespeare's *Troilus and Cressida*, I. iii. 97–107.
27 Quoted in Manning, *English People*, 56–7.
28 Greville, *Discourse Opening the Nature of Episcopacy* (1641), 2:93.
29 Case, 'Sermon before the House of Commons,' the second in his *Two Sermons Lately Preached at Westminster* (1642), 13, 16.
30 Ibid., 33.
31 Lawrence Stone, in his *Causes of the English Revolution, 1529–1642*, 52ff, regards Case's sermon as a call for 'revolution.' It really is much less.
32 'The Solemn League and Covenant' taken by the House of Commons, 25 Sept. 1643, in S.R. Gardiner, ed., *Constitutional Documents of the Puritan Revolution, 1625–1660*, 267.
33 'We shall with the same sincerity, reality and constancy, in our several vocations endeavour with our estates and lives mutually to preserve the right and privilege of the Parliaments ... We shall, also, according to our places and callings ... assist and defend all those that enter into this league and covenant ...' Ibid., 269, 270. The same type of formulation occurs in the Scottish National Covenant of 27 Feb. 1638, 'that we shall continue in the obedience of the doctrine and discipline of this Kirk, and shall defend the same according to our vocation and power all the days of our lives,' Gardiner, ed., ibid., 126; see also 133.
34 'Declaration of Some Proceedings of Lt.-Colonel John Lilburne,' in Haller and Davies, eds, *Leveller Tracts*, 118.
35 Ibid., 123. See also Price et al., 'Walwyn's Wiles,' 302–3.
36 Edward Gee (1613–60), *An Exercitation Concerning Usurped Powers* (1650), quoted in Marchamount Nedham, *Case of the Commonwealth of England Stated* (1650), 36. See also T. Hall, *Pulpit Guarded with XVII Arguments* (1651), 23.
37 Gee, *An Exercitation*, quoted in Nedham, *Case of the Commonwealth*, 37.
38 Nedham, *Case of the Commonwealth*, 37–8. On Nedham and others, see Skinner, 'History and Ideology in the English Revolution.' Nedham's position is

akin to that of the Puritan, Thomas Scott, almost thirty years earlier. Scott discussed what actions private persons might take in case of troubles in the commonwealth, and he concluded that one could do without a calling in 'extraordinary' circumstances because 'necessity supplies the place of an ordinary calling and warrants the undertaking of any action for the avoiding of a certain mischief ... to the state ...' Scott was very unusual in this type of claim, and there appear to be no other instances of such an assertion in the period in which he was writing. T. Scott, *Vox Populi, Vox Dei, Vox Regis*, 25.

39 J. Goodwin, *Right and Might Well Met.*

40 For background on John Goodwin, see Tolmie, *Triumph of the Saints*, 111ff, 143ff, 173ff, 187ff.

41 Walwyn, *Help to the Right Understanding of a Discovery Concerning Independency* (6 Feb. 1645), 3:197.

42 See Tolmie, *Triumph*, 169ff. The anti-Leveller tract *Walwyn's Wiles* (Apr. 1649) was subscribed to by Goodwin's co-pastor, John Price. The replies to this, *Walwyn's Just Defence* and also [Humphrey Brooke], *The Charity of Church Men* (28 May 1649), both attack members of Goodwin's congregation. See Haller and Davies, eds, *Leveller Tracts*, 330–98.

43 J. Goodwin, *Right and Might*, 2. Here Goodwin also makes reference to the 'Solemn League and Covenant.'

44 Ibid., 3–4. See also J. Goodwin, *Anti-Cavalierism* (1642), 2:222–3; J. Goodwin, 'Declaration of the English Army Now in Scotland' (1 Aug. 1650), 474–5; and Ireton at Putney, in Woodhouse, *Puritanism and Liberty*, 50.

45 J. Goodwin, *Right and Might*, 3.

46 Ibid., 9, 14, 15–16.

47 Ibid., 15, 12, 8.

48 See Walwyn, *Power of Love* (1643), 2:274; *Predication of Mr. Edwards: His Conversion and Recantation* (1646), 3:341; Overton, *Remonstrance of Many Thousand Citizens* (1646), 125.

49 Cf Manning, *English People*, 282–3.

50 Lilburne, *Work of the Beast* (1637), 2:16ff; *Come Out of Her My People* (1639), cf 1ff.

51 Cf Walwyn, *Vanity of the Present Churches* (Feb. 1649), 263.

52 Wildman, *Case of the Army* (1647), 86.

53 Walwyn, *Poor Wise-Man's Advocate* (1657), 132.

54 Wildman, *Call to All the Soldiers of the Army by the Free People of England* (1647), 443. See also Overton, *Appeale from the Degenerate Representative Body of Commons* (1647), 160, 179; Lilburne, *Mournful Cries of Many Thousand Poor Tradesmen* (Jan. 1648), 278.

55 Lilburne, *Manifestation* (Apr. 1649), 277–8.
56 Price et al., 'Walwyn's Wiles,' 302–3.
57 Walwyn, *Walwyn's Just Defence*, 383.
58 [Humphrey Brooke], *Charity of Church Men* (May 1649), 344.
59 Winstanley, *Truth Lifting Up His Head* (1649), 49–50.
60 [Diggers], *More Light Shining in Buckinghamshire* (1649), 627–33.
61 [Diggers], *Declaration of the Well Affected People of the County of Buckinghamshire* (May 1649), 643–4.
62 Winstanley, *Declaration from the Poor Oppressed People of England* (June 1649), 105. The theme is reiterated on 106.
63 Winstanley, *Watchword to the City of London and the Army* (1649), 131, 136, 137.
64 'Whether it be not a great breach of the National Covenant, to give two sorts of people their freedom, that is, Gentry and Clergy, and deny it to the rest.' Winstanley, *Letter to Lord Fairfax* (June 1649), 291.
65 [Diggers], *More Light*, 639.
66 Winstanley, *New Year's Gift Sent to the Parliament and Army* (Jan. 1650), 170–1. Compare Falstaff in I Henry IV, I. ii. 114–17:
   PRINCE HENRY: I see a good amendment of life in thee; from praying to purse-taking.
   FALSTAFF: Why, Hal, 'tis my vocation, Hal; 'tis no sin for a man to labour in his vocation.
67 Winstanley, *Fire in the Bush* (1649 or 1650), 227. See also 264.
68 On condemnation of Ranters and 'community of women' see Winstanley's *Vindication of Diggers* (Feb. 1650), 400.
69 Winstanley, *Fire in the Bush*, 246, 263.
70 Winstanley, *Law of Freedom in a Platform* (Nov. 1651), 386ff.
71 Ibid., 324ff.
72 Winstanley, *New Law of Righteousness* (Jan. 1649), 184.
73 Ibid., 188.
74 Quoted in Manning, *English People*, 296. See also Lilburne, *Manifestation* (Apr. 1649), 276ff; Lilburne, *Legall Fundamentall Liberties* (1644), 449. Overton appeared at times to be a little more sympathetic to views of a Digger type, see his *Appeale from the Degenerate Representative Body of Commons* (1647).
75 Walwyn, *England's Troublers Troubled* (1648), 6–7.
76 Lilburne, *Manifestation*, 277.
77 Ibid., 279.
78 Ibid., 280.

79 Walwyn, *Walwyn's Just Defence*, 387. On the relation of the Levellers to various classes and groups see Manning, *English People*, 313ff.

80 Leland Ryken in his *Work and Leisure in Christian Perspective* criticizes me for saying in *Labour of Love: Essays on Work* that the Puritans uncritically accepted the vocational structure of their day, cf 98, 113. He gives examples of Puritans criticizing unlawful callings and pointing out that some callings are more useful than others. But those remarks are beside the point. A feature of Puritan (and Leveller) views is that they identify divine callings with (some) aspects of the social division of labour.

81 Pocock, *Machiavellian Moment*, 336ff. See also Hanson, *From Kingdom to Commonwealth: The Development of Civic Consciousness in English Political Thought*.

7 Economics and Calling

1 Dunn, *Political Thought of John Locke*.

2 Macpherson, *Political Theory of Possessive Individualism*. I have discussed the debate between Dunn and Macpherson in my 'John Locke: Between God and Mammon.' Versions of pp 84–6, 91–5 of this article are incorporated into this chapter.

3 See, for example, Ashcraft, *Revolutionary Politics and Locke's 'Two Treatises of Government,'* esp. 258ff, 268ff; 304ff; *Locke's Two Treatises of Government*, 304–5; Tully, *Discourse on Property: John Locke and His Adversaries*, esp. 174ff.

4 Locke, *Conduct of the Understanding*, 49; *Essay Concerning Human Understanding*, 1:101. See also *John Locke: Two Treatises of Government, Second Treatise*, para. 6.

5 Locke, 'Of Study,' 411; *Essay*, 1:190–2, 206–17, 296. See also *Conduct*, 26; *Letter Concerning Toleration*, 46–7.

6 Locke, 'Of Study,' 411.

7 Dunn, *Political Thought*, 219–28, 250–3.

8 Locke, *Letter Concerning Toleration*, 47. Compare Axtell, ed., *Educational Writings of John Locke*, 112, 197, 284, 314, 398, 407–11, 495; *Conduct*, 15, 26–7, 43, 82; *Essay*, 2:242, 296–300; Dunn, *Political Thought*, 227, 248, 252–3.

9 Locke, *John Locke: Two Treatises*, 118.

10 Dunn, *Political Thought*, 228.

11 Ibid., 217.

12 Weber, *Protestant Ethic and the Spirit of Capitalism*, 62; Locke, *Conduct*, 40; 'Commonplace Book,' MS Film 77, 310.

13 Locke, 'Of Study,' 408–11.

14 Locke, *Conduct*, 43.

15 Ibid., 26. See also 43 and *Essay*, 2:298.

16 Locke, 'Of Study,' 409. See also 411; *Essay*, 2:298.

17 Locke, *Conduct*, 26–7; *Essay*, 2:298; *Letter Concerning Toleration*, 52–3; 'Some Thoughts Concerning Reading and Study for a Gentleman' (1703), 398; 'Of Study,' 407, 411; 'Essay Concerning Recreation' (Mar. 1677), MS Locke, f 3, 351–7; 'Labor' (1693).

18 Locke, *Letter Concerning Toleration*, 39.

19 Locke, 'On the Difference between Civil and Ecclesiastical Power' (1673–4), MS Locke c. 27, fol. 29a; 'The Parallel,' MS Locke c. 27, fol. 29a. The two categories are placed side by side in the original.

20 Locke, 'Letter to Benjamin Furley' (Jan. 1688), 3:330–1; Lord King, ed., *Life and Letters of John Locke* (orig. 1829), 254–5.

21 Locke, 'Paraphrase and Notes on Paul's First Epistle to the Corinthians' (1 Cor. 7:20), 201; *Letter Concerning Toleration*, 52–3; 'Thoughts on Education,' 317; 'Of Study,' 407, 411; 'Letter to Clarke, 6 Feb. 1688,' 382–3.

22 Locke, 'Paraphrase and Notes,' 201; *Letter Concerning Toleration*, 33–5.

23 Locke, 'Of Study,' 411.

24 Locke, 'Dedication' of 'Thoughts on Education,' 112–13; 'Thoughts on Education,' 197, 314–15; 'Letter to Clarke, 6 Feb. 1688,' 380; 'Some Thoughts Concerning Reading and Study for a Gentleman,' 398.

25 Locke, 'Thoughts on Education,' 197; 'Some Thoughts Concerning Reading and Study for a Gentleman,' 398.

26 Locke, 'Letter to Clarke, 6 Feb. 1688,' 382–3.

27 Locke, 'Letter to Clarke' (27 Jan. 1688), 3:343–4; Dunn, *Political Thought*, 231–2.

28 Morrice, *Apology for School Masters* (1619); E. Bolton, *The Cities Advocate: Whether Apprenticeship Extinguisheth Gentry* (1629).

29 Margaret Cavendish, Duchess of Newcastle, *The Worlds Olio* (1655), quoted in Ustick, 'Changing Ideals of Aristocratic Character and Conduct in Seventeenth-Century England,' 158.

30 Locke, *Conduct of the Understanding*, 40.

31 Locke, *Letter Concerning Toleration*, 47. Similarly, James Tully in his *Approach to Political Philosophy: Locke in Contexts*, 47, maintains that Locke's notion of 'self-proprietorship' is in the first place being 'master of oneself in the sense of being able to govern oneself ethically, in the neo-stoic sense, and of exercising some form of jurisdiction over the self free from the control of others.' This is a political and ethical view rather than an economic one, cf Tully, *Approach*, 80–5.

32 Locke, *Letter Concerning Toleration*, 33–5.

33 Ashcraft seeks to show parallels between Locke's and the Dissenters' view on a

variety of topics; see his *Revolutionary Politics and Locke's 'Two Treatises of Government'*, ch. 2. On Locke's affinities with the latitudinarians, see Reventlow, *Authority of the Bible and the Rise of the Modern World*, 244ff.

34 Dunn, *Political Thought*, 255; Cragg, *From Puritanism to the Age of Reason*, 129, 134–5.

35 Fenton, *Treatise of Usury* (1611), 121. On Fenton's reliance on Calvin, see 61ff.

36 Anonymous, *Usury Arraigned and Condemned* (1625).

37 Blaxton, *English Usurer* (1634).

38 Cf Cook, *Unum Necessarium* (1648), quoted in Appleby, *Economic Theory and Ideology in Seventeenth-Century England*, 56; Potter, *Key of Wealth* (1650).

39 Malynes, *Canker of England's Commonwealth* (1601). Malynes was an Assay Master of the English Mint.

40 See Misselden, *Free Trade or the Means of Free Trade* (1622); *Circle of Commerce* (1623); Mun, *Discourse of Trade from England unto the East Indies* (1621); *England's Treasure by Foreign Trade* (1664); Appleby, *Economic Theory*, 36ff, 40ff, 191.

41 Misselden, *Circle of Commerce*, 17.

42 Digges, *Defence of Trade* (1615); Culpeper, *Tract against Usury* (1621); Letwin, *Origins of Scientific Economics*, 48.

43 See Child, *Brief Observations Concerning Trade* (1668) and *New Discourse on Trade* (1693), both in *Sir Josiah Child: Selected Works, 1668–1697*; Fortrey, *England's Interest and Improvement* (1673); Barbon, *Discourse on Trade* (1690); Davenant, *Political and Commercial Works* (1771); Petty, *Economic Writings* and *Petty Papers*; Appleby, *Economic Theory*, 69, 169–73, 187, 191; Letwin, *Origins*, 146–9; Thirsk and Cooper, eds, *Seventeenth-Century Economic Documents*, esp. 97–8. Hecksher, *Mercantilism*, describes what we have called 'technical' economic argument as essentially 'amoral,' cf 2:285–7. Letwin describes it as the coming of 'scientific economics,' *Origins*, esp. ch. 3.

44 Sir Dalby Thomas, *An Historical Account of the Rise and Growth of the West-India Colonies* (1690), 2, quoted in Appleby, *Economic Theory*, 133.

45 See references in Appleby, *Economic Theory*, 54–63, to John Moore, *The Crying Sin of England, of Not Caring for the Poor* (1653); *A Scripture Word against Enclosure* (1656); Joseph Lee, *Considerations Concerning Common Fields and Enclosures* (1654); *A Vindication of Regulated Enclosure* (1656); *A Vindication of the Considerations Concerning Common Fields and Enclosures* (1656). The debate is summarized in Appleby, and it is from this that I take the summary that follows in the text.

46 Lee, *Vindication of Regulated Enclosure*, 7, quoted in Appleby, *Economic Theory*, 61. See also 71.

47 Appleby, *Economic Theory*, 71.

48 This is strikingly illustrated by the juxtaposition of Locke's very different pieces 'Labor' (1693) and 'Venditio' (1695) in Patrick Hyde Kelly's, *Locke on Money*, 493–500. See also Tully's contrast between the 'self-proprietory' individual and the 'utilizable' individual, *Approach*, 79–89.

49 Vaughan, *John Locke: Economist and Social Scientist*; Letwin, *Origins*, 156, 163.

50 Hecksher, *Mercantilism*, 2:285.

51 Ibid., 286, 301.

52 See Letwin, *Origins*, 171ff; Appleby, 'Locke, Liberalism and the Natural Law of Money.' Petty held a similar view, see Letwin, *Origins*, 181; Chalk, 'Natural Law and the Rise of Economic Individualism in England,' 332.

53 Hundert, 'Making of Homo Faber: John Locke between Ideology and History,' 9. See also his 'Market Society and Meaning in Locke's Political Philosophy.' Tully, *Approach*, also holds that the basic framework of Locke's treatment of property is a 'workmanship model.'

54 Dunn, *Political Thought*, 222.

55 See Pearson, 'Religion of John Locke and the Character of His Thought,' 248.

56 See the similar comments by Ian Harris in his *Mind of John Locke*, 320. On Locke and the latitudinarians, see Ashcraft, *Revolutionary Politics*; Carroll, *Common-Sense Philosophy of Religion of Edward Stillingfleet, 1635–1699*, ch. 4 on Stillingfleet and Locke; Reventlow, *Authority of the Bible*.

57 Ashcraft, 'Locke's State of Nature: Historical Fact or Moral Fiction'; Batz, 'Historical Anthropology of John Locke.'

58 Locke, 'Of Study,' 411.

8 Calling and the Shaping of the Modern World

1 Greaves, *Society and Religion in Elizabethan England*, 395, 430.

2 Greaves, ibid., 379–81, finds 'differences of emphasis' wherein Puritans had a more 'pronounced emphasis on diligence in vocations.'

3 J. Sears McGee maintains that Puritans concentrated on the duties of the first table of the law while Anglicans concentrated on the second table: this produced a real difference in views of piety. See McGee, *Godly Man in Stuart England; Anglicans, Puritans and the Two Tables.*

4 Little, *Religion, Order and Law*, 96, 98, 111ff, 127, 133, 147 (Little's emphasis).

5 On Anglican and Puritan views of nature and grace, see New, *Anglican and Puritan.*

6 Quentin Skinner disputes the 'Weberian analysis of Calvinism as a revolutionary ideology' in his *Foundations of Modern Political Thought*, 2:322. In doing so he focuses particularly on politics and, more particularly, on theories of revolution. However, he appears to have had in mind the 'Weber thesis' as such, and

laments its 'sharp distinction between the social and political theories of the Catholics and the Calvinists in the course of the sixteenth century.' As far as social theories are concerned, the pattern of early-sixteenth-century vocational views is at odds with Skinner's assertion. Part of the problem may be due to the fact that the first two of the 'main aims' of *Foundations of Modern Political Thought* are in tension. The first aim is 'to offer an outline account of the principal texts.' The second is to show how 'the main elements of a recognisably modern concept of the state were gradually acquired' (1:ix). But for Skinner modern political thought and, in particular, the state, are described in a narrowly secular fashion. The state is 'the sole source of law and legitimate force within its own territory and ... the sole appropriate object of its citizens' allegiances.' The church cannot claim 'to act as a law making power coeval with rather than subordinate to the secular authorities.' The state must reject 'a duty to uphold godly as well as peaceable government' (1:x; 2:352). Hence John Knox did not have 'strictly speaking a *political* theory at all' since he relied on 'alleged religious obligations' (2:211; emphasis in original). Skinner has one goal to cover the principal texts and another goal to cover the appearance of secular texts while rejecting those with an explicit religious basis. The result is a kind of 'foundations of modern secular political thought,' which, while undeniably a major achievement, still gives only a partial picture. Skinner's secular views about the proper nature of political theory lead him to a consistent downgrading of the importance of religious influences and may contribute to his rejection of Weber's views, see my 'Quentin Skinner and the Secularisation of Political Thought.'

7 See Tyacke, *Anti-Calvinists: The Rise of English Arminianism, c. 1590–1640*; MacCulloch, 'Myth of the English Reformation'; Lake, 'Calvinism and the English Church, 1570–1635'; Russell, *Causes of the English Civil War*; Trevor-Roper, *Catholics, Anglicans and Puritans: Seventeenth Century Essays*, 44. But see also P. White, 'Rise of Arminianism Reconsidered.'

8 Julian Davies correctly criticizes a 'polarisation of grace and predestination' in analyses of Calvinism, cf 50, 92, 122, 299 of his *Caroline Captivity of the Church: Charles I and the Remoulding of Anglicanism*. Quite why he repeatedly describes this polarity as 'Weberian' is not clear. Charles Partee argues convincingly that if there was a central dogma in Calvin it was 'union with Christ'; see his 'Calvin's Central Dogma Again.' There can also be a tendency to treat divines as 'Calvinists' simply because they were predestinarians. Occasionally Tyacke, *Anti-Calvinists*, falls into this.

9 See Allison, *Rise of Moralism*; Toon, *Emergence of Hyper-Calvinism in English Nonconformity*; Armstrong, *Calvinism and the Amyraut Heresy*. Baxter said that the doctrine of universal redemption was believed by 'half the divines of England.' However, it is too strong to describe him, as John Spurr does, as 'neo-

Arminian,' see Spurr's *Restoration Church of England, 1646–1689*, 314. Spurr is illuminating on other aspects of the range of Calvinism and Arminianism.

10 See Sommerville, 'Anti-Puritan Work Ethic,' 75, 77; McGee, *Godly Man*, 240. Hawkes, 'Logic of Assurance in English Puritan Theology' and Beeke, *Assurance of Faith: Calvin, English Puritanism, and the Dutch Second Reformation* concentrate on doctrine rather than on psychology, but their surveys are illuminating. While Weber was incorrect in suggesting *why* Protestants stressed *continual labour*, yet the fact that they did so needs some explanation. The mere fact of a calling does not itself determine this way of living within one. One reason might be a by-product of the rejection of justification by works. It may be a short step from believing that no works can ever save you to feeling that no amount of work is ever enough. The attempted eradication of works righteousness in favour of justification by faith means that there is no inbuilt limit to the amount of work to be done; hence, work could become limitless.

11 Weber, *Protestant Ethic and the Spirit of Capitalism*, 183, 220, 228–9.

12 Tawney, *Religion and the Rise of Capitalism*, esp. ch. 4. As noted earlier, Miroslav Volf points out that a calling is not 'labour ... performed as ... an absolute end in itself ...' but is a means 'to glorify God'; see his *Work in the Spirit: Toward a Theology of Work*, 227. The notion of an end in itself is already a secularized version of the Protestant view.

13 Zaret, *Heavenly Contract: Ideology and Organisation in Pre-Revolutionary Puritanism*, argues that covenantal theology adapted to the contractual views held by the laity.

14 Perhaps the most striking example of this individualism is in that most popular of seventeenth-century works, Bunyan's *Pilgrim's Progress*. When Christian sets out on his journey he is alone, and he puts his fingers in his ears the better to ignore the pleas of his wife and children, who are begging him to come back. Christiana is left to come along in Book II, dragging the kids with her, while Christian is already in the heavenly city. Van Beek points out the growth of expressions involving the compound 'self' in Puritan writing – 'self-examination,' 'self-protection,' 'self-denial.' They are among the most 'self-ish' works ever written. See Van Beek, *Enquiry into Puritan Vocabulary*.

15 Lake, 'Calvinism and the English Church,' says 'there were differences of opinion in the early Stuart church over the theology of grace ... If we want to understand why there were and what that meant, we must look at issues other than the theology of grace ...' 75. No doubt such disputes were interwoven with many other concerns and interests, as indeed Lake and others show. But is the only meaning of such a dispute to be found elsewhere? Perhaps we should take more seriously the idea that people argued about the doctrines of grace because they were vitally concerned with the doctrines of grace. There are worse things to be

concerned about, and probably more people fight about them still than about many other disputes of the seventeenth century. The disputes which have shaped our identity are more than surrogates for other interests.

16 Taylor, *Sources of the Self: The Making of the Modern Identity*, 227. Taylor relies on secondary souces in this section of his massive discussion, and he occasionally makes errors – for example, seeming to regard Bishop Robert Sanderson as a Puritan, cf 224. Nevertheless, his discussion gets to the essential points and to their significance.

17 Luther, 'Estate of Marriage' (1522), *Luther's Works*, 45:40.

18 John Milton, *Paradise Lost*, VII:192–4, quoted in Taylor, *Sources of the Self*, 227.

19 Milton, *Paradise Lost*, IV:610–20.

Works Cited

Unless otherwise noted, the place of publication of primary works is London.

Manuscripts

Locke, John. 'A Commonplace Book.' Bodleian, MS Film 77.
– 'Essay Concerning Recreation.' Mar. 1677. Bodleian, MS Locke, f. 3. 351–7.
– 'On the Difference between Civil and Ecclesiastical Power.' 1673–4. Bodleian, MS Locke, c. 27, fol. 29a.
– 'The Parallel.' Bodleian, MS Locke, c. 27, fol. 29a.

Primary Sources

Adams, Thomas. *Works*. 3 vols. Edinburgh: James Nichol 1861–2.
Allestree, Richard, *The Whole Duty of Man*. 1657 or 1658. Reprinted London: William Pickering 1842.
Andrewes, Lancelot. *Works*. 6 vols. Oxford: James Parker 1846.
Anonymous. *Usury Arraigned and Condemned*. 1625. Reprinted in *The Usury Debate*. New York: Arno Press 1972.
Axtell, J.L., ed. *The Educational Writings of John Locke*. Cambridge: Cambridge University Press 1968.
Bancroft, Richard. *A Survey of the Pretended Holy Discipline*. 1593.
Barbon, Nicholas. *A Discourse on Trade*. 1690. Reprinted Baltimore: Johns Hopkins University Press 1934.
Barrow, Isaac. *Theological Works*. 9 vols. Cambridge: Cambridge University Press 1859.
Bastwick, John. 'Letter to Mister Wyks.' In *The Letany*. 1637.
Baxter, Richard. *A Christian Directory*. 4 vols. 1673.

– *Practical Works*. 23 vols. London: James Duncan 1830.
– *The Saints Everlasting Rest*. 1650. Reprinted London: T. Nelson 1860.
Bayne, Paul. *Exposition of Ephesians*. Nd., author died 1617. Reprinted Evansville: Sovereign Grace 1953.
Becon, Thomas. *Works*. 2 vols. Cambridge: Parker Society 1844.
Bernade, John. *The Tranquility of the Mind*. 1570. Reprinted New York: Da Capo 1973.
Beton, Thomas. *A Right Profitable Treatise*. 1500. Cambridge: Cambridge University Press 1905.
Betson, Martin. *Here Beginneth a Treatise to Dispose Men to Be Virtuously Occupied in Their Mind and Prayers*. 1500. Norwood: Walter Johnson 1972.
Beveridge, William. *Works*. 10 vols. Oxford: J.H. Parker 1847.
Bisse, James. *Two Sermons Preached*. 1581. Sig. B 5.
Blaxton, John. *The English Usurer*. 1634. Reprinted Norwood: Walter Johnson 1974.
Bolton, Edmund. *The Cities Advocate: Whether Apprenticeship Extinguisheth Gentry*. 1629. Reprinted Norwood: Walter Johnson 1975.
Bolton, Robert. *Works*. 4 vols. 1641.
[Brooke, Humphrey]. *The Charity of Church Men*. 1649. In *The Leveller Tracts*, edited by W. Haller and G. Davies, 330–49.
Brooks, Thomas. *Works*. 6 vols. Edinburgh: James Nichol 1966–7.
Bullinger, Heinrich. *Works*. 4 vols. Cambridge: Parker Society 1849.
Burroughs, Jeremiah. *The Rare Jewel of Christian Contentment*. 1648. Reprinted London: Banner of Truth Trust 1964.
Bury, Edward. *The Husbandman's Companion*. 1677.
Calvin, J. *Commentaries on a Harmony of the Evangelists, Matthew, Mark and Luke*. Grand Rapids: Eerdmans 1957.
– *Commentary on the First Epistle to the Corinthians*. Translated by J.W. Friezer. Grand Rapids: Eerdmans 1960.
– *Commentary on Philippians*. Grand Rapids: Eerdmans 1961.
– *Corpus Reformatorum Calvani Opera*. Braunschweig: C.A. Schwetschke et Filium, 1863–1900. Reprinted New York: Johnson Reprint Corporation 1964.
– *Institutes of the Christian Religion*. Philadelphia: Westminster Press 1955.
Carleton, George. *Jurisdiction Regall, Episcopall, Papall*. 1620.
Case, Thomas. *Two Sermons Lately Preached at Westminster*. 1642.
Chaderton, Lawrence. *Sermon on Romans 12, v. 3–8*. 1584. In E.H. Emerson, *English Puritanism from John Hooper to John Milton*, 105–9. Durham, N.C.: Duke University Press 1968.
Charnock, Stephen. Discourse upon the Existence and Attributes of God. 1680. Reprinted New York: Robert Carter and Bros 1874.

Cheke, John. *The Hurt of Sedition.* 1549. Reprinted Menston: Scolar Press 1971.

Child, Sir Josiah. *Sir Josiah Child: Selected Works, 1668–1697.* Farnborough: Gregg Press 1968.

Chillingworth, William. *Works.* 3 vols. Oxford: Oxford University Press 1838.

Clarkson, David. *Sermons and Discourses.* 1696.

Cleaver, Robert. *A Godly Form of Household Government.* 1600.

Cooper, Thomas. *An Admonition to the People of England.* 1589. Reprinted Birmingham: Arber Reprints 1882.

Cosin, John. *A Collection of Private Devotions.* 1627. Reprinted New York: Oxford University Press 1967.

– *Works.* 5 vols. Oxford: James Parker 1874.

Cowdrey, Robert. *A Table Alphabetical.* 1604. Reprinted New York: Da Capo 1970.

Cranmer, Thomas. *Works.* 2 vols. Cambridge: Parker Society 1846.

Cranmer, Thomas, ed. 'Certain Sermons ...' In *In God's Name*, edited by J. Chandos, 62–7.

Crashawe, William. *The Sermon Preached at the Cross.* 1608.

Crowley, Robert. *The Select Writings of Robert Crowley.* Edited by L.M. Cowper. London: Early English Text Society 1877.

– *The Voice of the Last Trumpet ... Calling All Estates of Men to the Right Path of Their Vocation.* 1549.

– *The Way to Wealth: Wherein Is Taught a Remedy for Sedition.* 1550.

Cruso, Timothy. *The Usefulness of Spiritual Wisdom.* 1689.

Cudworth, Ralph. *A Sermon before the House of Commons.* 1647. Reprinted New York: Facsimile Text Society 1930.

Culpeper, Thomas. *A Tract against Usury.* 1621. Reprinted Norwood: Walter Johnson 1974.

Davenant, Charles. *Political and Commercial Works.* 5 vols. Edited by Sir Charles Whiteworth. 1771. Reprinted Farnborough: Gregg Press 1967.

Dering, Edward. *Works.* 1597. Reprinted New York: Da Capo 1972.

[Diggers]. *A Declaration of the Well Affected People of the County of Buckinghamshire.* 1649. In *Works of Gerrard Winstanley*, edited by George Sabine, 643–7.

– *More Light Shining in Buckinghamshire.* 1649. In *Works of Gerrard Winstanley*, edited by George Sabine, 627–40.

Digges, Sir Dudley. *The Defence of Trade.* 1615. Reprinted New York: Da Capo 1968.

Dod, John, and Robert Cleaver. *Household Government.* 1621.

– *A Plain and Familiar Exposition of the Ninth and Tenth Chapters of Proverbs.* 1612.

Donne, John. *Sermons of John Donne.* Edited by T. Gill. New York: Meridian 1958.

– *Works*. 6 vols. London: James Parker 1839.

Downame, John. *The Christian Warfare*. 1604.

– *A Guide to Godliness*. 1622.

– *The Plea of the Poor*. 1616.

Eckhart, Meister. 'The Contemplative and the Active Life.' In *Late Medieval Mysticism*, edited by R.C. Petry, 193–9. Philadelphia: Westminster 1957.

Elyot, Sir Thomas. *The Book Named the Governor*. 1531. Reprinted London: Dent 1962.

Feltham, Owen. *Resolves, A Duple Century*. 1628. Reprinted Norwood: Walter Johnson 1975.

Fenton, Roger. *A Treatise of Usury*. 1611. Reprinted Norwood: Walter Johnson 1975.

Ferrar, Nicholas. *The Ferrar Papers*. Edited by B. Blackstone. Cambridge: Cambridge University Press 1938.

Field, John. *A Godly Exhortation*. 1583.

Filmer, Robert. *Patriarcha and Other Political Works*. Edited by P. Laslett. Oxford: Blackwell 1949.

– *Quaestio Quodlibetica*. 1653. Reprinted in *The Usury Debate*. New York: Arno Press 1972.

Flavel, John. *Divine Conduct*. 1678.

– *Works*. 5 vols. London: Banner of Truth Trust 1968.

Floyd, Thomas. *The Picture of a Perfit Commonwealth*. 1600.

Fortrey, Samuel. *England's Interest and Improvement*. 1673. In *Early English Tracts on Commerce*, edited by J.R. McCulloch, 211–69. Cambridge: Cambridge University Press 1954.

Frank, Mark. *Works*. 2 vols. Oxford: Oxford University Press 1849.

Frith, John. *The Fathers of the English Church, Vol. I. John Frith*. London: John Hatchard 1807.

– *Works of John Frith*. Edited by N.T. Wright. Abingdon: Sutton Courtenay Press 1978.

– *The Works of Tyndale and Frith*. London: Ebenezer Palmer 1831.

– *Writings of Tindal, Frith and Barnes*. Philadelphia: Presbyterian Board of Education 1890.

Fuller, Thomas. *Collected Sermons*. 2 vols. London: Unwin 1891.

– *The Holy State and the Profane State*. 2 vols. 1642. Reprinted New York: Columbia University Press 1930.

Gardiner, Stephen. *De Vera Obedienta*. 1535. Leeds: Scolar Press 1966.

– *Letters*. Edited by J.A. Muller. Cambridge: Cambridge University Press 1933.

– *Obedience in Church and State: Three Political Tracts by Stephen Gardiner*. Edited by P. Janelle. Cambridge: Cambridge University Press 1930.

Gataker, Thomas. *Two Sermons Tending to Direction for Christian Carriage*. 1623.

Goodman, John. *The Penitent Pardoned*. 1694.

Goodwin, John. *Anti–Cavalierism*. 1642. In *Tracts on Liberty in the Puritan Revolution, 1638–1647*, vol. 2, edited by W. Haller, 215–27.

– *Right and Might Well Met*. 1649.

Goodwin, Thomas. *An Exposition of Ephesians 1.1–2.10*. 1681. Reprinted Evansville: Sovereign Grace 1958.

– *Works*. Edinburgh: James Nichol 1865.

Gouge, Thomas. *The Surest and Safest Way of Thriving*. 1673.

Gouge, William. *God's Three Arrows*. 1631.

– *Of Domesticall Duties*. 1626.

Greene, John. A Refutation of the Apology for Actors. 1615.

Greenham, Richard. *Works*. 1612.

Greville, Robert. *A Discourse Opening the Nature of Episcopacy*. 1641. In *Tracts on Liberty in the Puritan Revolution, 1638–1647*, vol. 2, edited by W. Haller, 37–163.

Grindal, Edmund. *Works*. Cambridge: Parker Society 1843.

Gurnall, William. *The Christian in Complete Armour*. 1655. Reprinted London: Banner of Truth Trust 1969.

Hake, Edward. *A Touchstone for This Time Present*. 1574.

Hales, John. 'Righteous Mammon.' In *In God's Name*, edited by J. Chandos, 218–22.

– *Works*. 3 vols. New York: AMS Press 1971.

Hall, Joseph. *Works*. 10 vols. Oxford: Oxford University Press 1863.

Hall, Thomas. *The Pulpit Guarded with XVII Arguments*. 1651.

Haller, W., ed. *Tracts on Liberty in the Puritan Revolution, 1638–1647*. 3 vols. New York: Columbia University Press 1934.

Haller, W., and G. Davies, eds. *The Leveller Tracts*. Gloucester, Mass.: Peter Smith 1964.

Hammond, Henry. *Sermons*. Oxford: James Parker 1845.

Harris, Robert. *God's Goodness and Mercy*. 1626.

Henry, Matthew. *Abridged Commentary*. London: Partridge nd.

– *Works*. London: Nelson 1847.

Herbert, George. *Works*. Oxford: Clarendon Press 1941.

Heywood, Oliver. *Works*. Edinburgh: John Vint 1820.

Hieron, Samuel. *All the Sermons of Samuel Hieron*. 1614.

– *Works*. 1635.

Hill, C., ed. *Winstanley: The Law of Freedom and Other Writings*. London: Pelican 1973.

Hill, Robert. *The Pathway to Prayer and Pietie*. 1613.

Hilton, W. 'Epistle on the Mixed Life.' In *The Law of Love: English Spirituality in the Age of Wyclif*, edited by D.L. Jeffrey, 229–35. Grand Rapids: Eerdmans 1988.

Hooker, Richard. *An Answer to a Supplication to the Privy Council*. Oxford: 1612.

– *Works*. 3 vols. Oxford: Oxford University Press 1845.

Hooper, John. *Works*. 2 vols. Cambridge: Parker Society 1843.

Hutchinson, Roger. *Works*. Cambridge: Parker Society 1842.

Jackson, Abraham. *The Pious Prentice*. 1640.

Jackson, Thomas. *Works*. 12 vols. Oxford: Oxford University Press 1844.

Jenny, John. *A Sermon Preached at the Funeral*. 1673.

Jewel, John. *Works*. 2 vols. 1583. Reprinted Cambridge: Parker Society 1847.

King, Henry. *A Sermon Preached at Paul's Cross*. 1621. Reprinted Norwood: Walter Johnson 1976.

King, Lord, ed. *The Life and Letters of John Locke*. Orig. 1829. Reprinted New York: Burt Franklin 1972.

Knewstub, John. *Lectures upon the Twentieth Chapter of Exodus*. 1578.

Latimer, Hugh. 'A Sermon of the Lord's Prayer.' In *English Reformers*, edited by T.H.L. Parker, 331–48. Philadelphia: Westminster Press 1966.

– 'Sermon of the Plough'; 'Inflation of Prices and Decay of Standards'; 'A Cure for Violence and Corruption.' In *In God's Name*, edited by J. Chandos, 12–15; 15–16; 17–25.

– *Works*. 2 vols. Cambridge: Parker Society 1844.

Lever, Thomas. *Sermons*. 1550. Reprinted London: Early English Text Society 1870.

Lilburne, John. *Come Out of Her My People*. 1639. Reprinted Exeter: The Rota 1971.

– *Legall Fundamentall Liberties*. 1644. In *The Leveller Tracts*, edited by W. Haller and G. Davies, 399–449.

– *A Manifestation*. 1649. In *The Leveller Tracts*, edited by W. Haller and G. Davies, 278–84.

– *The Mournful Cries of Many Thousand Poor Tradesmen*. 1648. In *Leveller Manifestoes of the Puritan Revolution*, edited by D.M. Wolfe, 273–8.

– *A Work of the Beast*. 1637. In *Tracts on Liberty in the Puritan Revolution, 1638–1647*, vol. 2, edited by W. Haller, 1–34.

Lilburne, John, et al. 'A Declaration of the English Army Now in Scotland.' 1 Aug. 1650. In *Puritanism and Liberty*, edited by A.S.P. Woodhouse, 474–5.

Locke, John. *Conduct of the Understanding*. New York: Burt Franklin 1971.

– *The Educational Writings of John Locke*. Edited by J.L. Axtell. Cambridge: Cambridge University Press 1968.

– *An Essay Concerning Human Understanding*. 2 vols. Edited by J. Yolton. London: Dent 1961.

– *John Locke: Two Treatises of Government.* Edited by P. Laslett. Cambridge: Cambridge University Press 1960.
– 'Labour.' 1693. In *Locke on Money*, 2 vols, edited by Patrick Hyde Kelly, 2:493–5. Oxford: Oxford University Press 1991.
– *A Letter Concerning Toleration.* Indianapolis: Hackett 1983.
– 'Letter to Benjamin Furley.' Jan 1688. In *The Correspondence of John Locke*, 8 vols, edited by J.S. de Beer, 3:330–1.
– 'Letter to Clarke.' 27 Jan. 1688. In *The Correspondence of John Locke*, 8 vols, edited by J.S. de Beer, 3:343–4.
– 'Letter to Clarke.' 6 Feb. 1688. In *The Educational Writings of John Locke*, edited by J.L. Axtell, 380–6.
– 'Of Study.' In *The Educational Writings of John Locke*, edited by J.L. Axtell, 405–22.
– 'A Paraphrase and Notes on Paul's First Epistle to the Corinthians.' (1 Cor. 7:20). In *John Locke: A Paraphrase and Notes on the Epistles of St. Paul to the Galatians, 1 and 2 Corinthians, Romans, Ephesians*, edited by Arthur Wainwright, 163–259. Oxford: Clarendon Press 1987.
– 'Some Thoughts Concerning Reading and Study for a Gentleman.' 1703. In *The Educational Writings of John Locke*, edited by J.L. Axtell, 397–404.
– 'Thoughts on Education.' In *The Educational Writings of John Locke*, edited by J.L. Axtell, 111–325.
– 'Venditio.' 1695. In *Locke on Money*, 2 vols, edited by Patrick Hyde Kelly, 2:496–500. Oxford: Clarendon Press 1991.
Lupset, Thomas. *Works.* In *The Life and Works of Thomas Lupset*, edited by J.A. Gee. New Haven: Yale University Press 1928.
Luther, Martin. *Luther's Works.* 55 vols. Vols 1–30 edited by J. Pelikan; vols 31–55 edited by H.T. Lehmann. Philadelphia and St Louis: Concordia and Muhlenberg 1955–86.
Malynes, Gerard de. *The Canker of Englands Commonwealth.* 1601. Reprinted Norwood: Walter Johnson 1977.
Manton, Thomas. *The Epistle of James.* 1693. Reprinted London: Banner of Truth Trust 1962.
Misselden, Edward. *The Circle of Commerce.* 1623. Reprinted New York: Da Capo 1969.
– *Free Trade or the Means of Free Trade.* 1622. Reprinted New York: Da Capo 1970.
More, Thomas. *Utopia.* In *The Yale Edition of the Complete Works of St. Thomas More*, 15 vols to date, edited by Edward Surtz and J.H. Hexter, vol. 4. New Haven: Yale University Press 1963–c. 1986.
Morrice, Thomas. *An Apology for School Masters.* 1619. Reprinted Norwood: Walter Johnson 1976.

Mun, Thomas. *A Discourse of Trade from England unto the East Indies.* 1621.

– *England's Treasure by Foreign Trade.* 1664.

Nedham, Marchamount. *The Case of the Commonwealth of England Stated.* 1650. Reprinted Charlottesville: University Press of Virginia 1967.

Newcombe, Henry. *Autobiography.* 1671. Reprinted London: Chetham Society 1852.

Norden, John. *A Pensive Man's Practice.* 1584. Reprinted New York: Da Capo 1972.

– *A Progress of Piety.* 1584. Reprinted Cambridge: Parker Society 1847.

Northbrooke, John. *A Treatise against Dicing, Dancing, Plays and Interludes.* 1643. Reprinted New York: AMS Press 1971.

Nowell, Alexander. *A Catechism.* Cambridge: Parker Society 1853.

Overton, Richard. *An Appeale from the Degenerate Representative Body of Commons.* 1647. In *Leveller Manifestoes of the Puritan Revolution*, edited by D.M. Wolfe, 157–95.

– *A Remonstrance of Many Thousand Citizens.* 1646. In *Leveller Manifestoes of the Puritan Revolution*, edited by D.M. Wolfe, 109–30.

Owen, John. *Works.* 17 vols. Philadelphia: Leighton Publications 1870.

Parker, Henry. *The Rich and the Poor.* 1493. Reprinted Norwood: Walter Johnson 1978.

Perkins, William. *The Whole Treatise of the Cases of Conscience.* 1606. Reprinted Norwood: Walter Johnson 1976.

– *The Work of William Perkins.* Edited by I. Breward. Appleford: Courteney Press 1970.

– *Works.* Cambridge: 1603.

Petty, Sir William. *Economic Writings.* Edited by C.H. Hull. New York: J.M. Kelly 1961.

– *The Petty Papers.* 2 vols. Edited by the Marquis of Lansdowne. London: Constable 1927.

Pilkington, James. *Works.* Cambridge: Parker Society 1842.

Ponet, John. *A Short Treatise of Politike Power.* Edited by Winthrop Hudson. Strasbourg 1556. Reprinted Chicago: University of Chicago Press 1942.

Poole, Matthew. *A Commentary on the Whole Bible.* 3 vols. 1685. Reprinted London: Banner of Truth Trust 1963.

Potter, William. *The Key of Wealth.* 1650. Reprinted New York: Johnson Reprint Corporation 1970.

Preston, John. *Life Eternal or, a Treatise of the Divine Essence and Attributes.* 1631.

– *The New Covenant.* 1630.

– *The Primer, or Book of Private Prayer.* In *English Historical Documents, Vol. 5, 1485–1558*, edited by C.H. Williams, 336–7.

– *Sermons Preached before His Majesty*. 1630.

Price, John, et al. *Walwyn's Wiles*. 1649. In *The Leveller Tracts*, edited by W. Haller and G. Davies, 286–317.

Prynne, William. *Histrio-Mastix*. 1633.

Richardson, Samuel. *The Cause of the Poor Pleaded*. 1653.

Rogers, Richard. *A Garden of Spiritual Flowers*. 1632.

– *Seven Treatises*. 1603.

Rogers, Thomas. *The Catholic Doctrine of the Church of England*. 2 parts. 1579; 1585. Reprinted Cambridge: Parker Society 1854.

Rolle, Richard. *The Amending of Life*. 1434. Reprinted London: Burns, Oates and Washbourne 1927.

Sanderson, Robert. 'Sermon in St. Paul's Church on I Corinthians 7.24.' 1621. In *The English Sermon*, 3 vols, edited by M.S. Smith, *Vol. I (1550–1650)*, 204–44. Cheadle, Cheshire: Carcanet Press 1976.

– *Works*. 6 vols. Oxford: Oxford University Press 1854.

Sandys, Edwin. *Sermons*. Cambridge: Parker Society 1841.

Scott, Thomas. *Vox Populi, Vox Dei, Vox Regis*. Utrecht 1624.

Scott, William. *An Essay of Drapery*. 1635. Reprinted Cambridge, Mass.: Harvard Business School 1953.

Sharp, John. *Sermon on I Timothy iv:8*. 1676.

Sherlock, Richard. *The Principles of Holy Christian Religion*. 1673.

Sibbes, Richard. *Beams of Divine Light*. 1639.

– *The Saint's Cordial*. 1637.

– *The Soul's Conflict with Itself*. 1637.

– *Works*. 8 vols. Edinburgh: James Nichol 1863.

Sibthorpe, Robert. *Apostolike Obedience*. 1627.

Snawsel, Robert. *A Looking Glass for Married Folks*. 1631. Reprinted Norwood: Walter Johnson 1975.

Some, Robert. *A Godly Treatise Concerning the Ministry*. 1588. Reprinted Norwood: Walter Johnson 1974.

South, Robert. *Sermons*. 4 vols. Oxford: Clarendon Press 1842.

Sparke, Michael. *The Crumbs of Comfort to Groans of the Spirit*. 1650; orig. 1623.

Sprat, Thomas. *The History of the Royal Society of London*. 1667.

Sprint, John. *Propositions Tending to Prove the Necessary Use of the Christian Sabbath*. 1607.

Starkey, Thomas. *A Dialogue between Pole and Lupset*. Edited by K.M. Burton. 1538. Reprinted London: Chatto and Windus 1948.

Steele, Richard. *The Husbandman's Calling*. 1668.

– *The Tradesman's Calling*. 1684.

Stillingfleet, Edward. *Works*. 2 vols. 1710.

Stubbes, Phillip. *Anatomy of Abuses.* 1583. Reprinted New York: Garland Publishing 1973.

Sutcliffe, Matthew. *Ecclesiastical Discipline.* 1590. Reprinted Norwood: Walter Johnson 1973.

– *The Examination of M. Thomas Cartwright's Late Apologie.* 1596.

Swinnock, George. *Works.* 5 vols. Edinburgh: James Nichol 1868.

Tauler, Johann. *Oeuvres Complètes.* 9 vols. Paris: Tralin 1911.

Taylor, Jeremy. *Holy Living and Holy Dying.* 1674. Reprinted London: Longmans, Green 1927.

– 'Of Christian Prudence.' In *In God's Name*, edited by J. Chandos, 484–6.

– *Whole Works.* 10 vols. London: Longman, Brown, Green and Longmans 1850–4.

Taylor, Thomas. *Christ's Combate and Conquest: Or the Lion of Judah.* Cambridge 1618.

– *Three Treatises.* 1633.

Tenison, Thomas. *A Sermon Concerning Discretion in Giving Alms.* 1681.

Thorndike, Herbert. *Works.* 6 vols. Oxford: James Parker 1853.

Tillotson, John. *Works.* 10 vols. London: R. Priestly 1820.

Traherne, Thomas. *Centuries of Meditation.* London: B. Dobell 1908.

– *Centuries, Poems and Thanksgivings.* 2 vols. Oxford: Oxford University Press 1958.

– *Christian Ethics.* 1657. Reprinted Ithaca: Cornell University Press 1968.

Trapp, John. *Commentary on the New Testament.* 1647. Reprinted Evansville: Sovereign Grace 1958.

Tyndale, William. *Doctrinal Treatises and Portions of Holy Scripture.* Cambridge: Parker Society 1848.

– *The Works of Tyndale and Frith.* London: Ebenezer Palmer 1831.

– *Writings of Tindal, Frith and Barnes.* Philadelphia: Presbyterian Board of Education 1890.

Walwyn, William. *England's Troublers Troubled.* 1648.

– *A Help to the Right Understanding of a Discovery Concerning Independency.* In *Tracts on Liberty in the Puritan Revolution, 1638–1647*, edited by W. Haller, 3:189–201.

– *The Poor Wise-Man's Advocate.* 1647. In *Freedom in Arms*, edited by A.L. Morton, 123–34. Berlin: Seven Seas Publishers 1975.

– *The Power of Love.* 1643. In *Tracts on Liberty in the Puritan Revolution, 1638–1647*, edited by W. Haller, 2:273–304.

– *A Predication of Mr. Edwards: His Conversion and Recantation.* 1646. In *Tracts on Liberty in the Puritan Revolution, 1638–1647*, edited by W. Haller, 3:339–48.

– *The Vanity of the Present Churches.* 1649. In *The Leveller Tracts*, edited by W. Haller and G. Davies, 253–75.

- *Walwyn's Just Defence*. 1649. In *The Leveller Tracts*, edited by W. Haller and G. Davies, 351–98.
Watson, Thomas. *A Body of Practical Divinity*. Edinburgh: Blackie and Son 1859.
- *A Plea for Alms*. 1658.
- *The Saint's Delight*. 1657.
Whately, William. *A Bride Bush*. 1619.
Whichcote, Benjamin. *Select Sermons*. New York: Scholar's Press 1977.
Whitgift, John. *Works*. 3 vols. Cambridge: Parker Society 1851.
Wildman, John. *A Call to All the Soldiers of the Army by the Free People of England*. 1647. In *Puritanism and Liberty*, edited by A.S.P. Woodhouse, 439–43.
- *The Case of the Army*. 1647. In *The Leveller Tracts*, edited by W. Haller and G. Davies, 65–87.
Willymat, William. *A Loyal Subject's Looking Glass*. 1604.
Wilson, Thomas. *Works*. 7 vols. Oxford: J.H. Parker 1849.
Winstanley, Gerrard. *A Declaration from the Poor Oppressed People of England*. 1649. In *Winstanley: The Law of Freedom and Other Writings*, edited by C. Hill, 99–108.
- *England's Spirit Unfolded*. 1650. Edited by G.E. Aylmer. *Past and Present* 6 (1958): 3–15.
- *Fire in the Bush*. 1649 or 1650. In *Winstanley: The Law of Freedom and Other Writings*, edited by C. Hill, 213–72.
- *The Law of Freedom in a Platform*. 1651. In *Winstanley: The Law of Freedom and Other Writings*, edited by C. Hill, 275–389.
- *A Letter to Lord Fairfax*. 1649. In *Works of Gerrard Winstanley*, edited by George Sabine, 381–92.
- *The New Law of Righteousness*. 1649. In *Works of Gerrard Winstanley*, edited by George Sabine, 149–279.
- *A New Year's Gift Sent to the Parliament and Army*. 1650. In *Winstanley: The Law of Freedom and Other Writings*, edited by C. Hill, 161–210.
- *Truth Lifting Up His Head*. 1649.
- *A Vindication of Diggers*. 1650. In *Works of Gerrard Winstanley*, edited by George Sabine, 394–403.
- *A Watchword to the City of London and the Army*. 1649. In *Winstanley: The Law of Freedom and Other Writings*, edited by C. Hill, 130–51.
- *The Works of Gerrard Winstanley*. Edited by George Sabine. New York: Russell and Russell 1965.
Wolfe, D.M., ed. *Leveller Manifestoes of the Puritan Revolution*. New York: Nelson 1944.
- Woolton, John. *The Christian Manual*. 1570. Reprinted Cambridge: Parker Society 1851.

Secondary Sources

Adams, Robert M. 'Vocation.' *Faith and Philosophy* 4 (1987): 448–62.

Agnell, G. *Work, Toil and Sustenance: An Examination of Views of Work in the New Testament.* Lund: Verbum 1976.

Allen, J.W. *A History of Political Thought in the Sixteenth Century.* London: Methuen 1960.

Allison, C.F. *The Rise of Moralism.* New York: Seabury 1960.

Althaus, P. *The Ethics of Martin Luther.* Translated by R.C. Schultz. Philadelphia: Muhlenberg Press 1972.

Appleby, J.O. *Economic Theory and Ideology in Seventeenth-Century England.* Princeton: Princeton University Press 1978.

– 'Locke, Liberalism and the Natural Law of Money.' *Past and Present* 71 (1976): 43–69.

Arendt, H. *The Human Condition.* New York: Doubleday 1959.

Armstrong, B.G. *Calvinism and the Amyraut Heresy.* Madison: University of Wisconsin Press 1969.

Ashcraft, R. 'Locke's State of Nature: Historical Fact or Moral Fiction.' *American Political Science Review* 62 (1968): 898–915.

– *Locke's Two Treatises of Government.* London: Unwin 1987.

– *Revolutionary Politics and Locke's 'Two Treatises of Government.'* Princeton: Princeton University Press 1986.

Bailey, D.S. *Thomas Becon.* London: Oliver and Boyd 1952.

Barth, K. 'Vocation.' In his *Church Dogmatics*, translated by A.T. Mackay, T.H.L. Parker, H. Knight, H.A. Kennedy, and J. Marks, vol. 3, part 4:595–647. Edinburgh: T. and T. Clark 1961.

Batz, W.G. 'The Historical Anthropology of John Locke.' *Journal of the History of Ideas* 35 (1975): 663–70.

Beardslee, W.A. *Human Achievement and Divine Vocation in the Message of Paul.* London: SCM 1961.

Beeke, Joel R. *Assurance of Faith: Calvin, English Puritanism, and the Dutch Second Reformation.* New York: P. Lang 1991.

Biéler, A. *La pensée économique et sociale de Calvin.* Geneva: Librairie de l'université 1961.

– *The Social Humanism of John Calvin.* Richmond: John Knox Press 1966.

Bouwsma, W.J. *John Calvin: A Sixteenth-Century Portrait.* Oxford: Oxford University Press 1988.

Breen, T.H. 'The Non-existent Controversy: Puritan and Anglican Attitudes on Work and Wealth, 1600–1640.' *Church History* 35 (1966): 273–87.

Brunner, Emil. *The Divine Imperative.* London: Lutterworth 1937.

Burford, A. *Craftsmen in Greek and Roman Society*. London: Thames and Hudson 1972.

Burgess, Glen. *The Politics of the Ancient Constitution, 1603–1642*. London: Macmillan 1992.

Butler, Dom C. *Western Mysticism*. New York: Barnes and Noble 1968.

Carroll, R.T. *The Common-sense Philosophy of Religion of Edward Stillingfleet, 1635–1699*. The Hague: Martinus Nijhoff 1975.

Chalk, A.F. 'Natural Law and the Rise of Economic Individualism in England.' *Journal of Political Economy* 59 (1951): 324–44.

Chandos, J. *In God's Name*. London: Hutchinson 1971.

Clebsch, W.A. *England's Earliest Protestants, 1520–1535*. New Haven: Yale University Press 1964.

Cohen, C. 'The Saints Zealous in Love and Labour: The Puritan Psychology of Work.' *Harvard Theological Review* 76 (1983): 455–80.

Collinson, P. 'A Comment: Concerning the Name Puritan.' *Journal of Ecclesiastical History* 31 (1980): 483–8.

– *Godly People: Essays on English Protestantism and Puritanism*. London: Hambledon Press 1983.

Compagnac, E.T. *The Cambridge Platonists*. Oxford: Oxford University Press 1901.

Constantin, C. 'The Puritan Ethic and the Dignity of Labour: Hierarchy versus Equality.' *Journal of the History of Ideas* 40 (1979): 543–61.

Cragg, G.R. *From Puritanism to the Age of Reason*. Cambridge: Cambridge University Press 1966.

Cranz, F.E. *An Essay on the Development of Luther's Thought on Justice, Law and Society*. Harvard Theological Studies, No. 19. Cambridge, Mass.: Harvard University Press 1964.

Davies, Julian. *The Caroline Captivity of the Church: Charles I and the Remoulding of Anglicanism*. Oxford: Clarendon Press 1992.

Deane, H.A. *The Political and Social Ideas of St. Augustine*. New York: Columbia University Press 1963.

Douglas, R.M. 'Talent and Vocation in Humanist and Protestant Thought.' In *Action and Conviction in Early Modern Europe*, edited by T.K. Rabb and J.E. Siegel, 261–98. Princeton: Princeton University Press 1969.

Dunn, J. *The Political Thought of John Locke*. Cambridge: Cambridge University Press 1969.

Edelstein, L. *The Meaning of Stoicism*. Cambridge, Mass.: Harvard University Press 1966.

Eisen, Arnold. 'Called to Order: The Role of the Puritan *Berufsmensch* in Weberian Sociology.' *Sociology* 13 (1979): 203–18.

Eisenstadt, S.N., ed. *The Protestant Ethic and Modernization.* New York: Basic Books 1968.

Ellul, Jacques. 'Work and Calling.' In *Callings!*, edited by James Y. Holloway and Will D. Campbell, 18–44. New York: Paulist Press 1974.

Emerson, E.H. *English Puritanism from John Hooper to John Milton.* Durham: Duke University Press 1968.

Engnell, I. 'Some Biblical Attitudes to Work. 1. Work in the Old Testament.' *Svensk Exegetisk Arsbok* 26 (1961): 5–12.

Ferrar, J., ed. *Eusebius: Demonstratio Evangelica.* New York: MacMillan 1920.

Finley, M.I. *Economy and Society in Ancient Greece.* London: Chatto and Windus 1981.

Foster, Stephen. *Their Solitary Way: The Puritan Social Ethic in the First Century of Settlement in New England.* New Haven: Yale University Press 1971.

Gardiner, S.R., ed. *The Constitutional Documents of the Puritan Revolution, 1625–1660.* 3rd ed. Oxford: Clarendon Press 1968.

Gartner, B. 'Some Biblical Attitudes to Work. 2. Work in the New Testament.' *Svensk Exegetisk Arsbok* 26 (1961): 13–18.

Geoghegan, A.T. *The Attitude toward Labour in Early Christianity and Ancient Culture.* Washington: Catholic University of America Press 1945.

George, C.H., and K. George. *The Protestant Mind of the English Reformation.* Princeton: Princeton University Press 1961.

Goldman, Harvey. *Max Weber and Thomas Mann: Calling and the Shaping of the Self.* Los Angeles: University of California Press 1988.

Grant, R.M. *Early Christianity and Society.* New York: Harper and Row 1977.

Gray, B.K. *A History of English Philanthropy.* London: P.S. King and Son 1905.

Gray, C.M. *Hugh Latimer and the Sixteenth Century.* Cambridge, Mass.: Harvard University Press 1950.

Greaves, Richard L. *Society and Religion in Elizabethan England.* Minneapolis: University of Minnesota Press 1991.

Green, R.W. *Protestantism, Capitalism and the Social Sciences.* Lexington: Heath 1973.

Gryglewicz, E. 'La valeur du travail manuel dans la terminologie grèque de la bible.' *Biblica* 7 (1956): 314–37.

Haigh, C., ed. *The English Reformation Revised.* Cambridge: Cambridge University Press 1987.

Haines, R.M. 'Church, Society and Politics in the Early Fifteenth Century as Viewed from an English Pulpit.' In *Studies in Church History*, vol. 12, edited by D. Baker, 143–57. Oxford: Blackwell 1975.

Hall, B. 'Puritanism: The Problem of Definition.' In *Studies in Church History*, vol. 2, edited by G.J. Cuming, 283–96. London: Nelson 1965.

Hancock, Ralph. *Calvin and the Foundations of Modern Politics.* Ithaca: Cornell University Press 1989.

Hanson, D.W. *From Kingdom to Commonwealth: The Development of Civic Consciousness in English Political Thought.* Cambridge, Mass.: Harvard University Press 1970.

Hardy, Lee. *The Fabric of This World.* Grand Rapids: Eerdmans 1990.

Harkness, G. *John Calvin: The Man and His Ethics.* New York: Holt 1931.

Haroutunian, J. *Piety versus Moralism.* New York: Harper and Row 1970.

Harris, Ian. *The Mind of John Locke.* Cambridge: Cambridge University Press 1994.

Hawkes, R.M. 'The Logic of Assurance in English Puritan Theology.' *Westminster Theological Journal* 52 (1990): 247–61

Hecksher, E. *Mercantilism.* 2 vols. London: Allen and Unwin 1935.

Hexter, J.H. *More's Utopia: The Biography of an Idea.* Princeton: Princeton University Press 1952.

Hill, C. *Change and Continuity in Seventeenth Century England.* London: Weidenfeld and Nicolson 1974.

– 'Protestantism and the Rise of Capitalism.' In *Essays in the Economic and Social History of Tudor and Stuart England,* edited by F.J. Fisher, 15–38. Cambridge: Cambridge University Press 1961.

– *Puritanism and Revolution.* London: Secker and Warburg 1958.

– *Society and Puritanism.* London: Secker and Warburg 1964.

– *Some Intellectual Consequences of the English Revolution.* Madison: University of Wisconsin Press 1980.

Hogrefe, P. *The Sir Thomas More Circle.* Urbana: University of Illinois Press 1959.

Holdsworth, Christopher. 'The Blessing of Work: The Cistercian View.' In *Sanctity and Secularity: The Church and the World,* edited by D. Baker, 59–76. Oxford: Blackwell 1973.

Holl, K. 'Die Geschichte des Worts "Beruf."' In his *Gesammelte Aufsätze zur Kirchengeschichte,* 3 vols, 3:184–219. Tübingen: J.C.B. Mohr 1931.

Hughes, P.E. *Theology of the English Reformers.* Grand Rapids: Eerdmans 1965.

Hundert, E.J. 'The Making of Homo Faber: John Locke between Ideology and History.' *Journal of the History of Ideas* 23 (1972): 3–22.

– 'Market Society and Meaning in Locke's Political Philosophy.' *Journal of Philosophy* 15 (1977): 33–44.

Jacard, P. *Histoire sociale du travail.* Paris: Payot 1960.

Jackson, R.S. *John Donne's Christian Vocation.* Evanston: Northwestern University Press 1976.

James, M. 'The Effect of the Religious Changes of the Sixteenth and Seventeenth Centuries in Economic Theory and Development.' In *Economic History of*

Europe since the Reformation, edited by E. Eyre, 5–111. Oxford: Clarendon Press 1937.

Johnson, R.S. *More's Utopia: Ideal and Illusion*. New Haven: Yale University Press 1969.

Jones, W.R. *The Tudor Commonwealth, 1529–1559*. London: Athlone Press 1970.

Kaiser, G. *Theology of Work*. Westminster, Md: Newman Press 1966.

Keynes, G. *A Bibliography of Dr. John Donne*. Cambridge: Cambridge University Press 1958.

Killeen, S.M. *The Philosophy of Labour According to Thomas Aquinas*. Washington: Catholic University of America Press 1939.

Kitch, M.J. *Capitalism and the Reformation*. New York: Barnes and Noble 1968.

Knappen, M.M. *Tudor Puritanism*. Chicago: University of Chicago Press 1939.

Knox, R.B. 'The Social Teachings of Archbishop John Williams.' In *Studies in Church History*, vol. 8, edited by G.J. Cuming and D. Baker, 179–85. London: Nelson 1972.

Lake, P. 'Calvinism and the English Church, 1570–1635.' *Past and Present* 114 (1987): 32–76.

– *Moderate Puritans and the Elizabethan Church*. Cambridge: Cambridge University Press 1982.

– 'Puritan Identities.' *Journal of Ecclesiastical History* 35 (1984): 112–23.

Lake, P., and M. Dowling, eds. *Protestantism and the National Church in Sixteenth Century England*. New York: Croom Helm 1987.

Lamont, W. 'Puritanism as History and Historiography: Some Further Thoughts.' *Past and Present* 44 (1969): 133–40.

Lehmann, H. 'Ascetic Protestantism and Economic Rationalism: Max Weber Revisited after Two Generations.' *Harvard Theological Review* 80 (1987): 307–20.

Lehmann, Hartmut, and Guenther Roth, eds. *Weber's Protestant Ethic: Origins, Evidences, Contexts*. Berkeley: University of California Press 1993.

Letwin, W. *The Origins of Scientific Economics*. London: Methuen 1963.

Lightfoot, J.B., ed. *The Apostolic Fathers*. London: Macmillan 1926.

Little, D. *Religion, Order and Law*. New York: Harper and Row 1969.

MacCulloch, Diarmaid. 'The Myth of the English Reformation.' *Journal of British Studies* 30 (1991): 1–19.

McGee, J.S. *The Godly Man in Stuart England: Anglicans, Puritans and the Two Tables*. New Haven: Yale University Press 1976.

Mackinnon, Malcolm H. 'Part I: Calvinism and the Infallible Assurance of Grace: The Weber Thesis Reconsidered'; 'Part II: Weber's Exploration of Calvinism: The Undiscovered Provenance of Capitalism.' *British Journal of Sociology* 39 (1988): 143–77; 178–210.

MacLure, M. *The Paul's Cross Sermons, 1534–1642*. Toronto: University of Toronto Press 1958.

Mcmichael, Jack R., and Barbara Taft, eds. *The Writings of William Walwyn*. Athens, Ga: University of Georgia Press 1989.

Macpherson, C.B. *The Political Theory of Possessive Individualism*. Oxford: Clarendon Press 1962.

Manning, B. *The English People and the English Revolution*. London: Heinemann 1976.

Manning, B., ed. *Politics, Religion and the English Civil War*. London: Arnold 1973.

Marc'hadour, G. '*Obediens usque ad Mortem*: A Key to St. Thomas More.' *Spiritual Life* 7 (1965): 205–22.

– 'Saint Thomas More.' In *Pre-Reformation Spirituality*, edited by J. Walsh, 224–39. London: Burns and Oates 1965.

– 'Thomas More's Spirituality.' In *St. Thomas More: Action and Contemplation*, edited by R.S. Sylvester, 123–59.

Marshall, G. *In Search of the Spirit of Capitalism*. London: Hutchinson 1982.

Marshall, P. 'John Locke: Between God and Mammon.' *Canadian Journal of Political Science* 12 (1979): 73–96.

– 'Quentin Skinner and the Secularisation of Political Thought.' *Studies in Political Thought* 2 (1993): 85–104.

– 'The Shape of the Modern Work Ethic.' In *Work in Canada*, edited by J. Peters, 5–24. Waterloo, Ont.: Interdisciplinary Research Seminar, Wilfrid Laurier University 1986.

– 'Substance and Method in Weber's Protestant Ethic.' *Tydskrif vir Christelike Wetenskap* (1991): 40–56.

– 'Vocation, Work and Rest.' In *Christian Faith and Practice in the Modern World*, edited by Mark A. Noll and David F. Wells, 199–217. Grand Rapids: Eerdmans 1988.

– 'Work and Vocation: Some Historical Reflections.' *Reformed Journal* (Sept. 1980): 16–20.

Marshall, P., et al. *Labour of Love: Essays on Work*. Toronto: Wedge 1979.

Martz, L.L. 'Thomas More: The Tower Works.' In *St. Thomas More: Action and Contemplation*, edited by R.S. Sylvester, 57–83.

Meilander, Gilbert. *Friendship: A Study in Theological Ethics*. South Bend: University of Notre Dame Press 1981.

Merrill, T.F. *William Perkins, 1558–1602*. Nieuwkoop: B. de Graaf 1966.

Michaelson, R.S. 'Changes in the Puritan Concept of Calling or Vocation.' *New England Quarterly* 26 (1953): 315–36.

Miegge, M. *I Talenti Messi a Profitto*. Urbino: Argalia 1969.

Miller, P., and H.T. Johnson, eds. *The Puritans*. 2 vols. New York: Harper and Row 1963.

Morgan, E.S. 'Review' of Kurt Samuelsson's *Religion and Economic Action*. *William and Mary Quarterly* 3rd ser., 20 (1963): 135–40.

Morgan, I. *The Godly Preachers of the Elizabethan Church*. Epworth: Epworth Press 1965.

Morrill, John. *The Nature of the English Revolution*. London: Longman 1993.

Morris, C. *Political Theory in England: Tyndale to Hooker*. London: Oxford University Press 1953.

Mossé, C. *The Ancient World at Work*. London: Chatto and Windus 1969.

Nelson, B. 'Weber's Protestant Ethic: Its Origins, Wanderings and Foreseeable Futures.' In *Beyond the Classics?*, edited by C.Y. Glock and P.E. Hammond, 71–130. New York: Harper and Row 1973.

New, J.F.H. *Anglican and Puritan: The Basis of Their Opposition, 1558–1640*. Palo Alto: Stanford University Press 1964.

The New Catholic Encyclopedia. Edited by Most Rev. William J. McDonald, et al. New York: McGraw-Hill 1967.

Oakes, Guy. 'The Thing That Would Not Die: Notes on Refutation.' in *Weber's Protestant Ethic: Origins, Evidences, Contexts*, edited by H. Lehmann and G. Roth, 285–94.

O'Brien, G. *An Essay on Medieval Economic Thinking*. London: Longmans, Green 1920.

O'Day, R. *The Debate on the English Reformation*. London: Methuen 1986.

O'Malley, J. 'Erasmus and Luther: Continuity and Discontinuity as the Key to Their Conflict.' *Sixteenth Century Journal* 5 (1974): 47–65.

Opie, J. 'The Anglicizing of John Hooper.' *Archiv für Reformation Geschichte* 59 (1968): 150–77.

Owst, G.R. *Literature and Pulpit in Medieval England*. Oxford: Blackwell 1961.

Packer, J.I. 'The Doctrine of Justification in Development and Decline among the Puritans.' In *Puritan and Reformed Studies Conference*, 18–31. London 1969.

Pangle, Thomas. *The Spirit of Modern Republicanism*. Chicago: University of Chicago Press 1988.

Partee, C. 'Calvin's Central Dogma Again.' *Sixteenth Century Journal* 18 (1987): 191–9.

Pearson, S.C. 'The Religion of John Locke and the Character of His Thought.' *Journal of Religion* 58 (1978): 244–62.

Pieper, J. *Leisure: The Basis of Culture*. New York: Random House 1963.

Pocock, J.G.A. *The Machiavellian Moment: Florentine Political Thought and the Atlantic Republican Tradition*. Princeton: Princeton University Press 1975.

Poggi, G. *Calvinism and the Capitalist Spirit: Max Weber's Protestant Ethic.* London: Macmillan 1987.

Redekop, Calvin. 'Mennonites, Creation and Work.' *Christian Scholar's Review* 22 (1993): 348–66.

Reidy, M.F. *Bishop Lancelot Andrewes.* Chicago: Loyola University Press 1955.

Reventlow, Henning Graf. *The Authority of the Bible and the Rise of the Modern World.* Philadelphia: Fortress Press 1985.

Richardson, A. *The Biblical Doctrine of Work.* London: SCM 1958.

Richardson, R.C. *The Debate on the English Revolution Revisited.* London: Routledge 1988.

Russell, Conrad. *The Causes of the English Civil War.* Oxford: Clarendon Press 1990.

Ryken, L. *Work and Leisure in Christian Perspective.* Portland, Or.: Multnomah 1987.

Samuelsson, K. *Religion and Economic Action.* New York: Harper and Row 1961.

Sasek, Lawrence A. *Images of English Puritanism: A Collection of Contemporary Sources, 1589–1646.* Baton Rouge: Louisiana State University Press 1989.

Scharmann, Th., G. Mensching, F. Lau, W. Freytag, W. Nordmann, and J. Fichtner. 'Beruf.' In *Die Religion in Geschichte und Gegenwart,* 8 vols, edited by J.C.B. Mohr, 1:1071–80. Tübingen: J.C.B. Mohr 1957.

Schlaifer, R. 'Greek Theories of Slavery from Homer to Aristotle.' *Harvard Studies in Classical Philology* 47 (1936): 165–204.

Schlatter, R.B. *Social Ideas of Religious Leaders, 1660–1688.* Oxford: Oxford University Press 1940.

Schmidt, K.L. 'klesis.' In *Theological Dictionary of the New Testament.* 9 vols, 1964–74. Vol. 2, TH-K, edited by A. Kittel, translated by A. Bromiley, 491–6. Grand Rapids: Eerdmans 1965.

Schuurman, Doug. 'Reformed Vocation under Assault.' Unpublished paper 1990.

Seaver, P. 'The Puritan Work Ethic Revisited.' *Journal of British Studies* 19 (1980): 35–53.

– *Wallington's World.* London: Methuen 1985.

Sevenster, J.N. *Paul and Seneca.* Leiden: E.J. Brill 1961.

Shaw, R.B. *The Call of God: The Theme of Vocation in the Poetry of Donne and Herbert.* Cambridge, Mass.: Cowley Publications 1981.

Skinner, Q. *The Foundations of Modern Political Thought.* 2 vols. Cambridge: Cambridge University Press 1978.

– 'History and Ideology in the English Revolution.' *Historical Journal* 8 (1965): 151–78.

Slavin, A.J. *Humanism, Reform and Reformation in England.* New York: Wiley 1969.

Smith, L.B. *Tudor Prelates and Politics*. Princeton: Princeton University Press 1953.

Smith, M.S. *The English Sermon, Vol. I (1550–1650)*. Cheadle, Cheshire: Carcanet Press 1976.

Sombart, W. *Der Moderne Kapitalismus*. Munich: Duncker and Humblot 1902.

Sommerville, C.J. 'The Anti-Puritan Work Ethic.' *Journal of British Studies* 20 (1981): 70–81.

– *The Secularisation of Early Modern England: From Religious Culture to Religious Faith*. New York: Oxford University Press 1992.

Spurr, J. '"Latitudinarianism" and the Restoration Church.' *Historical Journal* 31 (1988): 61–82.

– *The Restoration Church of England, 1646–1689*. New Haven: Yale University Press 1991.

Stone, L. *The Causes of the English Revolution, 1529–1642*. London: Routledge and Kegan Paul 1972.

Sylvester, R.S., ed. *St. Thomas More: Action and Contemplation*. New Haven: Yale University Press 1972.

Tawney, R.H. *Religion and the Rise of Capitalism*. Orig. 1926. New York: Harcourt, Brace and World 1954.

Taylor, Charles. *Sources of the Self: The Making of the Modern Identity*. Cambridge, Mass.: Harvard University Press 1989.

Thirsk, J., and J.P. Cooper, eds. *Seventeenth-Century Economic Documents*. Oxford: Clarendon Press 1972.

Todd, M. *Christian Humanism and the Puritan Social Order*. New York: Cambridge University Press 1987.

Tolmie, M. *The Triumph of the Saints*. Cambridge: Cambridge University Press 1977.

Tonkin, J. *The Church and the Secular Order in Reformation Thought*. New York: Columbia University Press 1971.

Toon, P. *The Emergence of Hyper-Calvinism in English Nonconformity*. London: The Olive Tree 1967.

– *God's Statesman*. Exeter: Paternoster 1971.

Trevor-Roper, Hugh. *Catholics, Anglicans and Puritans: Seventeenth Century Essays*. London: Secker and Warburg 1987.

Troeltsch, E. *The Social Teachings of the Christian Churches*. 2 vols. New York: Harper and Row 1956.

Tully, J. *An Approach to Political Philosophy: Locke in Contexts*. Cambridge: Cambridge University Press 1993.

– *A Discourse on Property: John Locke and His Adversaries*. Cambridge: Cambridge University Press 1980.

Tyacke, N. *Anti-Calvinists: The Rise of English Arminianism, c. 1590–1640.* Oxford: Oxford University Press 1988.

Underdown, David. *Revel, Riot and Rebellion: Popular Politics and Culture in England, 1603–1660.* Oxford: Clarendon Press 1985.

Ustick, W.L. 'Changing Ideals of Aristocratic Character and Conduct in Seventeenth-Century England.' *Modern Philology* 30 (1932–3): 147–66.

Van Beek, M. *An Enquiry into Puritan Vocabulary.* Groningen: Wolters-Nordhoff 1969.

Vaughan, K.I. *John Locke: Economist and Social Scientist.* Chicago: University of Chicago Press 1980.

Volf, Miroslav. *Work in the Spirit: Toward a Theory of Work.* New York: Oxford University Press 1991.

Von Greyer, Kaspar. 'Biographical Evidence on Predestination, Covenant, and Special Providence.' In *Weber's Protestant Ethic,* edited by H. Lehmann and G. Roth, 273–84.

Weber, M. 'Anti-critical Last Word on the Spirit of Capitalism.' Translated by W.M. Davis. *American Journal of Sociology* 83 (1978): 1105–31.

– *General Economic History.* New York: Collier Books 1961.

– *The Protestant Ethic and the Spirit of Capitalism.* Translated by T. Parsons. New York: Scribners 1958.

– *The Religion of China.* Glencoe: Free Press 1951.

– *The Sociology of Religion.* Boston: Beacon 1963.

– *Theory of Social and Economic Organization.* New York: Free Press 1947.

Westerman, W. 'Between Slavery and Freedom.' *American Historical Review* 50 (1945): 213–27.

White, H.C. *Social Criticism in the Popular Religious Literature in the Sixteenth Century.* New York: Columbia University Press 1951.

– *Tudor Books of Private Devotion.* Madison: University of Wisconsin Press 1951.

White, Peter. 'The Rise of Arminianism Reconsidered.' *Past and Present* 101 (1983): 55–78.

Williams, C.H., ed. *English Historical Documents, Vol. 5, 1485–1558.* London: Eyre and Spottiswoode 1967.

Wingren, G. 'The Concept of Vocation – Its Basis and Its Problems.' *Lutheran World* 15 (1968): 87–95.

– *Creation and Gospel.* Toronto: Edwin Mellen 1979.

– *Luther on Vocation.* Translated by C.C. Rasmussen. Philadelphia: Muhlenburg Press 1957.

Woodhouse, A.S.P., ed. *Puritanism and Liberty.* Chicago: University of Chicago Press 1951.

Wright, L.B. *Middle-Class Culture in Elizabethen England.* Ithaca: Cornell University Press 1958.

Yost, J.K. 'William Tyndale and the Renaissance Humanist Origins of the *Via Media.*' *Nederlands Archief voor Kerkgescheidenis* 41 (1971): 167–86.

Zaret, David. *The Heavenly Contract: Ideology and Organisation in Pre-Revolutionary Puritanism.* Chicago: University of Chicago Press 1985.

– 'The Use and Abuse of Textual Data.' In *Weber's Protestant Ethic,* edited by H. Lehmann and G. Roth, 245–72.

Zeeveld, W.G. *Foundations of Tudor Policy.* Cambridge, Mass.: Harvard University Press 1968.

Index